Trade and Empire in Early Nineteenth-Century Southeast Asia

WORLDS OF THE EAST INDIA COMPANY

ISSN 1752–5667

This series offers high-quality studies of the East India Company, drawn from across a broad chronological, geographical and thematic range. The rich history of the Company has long been of interest to those who engage in the study of Britain's commercial, imperial, maritime and military past, but in recent years it has also attracted considerable attention from those who explore art, cultural and social themes within an historical context. The series will thus provide a forum for scholars from different disciplinary backgrounds, and for those whose have interests in the history of Britain (London and the regions), India, China, Indonesia, as well as the seas and oceans.

The editors welcome submissions from both established scholars and those beginning their career; monographs are particularly encouraged but volumes of essays will also be considered. All submissions will receive rapid, informed attention. They should be sent in the first instance to:

Professor H.V. Bowen, Department of History and Classics, Swansea University, Swansea SA2 8PP

Previously published titles are listed at the back of this volume.

TRADE AND EMPIRE IN EARLY NINETEENTH-CENTURY SOUTHEAST ASIA

Gillian Maclaine and his Business Network

G. Roger Knight

THE BOYDELL PRESS

First published 2015
The Boydell Press, Woodbridge

ISBN 978-1-78327-069-9

The Boydell Press is an imprint of Boydell & Brewer Ltd
PO Box 9, Woodbridge, Suffolk IP12 3DF, UK
and of Boydell & Brewer Inc.
668 Mt Hope Avenue, Rochester, NY 14620–2731, USA
website: www.boydellandbrewer.com

A CIP catalogue record for this title is available from the British Library

The publisher has no responsibility for the continued existence or accuracy of URLs for external or third-party internet websites referred to in this book, and does not guarantee that any content on such websites is, or will remain, accurate or appropriate

This publication is printed on acid-free paper

Typeset by Fakenham Prepress Solutions, Fakenham, Norfolk NR21 8NN

CONTENTS

ACKNOWLEDGEMENTS

The University of Adelaide's Study Leave Fund has generously supported my research over a number of years, as has Margaret Hosking of the University's Barr-Smith Library. I am deeply indebted to many others (too numerous to name) in Australia, the UK and the Netherlands for their unstinting assistance, hospitality and advice over many years. My particular thanks, however, must go to James and Janet Greenfield for supporting and sustaining my interest in their distant ancestor, and to Gordon Brotherton (*primus inter pares*) for helping me to keep going in difficult circumstances over the last couple of years. Nor should I forget Peter Sowden, my editor at Boydell and Brewer, and Huw Bowen of the University of Swansea, editor of the series in which this volume appears, whose kind enthusiasm has contributed mightily to bringing 'Maclaine' into the light of day.

ABBREVIATIONS

AM	Angus Maclaine (GM's brother)
EIC	East India Company (GB)
GG in Rade	Besluiten Governor-Generaal in Rade [Decisions Governor General in Council]
GM	Gillian Maclaine
HCHO	*Handboek voor Cultuur-en Handelsondernemingen in Nederlandsch Indië* [Handbook of Plantation and Mercantile Enterprises in the Netherlands Indies]
JG	John Gregorson (GM's uncle and MM's brother)
MK	Archief Ministerie van Koloniën [Ministry of Colonies]
MM	Marjorie Maclaine (GM's mother and GJ's sister)
NA	[Netherlands] Nationaal Archief [National Archives]
NHM	Nederlandsche Handel-Maatschappij [Netherlands Trading Association]
NHMA	Archief Hoofd Kantoor [Head Office] NHM
NIVAS	Nederlandsch-Indische Vereeniging voor de Afzet van Suiker [Netherlands Indies Association for the Sale of Sugar]
0-M MSS	Osborne-Maclaine Papers
Vb.	Verbaal [Record of Proceedings] MK
VJSP	Vereenigde Javasuiker Producenten [United Java Sugar Producers Association]
VOC	Vereenigde Oost-Indische Compagnie [Dutch East India Company]

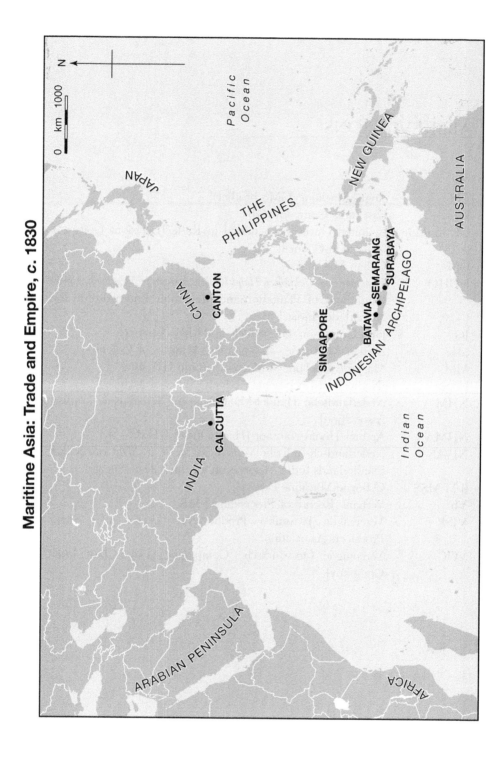

Maritime Asia: Trade and Empire, c. 1830

PREFACE

> We are interested in the way in which individuals and groups have created links to facilitate the movement of commodities, money, information and people across relatively long distances.[1]

It is to this context that the present volume is addressed, in so far it relates to an individual – and the enduring mercantile firm that he helped found – whose career was enmeshed not only in maritime empire in Southeast Asia but also in some of the early nineteenth-century world's most dynamic commodity chains. As such, it constitutes a history of the nexus between a particular person and a complex and evolving commercial system that was both imperial and global. The focus is on the young émigré Scot Gillian Maclaine and his activities as a trainee in a London 'East India' mercantile house and subsequently in colonial trade and plantation in the erstwhile Netherlands Indies (present-day Indonesia) – and on the island of Java in particular – during the opening decades of the nineteenth century.

The book is more than a biography, however, since the story of Maclaine's activities as both merchant and planter intersects with key debates about the dynamics of Western imperialisms in Asia; the imperatives of commodity chains and the character of 'diaspora' commercial networks; and the associated – and problematic – nexus between colony and metropole. It is distinctive in that it essays an in-depth, 'micro-level' account of developments that are known to historians primarily on a broad 'macro-level'. Some similar studies exist in relation to European mercantile activities in the Indian sub-continent and China during the nineteenth century.[2] However, none have been essayed

---

1 Shinya Sugiyama and Linda Grove, 'Introduction', in Shinya Sugiyama and Linda Grove (eds), *Commercial Networks in Modern Asia* (Richmond: Curzon, 2001), p. 2.

2 Notable among them are: Anthony Webster, *The Richest East India Merchant. The Life and Business of John Palmer of Calcutta, 1767–1836* (Woodbridge and Rochester, NY: The Boydell Press, 2007); Anthony Webster, *The Twilight of the East India Company 1813–1858* (Woodbridge and Rochester, NY: The Boydell Press, 2009); H.V. Bowen, 'Britain in the Indian Ocean Region and Beyond: Contours, Connections and the Creation of a Global Maritime Empire', pp. 45–67 in H.V. Bowen, E. Mancke and J.G. Reid (eds), *Britain's Oceanic Empire: Atlantic and Indian Ocean Worlds c.1550–1850* (Cambridge: Cambridge University Press, 2012);

hitherto in relation to the Southeast Asian region in which Maclaine operated during the period with which the present study is concerned.[3]

Maclaine was a major, yet a now virtually unknown, figure[4] and the creator in the 1820s of a European mercantile network in Asia, centred on the Batavia (Jakarta) firm of Maclaine Watson, that long outlasted its founder. It became, over the century and a half of its existence, one of colonial Indonesia's key commodity traders and, as such, very heavily involved in the trade in sugar that constituted the single most valuable of the Java's exports and secured the Netherlands Indies a position at the apex of the huge international market for this form of sweetener. It was a formidable record, but a poorly documented one. Maclaine Watson's London office (in Fenchurch Street) appears to have survived the Blitz of 1940, but the firm's London archive subsequently disappeared, while that of its Jakarta (Batavia) head-office – so it would seem – suffered a similar fate around the time that it passed into the hands of the

J. Forbes Munro, *Maritime Enterprise and Empire. Sir William Mackinnon and his Business Network, 1823–1893* (Woodbridge: The Boydell Press, 2003); S.D. Chapman, *Merchant Enterprise in Britain. From the Industrial Revolution to World War 1* (Cambridge: Cambridge University Press, 1992); Alain Le Pichon, *China Trade and Empire. Jardine Matheson & Co. and the Origins of British Rule in Hong Kong, 1827–1843* (Oxford and New York: Oxford University Press for the British Academy, 2006).

3   Recent work has concentrated predominantly on late nineteenth-century developments, e.g. Nico van Horn, 'Het Indische handelshuis Bauermann in de negentiende eeuw', *NEHA-jaarboek voor economische, bedrijfs- en techniekgeschiedenis*, 60(1997), pp. 137–58. The most formidable contribution to the general field (though again primarily focused on events post-1870) is Alexander Claver, *Dutch Commerce and Chinese Merchants in Java. Colonial Relationships in Trade and Finance, 1800–1942* (Leiden and Boston, MA: Brill, 2014). An earlier work [W.F.M Mansvelt], *De eerste Indische Handelshuizen* (Batavia: Mededeeling No. 168, Departement van Economische Zaken, Centraal Kantoor voor de Statistiek, 1938) is no more than a preliminary sketch. On mercantile matters more generally, see e.g. the notable contributions of Ton de Graaf, *Voor Handel en Maatschappij. Geschiedenis van de Nederlandsche Handel-Maatschappij, 1824–1964* (Amsterdam: Boom, 2012); William Gervase Clarence-Smith, 'The Rise and Fall of Hadhrami Shipping in the Indian Ocean, c1750–c1940', pp. 227–58 in David Parkin and Ruth Barnes (eds), *Ships and the Development of Maritime Technology across the Indian Ocean* (London: Routledge-Curzon, 2002); Frank Broeze, 'The Merchant Fleet of Java, 1820–1850', *Archipel*, 18 (1979), pp. 251–69; Gerrit Knaap, *Shallow Waters, Rising Tide; Shipping and Trade in Java around 1775* (Leiden: KITLV Press, 1996) and Heather Sutherland and Gerrit Knaap, *Monsoon Traders; Ships, Skippers and Commodities in Eighteenth-Century Makassar* (Leiden: KITLV Press, 2004).

4   The 'centenary history' of the firm that Maclaine co-founded, *The First One Hundred Years. 1827–1927. Maclaine Watson & Co. MacNeill & Co. Fraser Easton & Co.* nd, np [1927] is a sixteen-page pamphlet. Apart from that, there exists only a short, pioneering essay on Maclaine himself by the late Frank Broeze: 'A Scottish Merchant in Batavia (1820–1840). Gillean [*sic*] Maclaine and Dutch Connections', pp. 393–414 in Ina Baghdiantz McCabe, Gelina Harlaftis and Ionna Pepelasis Minoglou (eds), *Diaspora Entrepreneurial Networks. Four Centuries of History* (Oxford and New York: Berg, 2005).

Indonesian government in the mid-1960s.[5] As a private company, moreover, Maclaine Watson left no published Annual Reports and the like. It is not without irony, indeed, that we know far more about the foundation of the firm in the 1820s and 1830s than we seem ever likely to know about its subsequent history. As well as a substantial number of contemporary records relating to the bankruptcy of his erstwhile London partners, a great many of Gillian Maclaine's own letters 'back home', extending more or less continuously from 1816 until 1839, have survived in various locations in the UK.[6]

What makes Maclaine's letters of particular interest, however, is more than their mere survival value. While they are rich in information about the commodity chains in which he was enmeshed throughout a career that began at the age of eighteen, they are not 'business letters' per se but instead exert a much broader fascination as the letters of a businessman to non-business people. They were addressed for the most part to members of a family of well-educated, highly literate individuals – Maclaine's mother, uncle and sole brother were the chief recipients – of the gentry class of the western Highlands of Scotland. While these people were very interested indeed in his doings, by the up-and-downs of his mercantile and plantation ventures, and by the sometimes exotic milieu in which he operated, their interest in mundane data on the number of bales of cotton goods, hundredweights of coffee and so on was distinctly limited. A consummate letter writer who was drilled in the art by his mother from an early age, Maclaine did his best to oblige. Accordingly, the book is emphatically not a 'company history': rather, it is a narrative of an individual's career in business and plantation. At the same time, however, its account of Maclaine's life is tightly located in an altogether broader historical framework – and enlivened by its subject's acute personal observations about mercantile operations in London and 'the East', colonial plantation ventures, and the Scots 'diaspora' of which he was part.

---

5   An invaluable, short appendix in Nicholas Crickhowell, *The Rivers Join. The Story of a Family* (Victoria, BC: Trafford Publishing, 2009) contains vital information about the dramatis personae of Maclaine Watson and associated Java companies through well into the twentieth century. Lord Crickhowell has also been assiduous in collecting material relating to the firm's later history, and I am much in his debt for kindly communicating these to me.

6   These letters are in the Greenfield MSS (in private hands in the UK – part listed as 'Gregorson of Ardtornish', National Register of Archives (Scotland) Survey no. 1285) – and in the Osborne-Maclaine papers D3330 in Gloucestershire Archives (previously Gloucester Records), Gloucester, UK. I would like to take this opportunity of thanking James and Janet Greenfield for their invaluable assistance, hospitality and may acts of kindness over the last several years. My heartfelt thanks also go to the helpful and patient archivists at Gloucester Records for their generous support over a number of visits to their archive between 2009 and 2013.

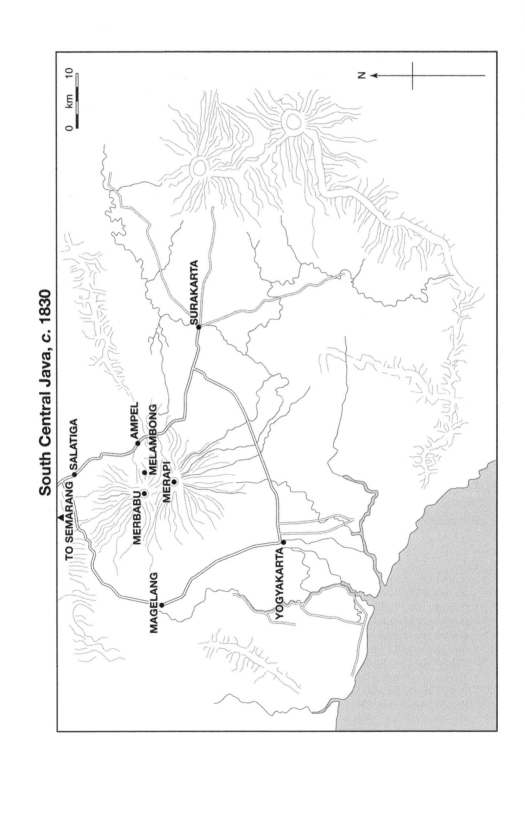

South Central Java, c. 1830

One

_____

INTRODUCTION: A SCOTS ÉMIGRÉ, IMPERIAL SYSTEMS AND GLOBAL COMMODITIES

Gillian Maclaine (he spelled his first name that way throughout his life) light-heartedly styled himself early in his career in the East as a 'Scotch Adventurer'. Yet, this was too modest a designation for an individual who went on to found a major and enduring mercantile business in colonial Indonesia and who, when he first arrived on the island of Java at the beginning of the 1820s, was both well educated and had several years of commercial experience behind him in the UK. Like many of his European counterparts, his career located him in the realms of Western empire-building in nineteenth-century Asia. More specifically, as we shall see, like so many of his British contemporaries, his own personal trajectory was framed within the context of the ongoing history of the British East India Company (EIC) that formed a ubiquitous presence in the world in which Maclaine operated. Even so, his location there was distinctive – though hardly unique – in so far as his activities as both merchant and planters straddled two very different empires: the British one from which he heralded and the Dutch one in the Netherlands Indies where he worked and settled. The imperial context in which he was enmeshed, however, was integrated with a global one that, in part, subsumed it.

For Maclaine was not only positioned, at times somewhat awkwardly, along one of the nineteenth century's (lesser) imperial fault lines. At least as crucially, he was positioned along commodity chains that extended between the Americas, Europe and the heartlands of Asia and whose key dynamics, though far from independent of 'empire', nonetheless exhibited a substantial degree of autonomy from it. At the same time, however, Maclaine's engagement in commodity chains is easily misunderstood, particularly so, indeed, if those chains are viewed (predominantly or exclusively) in terms of a 'World System' that subordinated a (colonial) 'periphery' of raw material production to a (metropolitan) manufacturing 'core'.

In fact, Maclaine's activity on the colonial 'periphery' of empire complicates significantly any notion that he was thereby subservient to, or simply the agent of, metropolitan 'core' interests in whatever form. His career in the Indies certainly started that way. Nevertheless, it continued and ended with a slewing-off of bilateral ties with his erstwhile metropole, and the establishment of a successful – and long-enduring – colonial business network solidly based in Asia and dependent (albeit to varying degrees over time) on intra-Asian trade. Inter alia, Maclaine's story raises questions about the explanatory value of 'World Systems' in general, suggesting that they fail to allow for the sheer diversity of global patterns of production and distribution, and for the power of agency on the periphery. In this latter context, moreover, the history of Maclaine Watson – both during its founder's life time and subsequently – relates to a broad and ongoing debate about the global importance of *inter-Asian* trade per se, as distinct from bilateral, intercontinental trade between a Western 'core' and Oriental 'peripheries'.

Gillian Maclaine: Life and Times

Gillian Maclaine was born on the island of Mull off the west coast of Scotland in 1798. At the age of twelve, he was sent to the grammar school at Oban, the main urban centre and chief port of the Western Highlands, and from there went on to the University of Glasgow. This was followed by an informal apprenticeship in business in an East India commercial house in London. By the age of twenty-two, however, Maclaine found himself across the other side of the world, on the island of Java, the 'garden of the East' and the key Dutch possession in the erstwhile Netherlands Indies. A precocious start as both a merchant and planter culminated in 1827 in the foundation of a business partnership under the name of 'Maclaine Watson' in the colonial capital of Batavia. At the very start of their history Maclaine Watson dealt primarily in cotton goods and coffee (though this was soon to change). Cotton goods were imported from the UK and sold locally, whereas coffee was grown in Java itself for sale in various destinations in the West. Notionally, there was a nice symbiosis between two commodities that paid for each other. In fact, matters developed very differently, and serious commercial difficulties, together with Maclaine's ill-health, almost brought the fledgling business to grief at the end of the 1820s, but eighteen months spent (mostly) in the UK restored both his constitution and his fortunes.

Returning to Java in 1832, Maclaine had the perspicacity and romantic good fortune to marry a young woman whom he had met on board ship from Rotterdam. Her family was exceptionally well connected in official circles in Java: a point of some significance because the Dutch colony was in thrall to an officialdom that had inherited some of the prejudice against 'private' business of its monopolistic Dutch predecessor. A good marriage helped in rebuilding Maclaine's commercial fortunes, but so too did an infusion of capital into the firm from a wealthy fellow Scot. Likewise of importance was a substantial but short-lived revival of the trade in cotton goods from the UK.

Most significant of all, however, was a major diversification of the firm's operations, that left it far less dependent on bilateral commercial relations with Europe than had previously been the case, and the formation of an embryonic mercantile network that extended both to other major ports in the Indies and northward to Singapore. In tandem, Maclaine succeeded in gathering around himself a number of very capable business partners – many of them fellow Scots – and became increasingly adept at navigating the considerable commercial hazards attendant on doing business in the East.

The upshot of these developments was that Maclaine Watson prospered, as it had not done earlier. So much so, indeed, that in 1840 Maclaine and his immediate family set sail for Scotland, since he was now in a strong enough financial position to set up as a landed proprietor in the Highlands, something that had been his ambition since his departure for London some two and half decades earlier. But it was not to be: somewhere in the Indian Ocean, probably not so very far from Mauritius, his ship went down in a storm, and all aboard perished.

Maclaine Watson, however, did not perish with its founder. On the contrary, it demonstrated a remarkable longevity. The firm's connection with Gillian Maclaine's own family in the Highlands had been severed by the end of the 1840s. So too had any connection with Edward Watson, Gillian Maclaine's chief business partner in Batavia. Nonetheless, the enterprise continued as a family firm, though now as one run by a coterie of Highland families – and their English and Dutch collaborators – whose links with Maclaine Watson dated back to the 1820s but who were not the founder's kith and kin. These families stayed at the helm of Maclaine Watson for the next hundred years, and inter alia ensured that the firm remained true to its original moorings in the East: although the firm opened a London office in the 1880s, its headquarters remained firmly located in Batavia. Over the course of time, the enterprise there transformed itself into one of Java's biggest sugar exporting firms, though as Java sugar began to fade from the world market during the 1930s, diversification into other commodities kept it in business. It remained functioning, with an interlude during the Second World War, until 1964, when its operations in the archipelago were nationalised by the Indonesian government. Elsewhere, the company's record finally petered out late in the twentieth century. The commercial enterprise that Gillian Maclaine had begun more than one hundred and forty years earlier had proved, in short, to be one of remarkable longevity. Indeed, very few of the European mercantile firms operating in 'the Indies' in the late colonial era could lay claim to a similar record.

A World 'Compact and Connected'

Gillian Maclaine was a tiny cog in a vast 'machine' that reflected an astonishing degree and scale of maritime interconnectedness. That degree and scale was, of course, a phenomenon that had deep historical roots. As has been expounded by Linda Colley, for instance, the mid-eighteenth century in particular witnessed one of those 'global moments' in which a 'sense that the world was becoming visibly more compact and connected was pronounced', and in which the sea, in particular, far from being a distancing factor, became 'the prime vehicle and emblem of connectivity'.[1]

Even so, during the first half of the nineteenth century, fuelled above all by the power of steam, the evolution of this 'connectivity', both on land *and* sea, remains remarkable – and a remarkable feature of Gillian Maclaine's own lifetime. In 1816 he first reached London from Scotland by sail: fifteen years later (as he proudly informed his uncle) he accomplished the journey from the Highlands to the southern metropolis in a mere sixty-four hours, taking steamers from the Highlands to Glasgow and thence onward to Liverpool. From there he made his way by the newly opened railway – the first of its kind in the world – to Manchester. He was then forced back to the stagecoach, but in another seven years (1838) could have reached his final destination train via a rail network that linked the industrial northwest to Birmingham and thence on to London.[2]

Connectedness, moreover, was by no means confined to Western Europe. Maclaine's voyages to Java – there were two of them – both took place by sail on a route around Africa that took between three and four months to complete. Had he lived another five or six years, he could have made the journey by steamer in a matter of five or six weeks via the Egyptian land bridge and the so-called Overland route.[3] Indeed, this is precisely what his

[1] Linda Colley, *The Ordeal of Elizabeth Marsh* (London: Harper Collins, 2007), pp. xxiv–xxv.
[2] Gillian Maclaine [hereafter GM] to John Gregorson [hereafter JG] London, 8.2.1831 Greenfield MSS (in private possession, UK): 'I had delightful weather traveling & got over the ground cleverly as you shall learn. I left Greenock in the Liverpool Steam Packet at half past two in the morning of the 26th and reached Liverpool at 7 on the morning of the 27th. Started by Steam on the railroad same day at 1, reached Manchester 20 minutes before 3 – started from Manchester at half past 8 P.M. & arrived at the *Belle Sauvage*, Ludgate Hill, London at 7 P.M. on the 28th.... Thus performing the journey from Greenock to London in 64 hours, including 5 hours I stopped in Liverpool and about 5 at Manchester!!'
[3] For contemporary accounts of the Overland route in the mid-nineteenth century, see F.

brother Angus Maclaine did in 1846, en route to his sheep farm in Australia, but calling on the way at Batavia to finalise the transfer of the fortune to which he had become heir.

Commerce followed similar patterns, with the important exception that it was not until the opening of the Suez Canal in 1869 that cargoes began to catch up with passengers on the Middle Eastern route between Europe and Asia. Until then, there could be no question of anything but the smallest parcels of the most valuable goods accompanying people. Nonetheless, as its full title implies, the Overland *Mail* route did mean a radical speeding up of commercial information, decades before the arrival of the telegraph at the end of the 1860s. While Maclaine was still alive, his letters to the people with whom he did business in London and Glasgow would have taken an average of three and a half months to arrive – and even their 'posting' in Java had to be carefully synchronised with the irregular sailing of cargo boats to London, Rotterdam or Amsterdam. By the mid-1840s, however, within scarcely five years of Maclaine's death, his surviving partners in Batavia could begin to rely on a regular mail service (though Singapore) that reduced the time lag for information about commodity supply and demand to around six weeks or even less.

The British and the Dutch: The EIC, the VOC and its Successors and Tensions of Empire in Maritime Southeast Asia[4]

Increasingly 'compact and connected' Gillian Maclaine's world may indeed have been: it did not signify, however, that it was without major fissures. Like many of his European counterparts and contemporaries, Maclaine's career

Junghuhn, *Terugreis van Java naar Europa met de zoogenaamde Engelsche Overlandpost, in de Maanden September tot October 1848* (Zalt-Bommel: Joh, Norman & Zoon, 1851), pp. 4–14: Jhr. Mr W.T. Gevers Deynoot, *Herinneringen eener Reis naar Nederlandsch Indie in 1862* (The Hague: Nijhoff, 1864), pp. 1–25. For a recent overview, see Femme Gastra, 'The Experience of Travelling to the Dutch East Indies by the Overland Route, 1844–1869', pp. 120–37 in Gordon Jackson and David M. Williams (eds), *Shipping, Technology, and Imperialism: Papers Presented to the Third British-Dutch Maritime History Conference* (Aldershot: Scholar Press/Brookfield, VT: Ashgate, 1996). For prior history, see Holden Furber, 'The Overland Route to India in the Seventeenth and Eighteenth Centuries', *Journal of Indian History*, 29 (1951), pp. 105–33.

4 The following account draws gratefully on Nicholas Tarling, *Anglo-Dutch Rivalry in the Malay World 1780–1824* (Cambridge: Cambridge University Press, 1962); Tarling, 'The Prince of Merchants and the Lion City', *Journal of the Malaysian Branch of the Royal Asiatic Society*, 36, 1 (1964), pp. 20–40; E.H. Kossmann, *The Low Countries, 1780–1940* (Oxford: Clarendon Press, 1978); Antony Webster, *Gentlemen Capitalists: British Imperialism in Southeast Asia, 1770–1890* (London and New York: Tauris Academic Studies, 1998); H.V. Bowen, *The Business of Empire: The East India Company and Imperial Britain, 1756–1833* (Cambridge: Cambridge University Press, 2006); Anthony Webster, *The Twilight*; Bowen, Mancke & Reid, *Britain's Oceanic Empire*.

located him in the realms of Western empire-building in Asia at a time of considerable frontier expansion and imperial consolidation, with all the external and internal tensions inherent therein.[5] Maclaine's actual location, however, was a highly distinctive (though hardly unique) one that saw him straddled between two different empires: the British one from which he heralded (and with which he remained closely connected) and the Dutch one in the Netherlands Indies where he worked and settled. As will be argued, although the relations between the two were sometimes antagonistic, it was also the case that rivalry and potential for conflict was tempered by the need for mutual accommodation.

Until the latter's collapse at the very end of the eighteenth century, Anglo-Dutch imperial and commercial rivalries in Asian waters took place within the framework of the (British) East India Company and the VOC (Vereenigde Oost-Indische Compagnie) or Dutch East India Company. The VOC went under as part of the more general disintegration of the *ancien régime* in Holland in the wake of the French revolutionary wars. Its British counterpart, however, survived another half century or more, and provided the essential background – and often very much more than that – in which Maclaine and his British contemporaries conducted their business not only in the East but also in London. Although the Honourable Company lost its monopoly on trade to the Indian subcontinent in 1813 and subsequently experienced the 'privatisation' of its trade to China some two decades later, it remained a formidable presence, operating in a sometimes uneasy symbiosis with 'private' UK mercantile interests.

Inter alia, it was the invasion and conquest of Java by Company forces in 1811 that paved the way for Maclaine's subsequent career there, insofar as it opened up the island to a degree of British mercantile penetration that was not extinguished by the colony's return to Dutch control in 1816 (as part of a post-Napoleonic settlement in Europe designed to bolster the newly formed Kingdom of the Netherlands against any future expansionist designs on the part of the French). The subsequent foundation of Singapore (however 'unauthorised') by one of its representatives demonstrated clearly enough that the Company remained a significant presence in Maritime Southeast Asia long after its withdrawal from Java, and incidentally provided Maclaine with another theatre of commercial activity. Moreover, as we shall see, it was the Company's role as a major supplier of Indian-produced opium to the world market that had an important influence in Maclaine Watson's mercantile fortunes during the final decade of its founder's life.

Alongside and permeating this larger geopolitical framework of the

---

[5]   For a classic overview, see John Darwin, *The Empire Project. The Rise and Fall of the British World System* (Cambridge: Cambridge University Press, 2012).

Company's influence on Maclaine's mercantile trajectory, moreover, was an altogether more mundane but equally vital one. When, for example, Maclaine first sailed to the Indies in 1820, he did so on board a ship captained by a man who had formerly been in the Company's service, and observed that on board 'everything is carried on quite in the Company style. I am pretty certain that there is not a smarter private trader out of London.'[6] As we shall see, moreover, the senior partner in the house in which he served his 'apprenticeship' in London, far from coincidentally, was an individual who had cut his commercial teeth as a ships' surgeon in the Company's service, while Maclaine himself, returning in some haste to the UK as a sick man at the beginning of 1830, found a berth on one of the Company's ships en route from Canton to London. Once in London, furthermore, he found providential financial backing from a man who was also a Company stockholder.

For all that the multifaceted world of East India Company played an inescapable part in Maclaine's own history, however, the fact that he chose to establish himself outside its immediate realm was of critical importance. Arriving at Batavia in 1820, he found himself in a Dutch colony presided over by a Dutch Governor-General and by a potentially formidable Dutch colonial officialdom. Still only half-formed at this stage in its evolution, the nascent Indies bureaucracy was nonetheless the inheritor of a set of lordly political and social assumptions both from its monopolistic VOC predecessor and from the pre-colonial Javanese state that it was in the process of supplanting. It was also the inheritor, moreover, of nearly two centuries of Anglo-Dutch maritime rivalry on the High Seas that had several times erupted into war, the last as recent as 1780–84. Maclaine, in short, found himself in a potentially unfriendly environment: a stranger in 'some-one else's colony'.

Java's return to the Dutch in 1816 (along with most other Dutch possessions in maritime Southeast Asia) had seen the withdrawal from the island of EIC personnel, both military and civilian. Nonetheless, the Company retained a foothold at Bencoolen on the west coast of neighbouring Sumatra – and an imperial interest in the region as whole, not least because of its key position between India and China and because of the extent of British-Indian mercantile investment in maritime Southeast Asia itself. Bencoolen was a backwater, but in 1819 the Company's Governor there, Sir Stamford Raffles, who had been Lieutenant-Governor of Java under the British occupation, went on to found a new settlement at Singapore. Scarcely 900 kilometres to the north and better commercially positioned on Southeast Asia's major

6 GM to Marjorie Maclaine [hereafter MM] ('off Beachy Head'), 21.4.1820. Osborne-Maclaine MSS [hereafter O-M MSS], Gloucester Records, Gloucester, UK.

east–west sea-lane than was Batavia, it soon became a major entrepot for traders of all nationalities.

Moreover, while British officials and troops had left Java in 1816, a number of British trader and planters had stayed on. There can be little doubt that they formed the most dynamic European element in the commercial life of an island that was otherwise dominated by Indies (Indonesian)-Chinese, Arab and Armenian traders and capitalists. Their Dutch counterparts were both few in number and, for the most part, lacking in the requisite mercantile connections with Europe or Asian commercial centres.

The situation was potentially one, in short, in which the Dutch flag flew over a colony whose commercial sinews were in cosmopolitan, 'alien' hands. Antagonism on this score, with regard to 'foreign' Europeans at least, was by no means universal among Dutch officials, some of whom were distinctly Anglophile in their outlook. Even so, a series of incidents and developments during the 1820s suggested a degree of defensiveness on the part of the Dutch, who initially refused to recognise the legitimacy of the new settlement at Singapore and agitated for its abandonment in negotiations with the British government. The Batavia authorities' contemporaneous action against the spread of European plantation enterprise in South Central Java at around the same was partly justified in official circles in terms of the need to curb the foreign (i.e. British) presence in the island's interior. Most significant of all, however, in 1824 the Dutch home government was instrumental in establishing a trading company – the Netherlands Trading Association (Nederlandsche Handel-Maatschappij) or NHM – with the avowed purpose of preventing British domination of Java's overseas commerce, and conferred on it privileges that presaged, so it might appear, a revival of the monopolistic pretensions of the VOC.[7]

Nonetheless, in the same year, the Treaty of London, signed after much haggling between the Dutch and their British counterparts, promised an accommodation of sorts between British and Dutch interests in Asia. British claims on Bencoolen were abandoned, but in return the Dutch had to recognise Singapore – and, implicitly, accept British hegemony on the vital east side of the Malacca strait. On the European front, however, the

---

[7] Founded in 1824, the NHM became the biggest European business-house operating in the colony in the mid-nineteenth century and both the commercial agent of the Indies government and (until 1850) its bankers. As such, the company enjoyed what seemed, at times, the status of a quasi-governmental enterprise. By virtue of their political connections, as well as the large amount of capital at their disposal – nominally 34.5 million guilders, subscribed by mostly Dutch stockholders – and the wide scope of their business, it played a dominant role in the commercial life of the Indies (and a major role in the Netherlands itself). For an authoritative recent overview of the company's history, see De Graaf, *Voor Handel en Maatschappij*.

'Belgian' revolt against the Dutch crown at the end of the decade signalled the nineteenth-century nadir of Anglo-Dutch relations. For a variety of reasons, London took the side of the 'rebels' and it might even have come to war – but did not. Matters were not finally resolved, however, until 1839, when the Dutch finally resigned themselves to the independence of their erstwhile southern provinces and relations with the UK were normalised.

Even so, such tensions of empire as existed in Southeast Asia between the Dutch and the British were mitigated by a number of factors. There were significant synergies, and accommodation was as an important a theme as was (potential) conflict. Hostility to British commercial 'pretensions' in region, for example, did not stop the Indies government from embarking in the mid-1820s on a grand scheme for raising a massive loan in Calcutta designed to tide over the crisis-ridden Indies treasury and to be brokered by the great British-Indian merchant and financier John Palmer. The negotiations eventually proved abortive – though not before Palmer himself had paid a visit to Java and had no doubt wined and dined with Dutch officials as well as resident British merchants.[8] The Palmer Loans Affair remained, nonetheless, an indication of the mutualistic (as well as the sometimes conflicted) aspects of the Dutch and British imperial presence in Asia – as well as of the serious divisions over policy manifest in the inner councils of the Indies government and in relations between Batavia and The Hague.

Within a larger context, moreover, the Dutch had perforce to accept that British (and other foreign European) mercantile houses played a continuing and significant role in the import-export trade of the Indies. Subsequently, the Dutch also needed skilled British personnel to help ensure the successful industrialisation of the large-scale commodity production of sugar that was a key dimension of the mid-nineteenth century *Cultuurstelsel* or System of (State) Cultivations that was introduced in 1830 to stave off the colonial state's imminent bankruptcy.[9] It was no accident that even the NHM, the Dutch company founded in 1824 (as we have just seen) to bolster Dutch trade with the Indies and fight off British competition, found itself employing an

---

[8]   For authoritative analysis of the negotiations between John Palmer and the Indies government, see Nicholas Tarling, 'The Palmer Loans', *Bijdragen tot de Taal-, Land-en Volkenkunde*, 119 (1963), pp. 161–88.

[9]   See Ulbe Bosma, "Het Cultuurstelsel en Zijn Buitenlandse Ondernemers", *Tijdschrift voor Sociale en Economische Geschiedenis*, 2, 2 (2005), pp. 3–28. Bosma's argument – that 'a group of migrants of foreign [i.e. non-Dutch] origin played a crucial role in the functioning of the Cultivation System' and that 'the pioneers in both trade and plantation were emphatically a multi-national crowd' – is impressively underpinned by data from the colonial archives relating to European and Armenian immigration into the Indies during the first half of the nineteenth century. See also E.C.M. van Enk, 'Britse Koopleiden en de Cultuurs op Java. Harvey Thompson (1790–1837) en Zijn Financiers' (PhD dissertation, Vrije Universiteit, Amsterdam, 1999).

Englishman at the helm of the great industrially equipped sugar factory that it created in central Java in the 1850s as a model for the rest of the island's colonial sugar producers.[10] It is possible, of course, to overstate the degree of the accommodation between British interests and Dutch needs. Even so, there is a strong argument that Java from the 1820s through into the mid-century was a much more cosmopolitan colonial enterprise than has often been realised. It was one in which, as we shall see, Maclaine and his associates featured prominently.

Commodity Chains: Cotton, Coffee and Opium

The nexus between imperial history and the evolution of worldwide commodity chains that linked producers through international trade to markets and consumers is a central theme of Gillian Maclaine's story.[11] Insofar as they transcended empire and its confines, the commodity chains in which Maclaine and those like him were enmeshed were global rather than imperial in character. Of course, during the course of the nineteenth century commodity chains intersected with imperial concerns at virtually every juncture. Even so, though far from autonomous, such chains had complex dynamics that cannot be simply subsumed under the mantle of empire. In this context, Maclaine's activities illuminate what Jon Curry-Machado has recently remarked upon as a 'transnational, trans-imperial perspective' that extends beyond already widely recognised 'mutually reinforcing relationship between "commodities" and "empires"' to a consideration of 'how porous such geopolitical boundaries were when it came to the production and trade of global commodities'.[12] Inter alia, the history of the foundational years of Maclaine Watson alerts us to the constant interplay of tensions along commodity chains that were always 'works-in-progress' whose links, far from being permanently forged, were subject to disruption from a multiplicity of causes.

Essentially, there were three commodity chains in which Gillian Maclaine and his associates had a stake. The first involved them in the importation and

[10] G. Roger Knight, 'Technology, Technicians and Bourgeoisie: Thomas Jeoffries Edwards and the Industrial Project in Sugar in Mid-Nineteenth Century Java', pp. 31–52 in Ulbe Bosma, Juan Giusti-Cordero and G. Roger Knight (eds), *Sugarlandia Revisited: Sugar and Colonialism in Asia and the Americas, 1800 to 1940* (London and New York: Berghahn Publishers, 2007).

[11] See in particular, Jennifer Bair, 'Global Commodity Chains: Genealogy and Review', pp. 1–34 in Jennifer Bair (ed.), *Frontiers of Commodity Chain Research* (Stanford, CA: Stanford University Press, 2009).

[12] Jonathan Curry-Machado, 'Preface … and Introduction', pp. viii–ix, 5, in Curry-Machado (ed.), *Global Histories, Imperial Commodities, Local Interactions* (Basingstoke: Palgrave Macmillan, 2013).

distribution of cotton cloth for local manufacture into apparel, and the other two saw them engaged in the drug trade as dealers in caffeine (in the form of coffee beans) and opium. Of the three, it is cotton goods that stand out, not only because of the sheer ubiquity of the commodity but also because of the *extent* of the global reach of the chain in which it was bound up.

What took Maclaine from London to Java in 1820 was, quite literally, a shipload of cotton goods that most probably originated in the industrial mills of Glasgow, some hundred miles or more to the south of his own Highland birthplace. Yet, the raw material from which they were manufactured came from much further afield, primarily the Americas.[13] Likewise, Java was far from being the terminal point of the commodity chain in which Maclaine and his firm became enmeshed. As we shall see, a significant proportion of the cotton piece goods that Maclaine imported into Java were shipped from there throughout the 'Eastern Isles' of the Indonesian archipelago, while other shipments reached Manila in the Philippines and Canton in southern China. The trade was also opening up, moreover, in the form of shipments of British manufactured cottons that reached the new European outposts on the Australian landmass and in the adjoining Pacific.[14]

The crucial point about the cotton commodity chain, however, was that during Maclaine's own lifetime it was famously in the throes of a rapid and dramatic transformation that saw the Indian subcontinent, previously the world's largest producer-exporter of the commodity, turned into perhaps the world's single largest cotton goods *importer*. Driven above all by the continually falling price of slave-grown raw cotton from the Americas, seconded by technological advances, and buttressed by an imperial political economy of trade, the industrialised factories of Lancashire and Scotland (with some subsidiary developments in continental Europe) took over from Indian

---

[13] On Glasgow cotton goods manufacture, and the provenance of the industry's raw material, see Anthony Cooke, *The Rise and Fall of the Scottish Cotton Industry* (Manchester and New York: Manchester University Press, 2010). Cooke (pp. 45ff) remarks that late in the eighteenth century, 'The West Indies and South America dominated [raw] cotton imports into Scotland', but that thereafter slave-grown cotton from the southern United States played an increasingly important role. Indeed, by 1811 raw cotton from the United States accounted for 46 per cent of imports along the Clyde.

[14] Supplying the Australian market – possibly with 're-exported' cotton goods and most certainly with 'Asian' produce such as sugar and rice – was potentially lucrative business for 'Country Traders' (see below) operating out of Asian ports. In Maclaine's case, commercial ventures in the Australian colonies extended to the purchase of land for the purpose of producing commodities, viz. sheep's wool. At a slightly later date, operating out of Calcutta, Mackinnon and his associates (see below) were also keen to explore the Australian market; Mackinnon himself visited Australia, but got his fingers burnt when companies with which he was associated in Sydney and Melbourne collapsed. See Munro, *Maritime Enterprise and Empire*, pp. 26–28.

producers as the key manufacturing 'nodes' (to adopt the terminology of World Systems analysis – see below) of cotton's global commodity chain. The consequence of these several developments, as D.A. Farnie argued more than a quarter of a century ago, was that 'the traditional balance of the textile trade between East and West was decisively and apparently permanently overturned in favour of Europe'.[15]

If it was cotton that brought Maclaine to Java, however, it was coffee that kept him there, at a key nodal point of a commodity chain of considerable antiquity and significance.[16] Viewed as a chain, coffee was a good deal more rudimentary than cotton – indeed, in present-day thinking about commodity chains it might even be refused the designation altogether, insofar as it had (at this stage in its history) no core industrial node. Producers and traders on the periphery supplied the core with a product that needed virtually no further processing (beyond the artisan roasting and grinding of the beans – and even that might be dispensed with) before it reached consumers. The instant coffee industry and all it implied for the character of the global commodity chain in coffee was still on the distant horizon. Likewise in contrast to cotton, coffee was a chain whose production nodes – characterised virtually exclusively by low cost labour inputs, the absence of high technology and correspondingly relatively minimal requirements for capital – were worldwide in their location, while their prime distribution and consumption nodes were located in Western Europe and North America. Pushing this contrast yet further, during the opening decades of the nineteenth century, coffee remained essentially 'an urban luxury good'.[17]

Even so, the coffee commodity chain did parallel its cotton counterpart in one important respect. With the emergence of Brazil as the main source of world production, it too was undergoing a major transformation in the opening decades of the nineteenth century. Prior to that, the cultivation of the coffee bean had first spread from its African origins into Arabia and Asia.

---

[15] D.A Farnie, *The English Cotton Industry and the World Market 1815–1896* (Oxford: Clarendon Press, 1979), p. 96. Farnie's detailed analysis, on which I have drawn in this paragraph, appears on pp. 96–134.

[16] One of its leading historians writes of its 'five hundred year sweep of history' and argues that 'coffee differs from many other tropical commodities: it is a food whose variations in taste are valued; it is less perishable than many tropical fruits; it is a psychoactive drug because of caffeine; and it has enjoyed a long partnership with humans'. See Steven Topik, 'Historicizing Commodity Chains. Five Hundred Years of the Global Coffee Commodity Chain', pp. 37–51 in Bair, *Commodity Chain Research*. For a general overview, see Steven Topik and William Gervase Clarence-Smith, 'Introduction. Coffee and Global Development', pp. 1–17 in William Gervase Clarence Smith and Steven Topik (eds), *The Global Coffee Economy in Africa, Asia and Latin America, 1500–1989* (Cambridge: Cambridge University Press, 2003).

[17] Topik, 'Historicizing Commodity Chains', p. 43.

It now took pride of place in the Americas, and though coffee remained an essentially multi-sourced commodity chain to an extent that its cotton goods counterpart (for much of the nineteenth century) was not, the sheer quantity of American coffee coming onto the market – by 1850 Brazil accounted for over half the world's recorded output[18] – meant that production areas elsewhere lost any price-setting advantage that they had earlier enjoyed. Maclaine, as we shall see, was to discover this to his cost.

Opium was the basis of the third commodity chain in which Maclaine Watson (so it would appear, since the evidence is speculative) became enmeshed. This particular chain – one which appears to have originated in the second half of the eighteenth century – linked peasant poppy growers in India (and counterparts in Turkey) to opium importers and consumers thousands of miles by sea to the east where it financed European purchases of Chinese goods, tea above all. In this context, at the beginning of the 1840s, the trade became the occasion of the first 'Opium War' between the UK and Peking that signalled the beginning of a hundred years of British commercial hegemony on the 'China Coast'. Under East India Company rule in the subcontinent, opium was a state monopoly: Indian cultivators of poppy had to process their raw material into dry cakes before delivery to Company agents or contractors, prior to its public sale at Company auctions in Calcutta. From there, the bulk of it was exported eastward, much of it to Canton, by private merchants rather than by the Company itself, which needed the cash raised from its sale in China to pay for its purchases there, but also needed to circumvent the (formal) prohibition placed on the drugs import by the Chinese authorities.[19] Even so, China was by no means the sole destination for the increasing quantities of opium manufactured in the Indian subcontinent under the auspices of the EIC from the mid-eighteenth century onward. As the business historian Anthony Webster argues, Southeast Asia was also an important point of sale, and 'though smaller than the China market, the region's consumption of the drug was significant', especially insofar as it provided a 'secondary … market … when the Chinese market was depressed or an alternative route into [that] market at times of resistance to opium imports by the Chinese state'.[20]

The essential conduit of this opium commodity chain that led through the maritime Southeast Asia into southern China was the so-called 'Country

---

[18] Topik, 'Historicizing Commodity Chains', p. 46.

[19] For the convoluted history of the EIC's connection with the cultivation and sale of opium in the subcontinent c. 1750–1813, see H.R.C. Wright, *East Indian Economic Problems in the Age of Cornwallis and Raffles* (London: Luzac, 1961), pp. 106–65. For its export eastwards, see Michael Greenberg, *British Trade and the Opening of China, 1800–42* (Cambridge: Cambridge University Press, 1951 [1969]), pp. 104–23; Le Pichon, *China Trade and Empire*, pp. 16–20.

[20] Webster, *Gentlemen Capitalists*, p. 57.

Trade'. Essentially a network of intra-Asian commercial circuits, the Country Trade appears to have originated among South Asian merchants trading eastward across the Indian Ocean, and must have had antecedents dating back to the fifteenth century or earlier. From the late eighteenth century European trading houses began to participate in the trade on a considerable scale, when it became the conduit for carrying cotton goods (eventually British cotton goods) and – of course – opium from India eastwards. Southeast Asian goods themselves also played a considerable albeit unquantifiable part in the trade.[21] It was their rapidly expanding involvement in this trade that may well have accounted for much of Maclaine Watson's prosperity during the last decade of its founder's life. It not only brought prosperity, but also demonstrated – if such a demonstration is indeed necessary – the degree of interface between European and Asian commercial ventures. Inter alia, the involvement in the opium trade of European mercantile houses, Maclaine Watson among them, would have been impossible without it.

Commodity Chains, World Systems Analysis and Developments on the Asian 'Periphery'

Despite the obvious utility of employing the concept of commodity chains to illuminate the fortunes of the mercantile (and plantation) enterprises in which Gillian Maclaine was engaged during the 1820s and 1830s, some serious problems remain. They relate, in particular, to the potential for distortion of the evolving history of Maclaine Watson created by a propensity to link commodity chains to World Systems analysis in ways that fail to account for what we shall see to be the firm's relative autonomy and independence.

Commodity chains are frequently referenced to concepts of World Systems in which (metropolitan) core areas or states are conceived as subordinating (colonial) peripheries and as playing a vital role in the articulation of such Systems.[22] The dynamics of the articulating process remain, nonetheless,

---

[21] South East Asian goods – trepang, spices, bird's nests and sugar, etc. – also bulked large in the Country Trade to China. See, for example, James Warren, *The Sulu Zone 1768–1898: The Dynamics of External Trade, Slavery, and Ethnicity in the Transformation of a Southeast Asian Maritime State* (Singapore: Singapore University Press, 1981); Heather Sutherland, 'Trepang and Wangkang: the China Trade of Eighteenth Century Makassar c. 1720s–1840s', *Bijdragen tot de Taal-, Land- en Volkenkunde*, 156, 3 (2000), pp. 451–72.

[22] For Worlds Systems analysis, see Immanuel Wallerstein's own succinct summary of his celebrated thesis: *World-Systems Analysis: An Introduction* (Durham, NC: Duke University Press, 2000). On the nexus between Commodity Chains and World Systems, see Gary Gereffi, Miguel Korzeniewicz and Roberto D. Korzeniewicz, 'Introduction: Global Commodity Chains', pp. 1–14 in Gary Gereffi and Miguel Korzeniewicz (eds), *Commodity Chains and Global Capitalism* (Westport, CT: Praeger, 1994).

problematic to a degree, as does 'the dominant historiography of World Systems with its clear-cut division between centre, periphery and semi-periphery'.[23] Inter alia, the periphery appears to be a substantially more complex subject than World Systems analysis originally proposed. To be sure, that analysis is neither totally homogeneous nor invariably dogmatic in its assertions. Gereffi et al., for example, suggest that 'within a commodity chain a *relatively* greater share of wealth *generally* accrues to core-like nodes than to peripheral ones'[24] while Wallerstein himself notes that 'the bare-bones imagery [of core and periphery] is much too simple'.[25] Even so, it is the precisely those 'bare-bones' that have had such an impress on scholarly literature, and which need to be fleshed with something altogether more nuanced.

As has been observed of the situation in the Latin American 'periphery', for example, existing colonial merchant firms might survive the onslaught of metropolitan finance capital, inter alia, by seeking refuge in specialist commodity trades, where their local knowledge, special requirements of the commodity and existing investment in technology might provide a barrier against takeover.[26] Much the same might be said of Java where, for instance, a world-class sugar industry grew up in the middle decades of the nineteenth century largely devoid of metropolitan financial control, together with a European mercantile community largely devoid of metropolitan 'parents'.[27] Within this context, the case of Maclaine Watson demonstrates, inter alia, the contested nature of the metropolitan–colonial tie and in so doing, raises

[23] Claude Markovits, *The Global World of Indian Merchants, 1750–1947* (Cambridge: Cambridge University Press, 2000), p. 295. For further discussion on this score, see e.g., Andrew Porter, '"Gentlemanly Capitalism" and Empire: The British Experience since 1750?', *The Journal of Imperial and Commonwealth History*, 18, 3 (1990), p. 270: 'It may be felt that under the influence of Gallagher and Robinson imperial historians' explanations have generally over-emphasized or misinterpreted the importance of the "periphery", but it is unhelpful to respond with an unqualified retreat to the metropole. Indeed, the terms "metropole" and "periphery" begin to expose their limitations as soon as one asks "whose metropole?" The answer is often far from self-evident.'

[24] Gereffi et al., 'Introduction', p. 2 [emphasis added].

[25] Terence K. Hopkins and Immanuel Wallerstein, 'Commodity Chains: Construct and Research', pp. 17–20, in Gereffi and Korzeniewicz, *Commodity Chains*.

[26] C. Jones, 'British Imperialism and the Argentine, 1875–1900: A Theoretical Note', *Journal of Latin American Studies*, 12, 2 (1980), pp. 437–44.

[27] Ulbe Bosma, 'Sugar & Dynasty in Yogyakarta', pp. 73–94 in Bosma et al., *Sugarlandia Revisited*; Ulbe Bosma, 'Het Cultuurstelsel en zijn Buitenlandse Ondernemers. Java tussen Oud en Nieuw Kolonialisme', *Tijdschrift voor Sociale en Economische Geschiedenis*, 2, 2 (2005), pp. 3–28. G. Roger Knight, 'Descrying the Bourgeoisie: Sugar, Capital and the State in the Netherlands Indies, c. 1840–1884', *Bijdragen tot de Taal-, Land- en Volkenkunde*, 163, 1 (2007), pp. 52–83; G. Roger Knight, 'Rescued from the Myths of Time: Toward a Reappraisal of European Mercantile Houses in Mid-Nineteenth Century Java, c. 1830–1870', *Bijdragen tot de Taal-, Land- en Volkenkunde*, 170, 1 (2014), pp. 313–41.

questions about the explanatory value of 'World Systems' in general, suggesting that they fail to allow for the sheer diversity of global patterns of production and distribution, and for the power of agency on the (Asian) periphery.

Old Companies and New Firms: the Global Re-organisation of Trade, 1800–60

It is to developments on that periphery to which we can now turn. Obviously enough, commodity chains were articulated at critical junctures by mercantile activity in both metropole and colony. In this context, the complex currents that Maclaine had to negotiate as merchant (and planter) in a foreign empire had a further dimension that related to major structural changes in the global commercial–financial nexus between metropole and colony. Simply stated, in relation to European mercantile operations in Asia three things were happening. The first was the demise – in the case of the EIC very much drawn out in contrast to the sudden collapse of the VOC, its erstwhile Dutch counterpart – of the great European monopoly companies that had previously dominated the scene. The second was the centralisation of commercial and financial power and authority on the metropole: one writer, discussing primarily the Anglo-sphere, has described the phenomenon as the 'London-isation of commerce'.[28] The third point – and one very much concomitant with this latter development – concerns the undermining of the autonomy of those colonial mercantile firms that had emerged in the wake of the great companies, together with the subsequent subordination of colonial mercantile activity to the dictates of metropolitan 'parents'.

In relation to the first point – the demise of great Companies that had monopolised large swathes of the colonial trade to (and within) Asia for the previous two centuries – Webster has recently advanced the thesis that 'The Twilight of the East India Company' was a development characterised by the conflicted yet also often overlapping interests of 'private' mercantile capital and of the Company's directors. It was further complicated, moreover, in the case of the Indian subcontinent by the collapse in the 1830s of the substantially autonomous agency houses of Calcutta and elsewhere that had grown up in a degree of complementarity with the EIC from the late eighteenth century onward. Even so, the secular trend was toward the replacement of monopoly concerns in the mercantile sphere with the competing interests of a variety of 'private' operators.[29]

In the Dutch sphere, meanwhile, a parallel and significantly earlier development to the demise of the EIC had occurred with the bankruptcy of the

---

[28] C. Jones as quoted in Darwin, *Empire Project*, p. 63.
[29] Webster, *The Twilight*, passim.

VOC at the very end of the eighteenth century. There, too, and primarily on the key Indonesian island of Java, new firms grew up in the wake of the demise of a monopoly trading enterprise. Of course, there were differences. Nonetheless, there were also clear parallels. In post-VOC Java, new commercial houses emerged in the shadow of the pretensions to maintain some aspects of its monopoly by the colonial regime that supplanted it. Not for nothing did the newly founded NHM (see above) gain the appellation in the Indies of '*Compagnie Kejil*' or 'Little Company' in reference to its VOC predecessor, with all that implied about the potentially adverse nexus between it and the colony's 'private' traders. What made the situation altogether more volatile, moreover, was that – as we have already seen – many of these 'private' traders were British rather than Dutch. Among them was the firm of Maclaine Watson founded in 1827 but subsuming an earlier mercantile business, Gillian Maclaine and Co, founded in Batavia some five years earlier.

The second and third of these developments – the increasing, mid-nineteenth century domination by metropolitan interests and the concomitant undermining of colonial autonomy – can best be dealt with conjointly. Broadly speaking, the argument is that around the middle of the nineteenth century metropolitan commercial and financial capital began to exert a hitherto unprecedented degree of control over the global periphery. It did so, inter alia, because of the way in which such control, fuelled by economic growth in the core, was facilitated by developments in communications and transport. [30] In particular, the case has been made that the mid-century decades saw 'a revolution in the *organisation* of British firms in Asia, and the nature of British economic relations with Asia' predicated, inter alia, on the replacement of an earlier generation of quasi-autonomous European mercantile houses with a new breed of enterprise much more in thrall to metropolitan financial and commercial interests than had been the case with their immediate predecessors: 'while this curtailment of independence was not total, it did mean that the new firms had to be much more responsive to the needs of their London parents, who in many cases had supplied [their] capital ...'[31]

The point is well taken. Yet, it is not the whole picture, any more than the 'core' and 'periphery' binary upon which it appears to rest is a satisfactory way of analysing the world economy. In fact, in some parts of the world at least, local (colonial) interests demonstrated a greater degree of continuing autonomy – were more resilient, more resistant to metropolitan takeover – than is sometimes supposed. The Dutch colonial empire was a case in point, characterised it might be argued (as was also the case with its Spanish

[30] E.g. Darwin, *The Empire Project*, p. 63.
[31] Webster, *The Twilight*, pp. 10–14, 91–92.

contemporary) by a weak 'core' and a strong 'periphery' – and by colonial–
metropolitan ties the nature of which largely belied notions of peripheral
'subjugation'. Maclaine Watson, as will be argued, was a prime case in point.

Intra-Asian Commerce and the 'Country Trade'

That degree of autonomy leads, in turn, to the issue of the *Asian* context
of European businesses like Maclaine Watson, and to a concomitant focus
on intra-Asian commerce, rather than on that which was carried on bilat-
erally between Asia and Europe or North America. Autonomy, it may be
suggested, had as an important corollary that mercantile firms based in the
Asian colonial 'periphery' might be more open than offshoots of metropolitan
concerns to the advantages of integrating into Asian commercial circuits
rather than basing their activities primarily or exclusively on inter-continental
trade. This was certainly the case, as we shall see, with Maclaine Watson.

As Huw Bowen has recently reminded us, when European ships first
rounded the Cape in the sixteenth century they found themselves in 'a
trading world that was mature and sophisticated, with an interlocking series
of regional circuits that facilitated the movement of commodities, people and
information … thereby connecting far-flung littoral societies and economies'.[32]
The maritime 'Country Trade' that had developed eastward from the ports of
the Indian subcontinent from around the sixteenth century onward has long
been recognised as an important dimension of these circuits and, as Claude
Markovits has convincingly argued with relation to later developments, such

> Asian networks did not form a kind of global sub-formation within the
> European-dominated international economy of nineteenth and early twentieth
> century Asia. Actually, each network found a place in the global system through
> a complex and prolonged process to which collaboration and conflict were
> intertwined themes.[33]

The grand narrative predicated on reappraisals of this kind – namely that
'International [commercial/mercantile] contacts between Asian countries …
[are] fundamental to the understanding of the region's economic modernisation
…'[34] – is something that can only be touched on in the present context, yet is

[32] H.V. Bowen, 'Britain in the Indian Ocean Region and Beyond: Contours, Connections and
the Creation of a Global Maritime Empire', in Bowen et al., *Britain's Oceanic Empire*, p. 54.
[33] Markovits, *Indian Merchants*, p. 19.
[34] Kaoru Sugihara, 'An Introduction', pp. 1–20 in Sugihara (ed.), *Japan, China and the Growth of
the Asian International Economy, 1850–1949* (Oxford: Oxford University Press, 2005). See also
Sugiyama and Grove, 'Introduction', pp. 1–14 in Sugiyama and Grove, *Commercial Networks*;

not irrelevant to an evaluation of the history of Maclaine Watson. Specifically, during the final years of its founder's life, the firm was engaged in the Country Trade to an extent that presaged its later evolution into a network of Asia-based mercantile concerns that, from the late nineteenth century onward, were founded, first and foremost, in intra-Asian trade. In short, and in however tentative fashion, the history of Maclaine Watson needs to be understood in terms not only of Maclaine's own long association with the UK (and Europe) but also in terms of his firm's positioning in a burgeoning world of Asian commerce.

A Mercantile Network of Family Firms

The more immediate point, however, concerns the structural characteristics of the mercantile business that Maclaine founded in 1827 with the establishment first of Maclaine Watson itself and subsequently of associated companies in Java itself and in Singapore. Some of the key points at issue are discussed succinctly in Forbes Munro's monumental work on *Maritime Enterprise and Empire* in the context of the Mackinnon mercantile enterprise, another chronologically somewhat later business with roots in a similar ethnic background to that in which the Maclaine concern was embedded. Inter alia, some of the key traits that Munro identifies include the absence of a 'parent' company; the 'compensating' existence of a cluster of firms in the hands of inter-related families or of more distant 'clan' members; and the defining presence of 'networks of corporate organisations as alternatives to the managerialist, hierarchical structure of big business'.[35]

Of course, the Mackinnon enterprise operated on a vastly grander scale in three or even four continents and under a chief whose business and political clout was of a totally different order to anything that Gillian Maclaine and his successors ever aspired to. Nonetheless, there are significant, albeit much humbler, parallels, since the essential point about Maclaine's own mercantile enterprises was that they evolved, from the 1820s onward, into a network of Asia-based mercantile concerns, rather than a single, hierarchically organised enterprise. Held together by the ties of consanguinity and by wider ethnic loyalties, the network was essentially made up of family firms, even though the families involved were not those of its founders, and included Dutchmen and Englishmen as well as the

Linda Grove and Mark Selden, 'Editors' Introduction: New Perspectives on China, East Asia and the Global Economy', pp. 1–11 in Takeshi Hamashita (edited Linda Grove and Mark Selden), *China, East Asia and the Global Economy* (London and New York: Routledge, 2008).

35 Munro, *Maritime Enterprise and Empire*, pp. 4–5 and 88–90.

inevitable Scots.[36] It formed, in short, an outstanding example of the extent to which (as business historian Geoffrey Jones has argued) 'families could be as successful as managers in owning and managing business concerns .... Socialization and strong corporate cultures could be as effective as hierarchy as a means of control of employees.'[37] The character of that 'corporate culture' is something to which we can now turn.

Calling Scotland 'Home': Diasporic Culture and the 'Scots in the East'

The importance of the role played by ethnic Scots is common currency in the history of the making of the *British* Empire. Munro, for example, writing about Mackinnon and his business ventures, noted the presence of primordial loyalties predicated on something more than simple consanguinity, and referred in telling fashion to a new '… enterprise network drawing deeply on an older sub-soil of Highland history and values'.[38] Expressed rather differently, 'the Scottish blend of commerce, shipping and Presbyterianism with either local capital or reinvestment of overseas financial returns was a powerful one'.[39]

Specific attention to 'the Scots in the East' has not been absent from discussion, ranging from accounts of the 'Shanghailanders' of the China coast[40] through to their counterparts in the Indian subcontinent.[41] In relation to the Scots in Java and elsewhere in the erstwhile Netherlands Indies, however, the pickings are very much slimmer. Obviously, the Scots' presence in a Dutch colony was likely to have been less pervasive than within the British Empire. It was also more likely, however, to have engendered a greater than usual sense of group solidarity. Moreover, during the twenty years that Maclaine was in Java (things almost certainly began to change around the mid-century) members of the Scots diaspora played a role in the commercial life of the Indies totally disproportionate to their small numbers.

[36] Crickhowell, *Rivers Join*, pp. 131–34.
[37] Geoffrey Jones, 'Alfred Chandler and the Importance of Organization', *Enterprise and Society*, 9, 3 (2008), pp. 419–21. Jones's broader argument is that, contrary to notions of the key role of the 'Visible Hand' of a hierarchical, impersonal management in successful business, that there was 'not "one best way" and no linear progression in organizational forms in business organization'.
[38] Munro, *Maritime Enterprise and Empire*, pp. 5–6.
[39] Porter, '"Gentlemanly Capitalism" and Empire', p. 277.
[40] E.g. Robert Bickers, 'Shanghailanders: The Formation and Identity of the British Settler Community in Shanghai 1843–1937', *Past and Present*, 159 (1998), pp. 161–211 (Bickers's analysis is by no means confined, however, to the Scots members of that community).
[41] E.g. James G. Parker, 'Scottish Enterprise in India, 1750–1914', pp. 191–219 in R.A. Cage (ed.), *The Scots Abroad* (London: Croom Helm, 1985), pp. 250–70; Phillip Constable, 'Scottish Missionaries, "Protestant Hinduism" and the Scottish Sense of Empire in Nineteenth and Early Twentieth Century India', *The Scottish Historical Review*, 86, 2 (2007), pp. 278–313.

Historically, of course (in the European and Middle Eastern context), the three great 'classical' diasporas have been those associated with Greeks, Jews and Armenians. Indeed, it has been argued that a rigorous definition of 'diaspora traders' refers to a 'distinct category ... engaged in international business ... based on trading companies [that] developed into networks of ethnic-religious groups that formed their own "unofficial" international market, [hence] enabling them to operate independently of the countries or states in which they were established'.[42] Development of any comparable trajectory for the 'Scots abroad' is complicated by their location – some might say privileged location – within the imperial complex of the nineteenth century's largest global superpower. To say the least, such people were not 'outsiders' to systems of power or faced with hegemonic commercial relations that somehow needed to be subverted or bypassed. The 'victim' status commonly attributed to the human objects of the Highland Clearances sits uneasily with the likes of McKinnon and Maclaine. To be sure, as Tom Devine has recently argued, the 'original etymological origins of the word ... [imply] a process of human dispersal that can be voluntary and opportunistic rather than necessarily governed by implacable expulsive forces'.[43] Even so, problems remain, not the least of them being that the Scots diaspora was far from being a unitary phenomenon. The gentry class origins of most of the people who constituted this particular group of 'Scots in the East' helped ensure that most of them remained in Asia for a limited period of time before returning home. Should this (as has been argued in another context) cast doubt on the 'legitimacy of the use of the category "diaspora" which involves a long-term separation from an imaginary or real homeland and is not really compatible with the phenomenon of transiency or sojourning'?[44]

Be that as it may, the importance, and distinguishing character, of ethnic-religious solidarity was high among the characteristics of the fellow countrymen with whom Gillian Maclaine associated in both London and Java. A crucial factor was their shared Calvinism (and these were the days before the Great Schism of 1843 rent the Scottish church). Maclaine himself, for instance, reported to his mother on his initial surprise at finding candles burning in the Dutch Reformed Church that he attended in Batavia (a

---

[42] Gelina Harlaftis, 'From Diaspora Traders to Shipping Tycoons: The Vagliano Bros', *Business History Review*, 81, 2 (Summer 2007), pp. 237–68. Quoting Geoffrey Jones (The *Evolution of International Business. An Introduction*, London: Routledge, 1995, p. 164), Professor Harlaftis argues, inter alia, that such companies facilitated international trade flows 'because they reduced search, negotiation and transaction costs in unfamiliar and risky environments'. See further McCabe et al., *Diaspora Entrepreneurial Networks*, passim.

[43] Tom M. Devine, *To the Ends of the Earth. Scotland's Global Diaspora, 1750–2010* (London: Allen Lane/Penguin Books, 2011), p. xiv.

[44] Markovits, *Indian Merchants*, pp. 4–5.

'Rome-ish' practice necessitated by the fact that services had to be held after dark, on account of the daytime heat).[45] More profoundly, proper religious observance was of keen interest in his correspondence with her, and we find him reassuring her that, except when business was unavoidably pressing, he kept the Sabbath free from mundane concerns. Moreover, he also reported that he had admonished the womenfolk of the Calvinist Dutch family into which he subsequently married for bringing their embroidery to the religious services held on board the ship taking them all to the Indies in 1832. Nonetheless, he was prepared to accept – contrary to usage in his part of the Highlands – that the piano might be open on Sundays.[46]

The Scots community in Batavia at the time of Maclaine's domicile there may not have had the formal sinews of church attendance – there was only what Maclaine termed 'an English chapel' and he evidently preferred going to the Dutch Calvinist Church. In short, the city's Scots community lacked the institutionalised religious observance that characterised its much larger counterpart in contemporary Calcutta, where the Scots Kirk had its own Minister.[47] Nonetheless, religious observance was and remained an important facet of diaspora identity. 'Piety', as Munro remarked in the case of Mackinnon, '… strengthened the bonds of trust based on kinship'.[48] Meanwhile, men – and it was only men whom he encountered in this context – were appraised in terms of their Highland countenances, handshakes and manners. In tandem, he evinced an honest delight in being able to communicate in Gaelic, a language that he had been at pains to acquire (ethnic credentials always being a work in progress) during his youth.[49]

In relation to doing business, however, as was famously the case with other diaspora communities, the fundamental aspect of this ethnic solidarity related to matters of trust. Ties of kith and kin combined with a wider sense of shared ethnicity to create, in Harlaftis's formulation, a 'framework that minimizes entrepreneurial risk and provides information flow [and allows] the establishment of transnational connections based on personal relations'.[50] As Maclaine was to discover, however, trust based on ethnic-religious solidarity

[45] GM to MM Batavia 28.12.1834. Greenfield MSS.

[46] Gillian Maclaine, 'Journal of a Voyage from Rotterdam to Batavia in 1832', entry for 24th April 1832, O-M MSS.

[47] Munro, *Maritime Enterprise*, p. 23.

[48] Munro, *Maritime Enterprise*, p. 33.

[49] Even before going to Java, moreover, he had admonished his brother (then a student in Glasgow) to work hard at his Gaelic: 'Unless you pay it considerable attention, you certainly cannot expect to write the language with any facility, much less to speak it fluently', GM to MM (with Postscript to AM) 15.6.1819 O-M MSS.

[50] See Harlaftis, 'Diaspora Trading Groups', pp. 240–41 for a succinct and richly referenced discussion on this score.

was not immune from the pitfalls inherent in the business in which he was engaged. Indeed, a misplaced trust in fellow Scots from his own part of the Highlands – family friends of his uncle – was nearly to ruin him. As we shall see, moreover, despite its ostensibly 'Scots' character, for critical periods in its mid- and late nineteenth-century history Maclaine Watson was by no means a concern run exclusively by people of Scottish ancestry. Even so, the milieu in which the young Gillian Maclaine grew up, and in which he served his apprenticeship before sailing to Java in 1820, was undoubtedly profoundly Scottish.

Two

MACLAINE'S 'APPRENTICESHIP': THE CITY OF LONDON AND THE COTTON TRADE WITH ASIA, 1816–20

> I am happy to inform you that I am daily growing fonder of the mercantile profession. It suits my inclinations more than any line of life I can think of. I find myself now considerably more interested in the Business as I commence to understand it a little better.[1]

By 1816 Gillian Maclaine, the man who went on to found Maclaine Watson, was in his eighteenth year. The elder child of an impoverished Highland laird, Allan Maclaine of Scallastle, he faced a common enough problem among those of his kind. The island of Mull, where his father had inherited a problematic claim to a small estate, together with the peninsula of Morvern on the adjacent mainland, was an economy and society in transition. Large-scale sheep farming was replacing crofter-rents and military service as the basis for the tenuous prosperity of the island's small gentry elite.[2] This posed problems for young men like Maclaine. Several of his paternal uncles had served in the British army, and a well-deserved reputation for military valour, in tandem with a presumably suitably dashing manner in Regency London, had brought two of them the prize of a rich wife. But the war with Napoleon was over and for the younger generation there were no similar opportunities. In this sense, and disregarding personal proclivities, it was no accident that Maclaine's only sibling went into the Church and that his foremost cousin, Donald Maclaine of Lochbuie, followed him into business. Nor did Maclaine's own immediate family circumstances make his prospects any more promising.[3]

---

[1] GM to JG 3.5.1817 O-M MSS.

[2] For Mull in general, see Jo Currie's indispensible *Mull. The Island and Its People* (Edinburgh: Birlinn, 2000).

[3] Currie, *Mull*, pp. 387–88, 424 and the many further references therein. In what follows, I have drawn gratefully on Dr Currie's generously shared knowledge of Gillian Maclaine and his family.

His father had been declared insane in 1800, two years after Gillian's birth and was to spend the remainder of his long life (he died in 1842) in an asylum near Edinburgh. In his absence, Gillian and his brother Angus were brought up by their mother, Marjory Gregorson and her as yet unmarried brother, John Gregorson of Ardtornish.[4] John Gregorson was a man of some substance, like his father before him *taksman* or bailiff and rent-collector for the Duke of Argyll in this part of the western Highlands. In 1819, when the famously profligate duke – his gambling debts were legendary – had to sell off large parts of his huge holdings in Scotland, Gregorson was able to raise enough money to buy Ardtornish House, the twenty-room mansion on Morvern in which he and his family lived, together with a large tract of land in the neighbouring coastal uplands. He became, in effect, a substantial sheep farmer.

This did not mean, however, that he was a rich man with capital to invest. Indeed, quite the contrary, since it looks as if sheep farming did not pay as well as he had hoped. Throughout the 1820s, he was obliged to borrow money on the security of his lands; in 1830, his properties were put into trust (though he continued to administer them); and around 1840 he experienced a major financial crisis that resulted in the sale of Ardtornish and his family's departure from Morvern to Tobermory on the north-east coast of Mull. In the circumstances, even at the time of his greatest apparent prosperity in the second decade of the century, his sister's two sons were clearly expected to make their own way in the world.

Nonetheless, Gregorson was able to help, through his connection with the McLachlans of Glensanda, whose property bordered on his own in the southern part of Morvern. Members of the McLachlan family were frequent visitors to John Gregorson at Ardtornish and were also evidently on intimate terms with Marjory Maclaine, Gregorson's sister and Gillian's mother. It was entirely characteristic that when Maclaine first wrote home from London, the McLachlan partners sent 'their kindest respects to all at Ardtornish'.[5] Indeed, the connection was close and convivial enough for Gillian, subsequently in Java, to have repeatedly to caution his mother to be more discreet in what was said over the dinner table about his business affairs.[6] In the

4   For Gregorson in this and the following paragraph, see in particular Philip Gaskell, *Morvern Transformed. A Highland Parish in the Nineteenth Century* (Cambridge: Cambridge University Press, 1980), pp. 28–29 and the subsequent references therein. See also: Norman MacLeod (edited Iain Thornber), *Morvern. A Highland Parish* (Edinburgh: Birlinn, 2002).

5   See GM to MM 28.12.1816. O-M MSS.

6   E.g. GM to MM Batavia 6.10.1826. O-M MSS: '... I earnestly beg you to keep my communications on these topics secret. What Mr. J. McLachlan Glensander heard at Ardtornish about our business concerns here gave rise to a disagreeable correspondence ... An occasion of this kind will not, I am satisfied, take place again ....'

meantime, however, the connection had provided an opening that he would not otherwise have had.

Like John Gregorson, Ewan McLachlan of Glensanda was a *taksman* for the Duke of Argyll, but several of his sons were involved in trade. Indeed, during the second decade of the nineteenth century, the brothers Patrick, Duncan and Hugh McLachlan – subsequently joined by John McLachlan – had established an 'East India House' in London, trading with the subcontinent in a variety of commodities, but primarily in cotton piece goods. It was with them that Gregorson sought an opening for Maclaine, then a student in Glasgow. Aware of his neighbour's growing business in the East, he evidently prevailed upon them to take his promising but penniless young nephew into their London office.

The McLachlan Brothers and their East India Business

The McLachlan brothers' establishment may not have been among the largest of its kind in the City but, as we shall see, it was certainly well connected in 'East India' circles there. Patrick McLachlan – he was evidently known to his familiars as Peter – was reputed to be the smartest and most urbane of the brothers, and very much the senior partner. Leastways, the eighteen-year-old Maclaine, who evidently stood in some awe of him, thought him so:

> I am not surprised that Mr. Peter should so completely command or rather sway his brothers, for he is infinitely their superior in every respect. In point of information and polished manners I cannot think of a comparison and I rather suspect he has more liberality of sentiment than the three of them put together.[7]

Patrick McLachlan's mercantile career had started when he was employed as a surgeon on East India Company ships, something that would have given him the chance to try his hand in trade, since – like the ships' officers – he was entitled to a certain, limited amount of cargo space whenever and wherever his ship sailed. William Jardine, the prominent opium smuggler and co-founder in the late 1820s of the great China Coast firm of Jardine Matheson, came from a similar background.[8] Like Jardine, Patrick McLachlan would have cut

---

7   GM to JG 22.12.1818. O-M MSS.
8   See Le Pichon, *China Trade and Empire*, pp. 21–22. As Le Pichon explains, the position as an officer on EIC ships brought with it the allocation of cargo space, dependent on rank. Like Jardine, Patrick McLachlan would hence have cut his teeth as a trader by dealing in small amounts of 'Eastern' produce brought back to the UK during his employment as a ship's surgeon. For Jardine Matheson in particular, see Richard J. Grace, *Opium and Empire* (Montreal and Kingston: McGill-Queen's University Press, 2014), pp. 78–160.

his teeth as a trader by dealing in small amounts of 'eastern' produce brought back to the UK during his period of Company employment. Also like Jardine, McLachlan travelled not only to the subcontinent, but also to China, having last been in Canton in 1805. He appears to have left the Company's employ some time after that; to have remained in India for a few years; and to have returned to the UK by 1811 with significant if not considerable commercial experience – and presumably a certain amount of capital.[9]

In consequence, in 1813, when the Company lost its monopoly on trade to and from India, he was well positioned to set up in business in London, in partnership with his brothers. As we shall see, he was also closely connected with a fellow Scot, Donald MacIntyre, who had commenced in business in the subcontinent as early as 1810. His Calcutta firm, MacIntyre & Co., was to figure prominently in the McLachlans' business affairs. From Maclaine's perspective, nonetheless, it was Patrick McLachlan who was the lynchpin of the entire enterprise. The nineteen-year-old admired him as a 'man of an excellent address' and reported to his mother (who had evidently give him a character sketch of his future employer before he left the Highlands) that McLachlan was indeed 'very clear-headed [and] of an orderly economical disposition', though he also thought he noted 'rather a mean artifice observable in every of his actions which does not at all correspond with his pious and sanctified appearance'.[10] Even so, 'Mr. Patrick certainly improves on acquaintance', he observed to his mother in May 1818, when he had been in the counting house for some eighteen months, 'and I often regret I have not more of his society. His abilities as a man of business are really astonishing. To his exertions the concern owes almost all its prosperity. At home and abroad he is the projector of most of their speculations.'[11]

Primarily, the 'speculations' to which Maclaine alluded were in the export of British cotton manufactures to the subcontinent and points further east. The years immediately following the end of the Napoleonic Wars were a boom time for London's East India merchants, particularly those engaged in the cotton goods trade. Between 1814 and 1820 British exports of cotton

---

[9]   For information about the McLachlan family of Glensanda – and for much else to do with Morvern – I am deeply indebted to Mr Iain Thornber of Lochaline, on whose unrivalled knowledge of the area's history I have drawn at a number of points in my discussion of McLachlan and his family background. On Patrick (aka Peter) McLachlan's career up to 1820, see: Select Committee of the House of Commons on the means of improving and maintaining Foreign Trade – East Indies and China, *Parliamentary Papers GB* 1821, vol. VI, 'Evidence of Patrick McLachlan', pp. 277–78 (hereafter cited as: 'McLachlan Evidence 1821').

[10]   GM to MM 24.3.1817. O-M MSS.

[11]   GM to MM 11.5.1818. O-M MSS (emphasis in original).

'piece goods' as they were termed increased from 800,000 to fourteen millions yards.[12] It was a development from which the McLachlan brothers, together with MacIntyre, sought to extract maximum advantage. Contingent on the radical transformation of the global commodity chain in cotton goods that took place (as we saw in the previous chapter) in the opening decades of the nineteenth century, the unprecedented flood of Western, pre-eminently British, manufactures onto Asian markets offered apparently limitless opportunities for businesses as well placed as theirs.

A Gentleman Capitalist in the Making: Patrick McLachlan and his Kind

From a base among the impoverished Highland gentry, Patrick McLachlan had successfully inserted himself into the gentlemanly capitalist world of City commerce, where, by the time that Maclaine got to know him, he was evidently well-established in East India mercantile circles. Like many in those circles, he not only involved in trade to 'the East' but also had become (it is uncertain quite how) the owner of a small sugar plantation in Jamaica which, along with his library, he bequeathed his only son, Alexander McLachlan, together with its 'slaves, cattle and stock …'.[13]

That son, meanwhile, as befitted a gentleman-in-the-making, had been sent first to Oxford,[14] and then had a commission bought for him in the Dragoons.[15] Nor was McLachlan's sole daughter neglected: 'an uncommonly clever, smart <u>lassy</u>', according to Maclaine, she was placed in an (unnamed) boarding school where she learnt to speak 'French as fluently as English …'[16] Much in line with this striving for status, McLachlan and his wife, Mary McLachlan – Maclaine admired the latter's facility on the piano

---

[12] Le Pichon, *China Trade & Empire*, p. 8.

[13] The will of *Alexander* McLachlan (made in the wake of Patrick McLachan's sudden death in 1824) includes: 'I bequeath to my sister Elizabeth Ridell McLachlan … also my Estate in Jamaica with the Slaves, Cattle, Stock, Improvements and Personal Effects thereon ….', National Archives UK, Kew, Probate 11/1687. How the elder McLachlan had come by his 'Estate' is at present uncertain; possibly through his wife, Mary, or possibly through his dealings with Colin Campbell (see text below). In 1836 Alexander McLachlan received compensation of £53 4s 5d for two slaves on St George 408, Jamaica. See www.ucl.ac.uk/lbs/search/McLachlan (accessed 31/5/14).

[14] GM to MM 8.1.1818 & GM to MM 15.7.1817. O-M MSS.

[15] GM to MM (fragment) 13.4.1819. O-M MSS. As of July 1820, Alexander McLachlan was a Cornet in the 3rd (or King's Own) Regiment of (Light) Dragoons. See *A List of the Officers of the Army and of the Corps of Royal Marines*, Great Britain, War Office at http://babel.hathitrust.org/cgi/pt?id=uc1.b2991585;view=1up;seq=4 (accessed 10/12/2014).

[16] GM to MM 19.8.1817. O-M MSS; GM to MM (fragment) 13.4.1819. O-M MSS (emphasis in original).

and her beautiful singing[17] – spent their vacations, sometimes together with their children, at fashionable Cheltenham Spa and Brighton.[18] Moreover, the family had taken up residence in a sought-after and salubrious part of outer London, a carriage ride away from the noise and stench of the City itself.

Stamford Hill, where Patrick McLachlan lived by the time that Maclaine got to know him, was more than simply salubrious, however. On the north-eastern outskirts of London, it was a neighbourhood where many wealthy merchants and bankers had their 'country' houses, among them no less a figure than Nathan Rothschild, the 'dominant presence' in the City for at least two decades prior to his death in 1836.[19] Did he ever call on the McLachlans? Most certainly, he knew one of their close acquaintances, the City businessman and financier Archibald Campbell (see below), well enough to set up a fund for his widow.[20] What is sure is that McLachlan's Stamford Hill house was the setting, as Maclaine – himself a frequent visitor – observed, for many 'select parties'. Among the regular invitees were old East India hands, one of whom, the young man reported, 'as far as I can judge, I think him the best informed man I ever saw'.[21]

By the 1820s, as was revealed by bankruptcy proceedings involving his surviving brothers at the beginning of the following decade,[22] Patrick McLachlan's City associates included the major East India houses of Palmer

---

17 GM to MM (fragment) 3.10.1817. O-M MSS.

18 E.g. GM to MM 15.7.1817. O-M MSS.

19 See David Kynaston, *The City of London. Volume 1. A World of its Own, 1815–1890* (London: Pimlico/Random House, 1995), pp. 53–55: 'but one man dominated the City in the early 1820s …. Rothschild had his country residence in Stamford Hill.' Nathan Rothschild lived there 1818–1835. It was at that time a very fashionable area. See Wikipedia, http://en.wikipedia.org/wiki/Stamford_Hill (accessed 10/12/2014).

20 Archibald Campbell apparently committed suicide after business failure in 1831 ('I fear his ways were crooked', Maclaine informed his uncle). It was reported that the great Jewish financier had 'raised a subscription for [his widow and children] lately in the City of 600 pounds & is most attached to them'. GM to JG, London, 8.2.1831. Greenfield MSS.

21 GM to MM 2.12.1817. O-M MSS.

22 Files of the Office of the Commissioners of Bankrupts and Court of Bankruptcy, National Archives UK, Kew, B3/3613. Papers relating to the bankruptcy of John McLachlan and Donald MacIntyre, Sun Court, Cornhill, London, merchants, bankrupts. 1831 (hereafter McLachlan/MacIntyre Bankruptcy 1831 B3/3613). See among the mass of documentation, 'Lett D. Debts due by the Bankrupt': Creditors of the Old Concern (ending 30 June 1825) were: Glyn Halifax (£1,594); Catherine McLachlan, Glensander (£302); Colin Campbell (£3,229); Murdoch Mackenzie, Stornaway – a partner in Bazett, Colvin Crawford & Co. – (£1,188); Palmers Mackillop (£6,155); McLachlan MacIntyre Concern 1826 (£7,329); McLachlan MacIntyre Concern 1829 (£1,756); and Estate of P. McLachlan – 'disputed' (£5,422). In total the debts of the Old Concern ending 30 June 1825 amounted to over £26,980.

Mackillop & Co.[23] and Bazett, Colvin Crawfurd & Co.[24] Nevertheless, it was the firm of Colin Campbell & Co. with whom the Messrs McLachlan appear to have been most closely and most enduringly connected. Though engaged in the East India business, the operations of this prominent London and Glasgow commercial enterprise were far from confined to Asia: indeed Colin Campbell and his partners – at one time or other they included Wilkinson Dent, William and James Macpherson, John Anderson and Archibald Campbell – had plantation interests in the West Indies and did business in both Rotterdam and Antwerp as well as in the UK.[25] Patrick McLachlan and his brothers, together with their associate Donald MacIntyre, likewise had continental European connections. Indeed, MacIntyre was in Hamburg (having previously been in Leipzig) drumming up business when news reached him of Patrick McLachlan's sudden death in 1825,[26] and the London partners evidently had ongoing mercantile connections in Elberfeld-Wuppertal as well as in Leipzig itself.[27]

Meanwhile, at least two of the Campbell partners were in business with the McLachlan brothers and Donald MacIntyre during the 1820s and, most probably, in the previous decade as well. One of them was William McPherson,[28] a man whose commercial interests had at one time taken him

---

[23] The chief partners were James Mackillop, the brothers John Horsley Palmer, a director of the Bank of England, and George Palmer, later Member for Essex South. The firm's Calcutta agency, which in 1831 was being run by Cullen, Thomas Hutton and Robert Browne, was the last of the major houses to fail, going under in January 1834. The London firm was styled Palmers, Mackillop, Dent and Company by 1838, and remained as such until the early 1860s, when it became Dent, Palmer and Company. Like Patrick McLachlan (and Colin Campbell), Mackillop was a plantation owner/financier in Jamaica in addition to his mercantile interests in India. See D.R. Fisher (ed.), *The History of Parliament: the House of Commons 1820–1832* (Cambridge, Cambridge University Press, 2009) under 'James Mackillop'.

[24] The firm was located in Old Broad Street, City of London, and its partners in 1833 were Richard Campbell Bazett, Murdoch Mackenzie (Stornaway), William Crawfurd, James Gathorne Remington and James Colvin.

[25] See http://www.ucl.ac.uk/lbs/person/view/45375 (accessed 30/8/2013).

[26] Donald MacIntyre to MM, London 25.6.1825. O-M MSS.

[27] Andrew Thompson or Tomsen of Elberfeld was among the mid-1820s creditors of McLachlan and MacIntyre, as were the Leipzig merchants C.F. Kretschmann and J.A. Schonkopff. See McLachlan/MacIntyre Bankruptcy 1831 B3/3613 'Lett D: Debts of the Bankrupt'.

[28] William McPherson appears in the McLachlan/MacIntyre bankruptcy documentation as their 'late partner' and specifically as a partner in the 1826 'Concern' with the two men. Together with his brother James McPherson, he was also identified in 1834 in the bankruptcy documentation as a 'late partner' in Colin Campbell and Co. See McLachlan/MacIntyre Bankruptcy1831 B3/3613. For Gillian Maclaine's visit to James McPherson in Rotterdam in 1831, the significance of which was that it provided further evidence of the longstanding connection between the McPhersons and Maclaine's erstwhile London business partners, see Chapter 4.

as far afield as Sydney (and whose brother and young family were to perish in the South China Sea in 1839), while the other was the high-living Archibald Campbell. The parties that Campbell gave at his mansion at Harrow-on-the-Hill (north-west of London) impressed the nineteen-year-old Maclaine not only with the company but also with the music performed by the most celebrated group of Scots musicians of the day, and the flattering attention that his host paid him:

> I was lately at a very grand dance at Harrow, much grander really than I had any idea Mr. Campbell would have given. The company assembled about nine o'clock in the evening and danced still about four in the morning. There was a very elegant supper – an abundance of Hock and Champagne. Gow and his band attended and gave the most exquisite music. I went up in a post-chaise … Immediately on arrival, after paying my respects to Mrs. Campbell, worthy Mr. Campbell asked me to dance a Highland reel with him, the only one he danced that evening.[29]

Maclaine's host on this occasion obviously did not believe in doing things by halves: 'Gow's celebrated band' entertained the King himself on a visit to Edinburgh in 1822,[30] and there is some indication that this was not the only one of Campbell's excesses that evening. In any case, a few days later Maclaine was reporting to his relatives at Ardtornish that 'Poor Mr. Campbell has been complaining ever since the dance at Harrow. I trust he will soon get better. Mrs. Campbell is now perfectly recovered.'[31]

Campbell was evidently not only familiar with the clan Maclaine but also well known to John Gregorson and his family, and a frequent caller at the McLachlan's City office: 'Mr. A. Campbell called today', Maclaine reported to his uncle in May 1819, 'He looks extremely well. I told him you were astonished at his never writing. He merely shook his head and made no reply as if ashamed of himself.'[32] Two years earlier and still very much a newcomer to the City, Maclaine had ventured a character sketch. Although he had not

---

[29] 'The reel was actually Mrs Macleod Rasay. I tripped it away – I thought I was in the Highlands again. You will be astonished to know that there were seven Maclaines there [he means extended family/clan members] Sir J. McLean, General Fitz R. McLean's son, Allen Pennicross and his uncle Torren etc etc.' GM to MM (fragment 3.10.1817). O-M MSS.

[30] E.A. Smith, *George IV* (New Haven, CT and London: Yale University Press, 1999), p. 202.

[31] GM to JG 4.10.1817. O-M MSS.

[32] GM to JG 26.5.1819. John Gregorson's mother was Elizabeth Campbell of Achnaba (d. 1819), wife of Angus Gregorson of Ardtornish (d. 1811); his great-grandmother (d. 1780) was Marjory Gregorson, daughter of Alexander Campbell of Airds; and his wife's mother was Jane Campbell of Airds. See 'Lismore Parish Church. External burial-aisle at the East End of the church. Gregorson/McGregor Panel Inscriptions', kindly transcribed (and communicated to me) by Mr Iain Thornber, 2012. This presumably explains the connection to Archibald Campbell.

dined chez Campbell, 'I find him very kind when I call and seldom it is he allows me to go without asking "Can I do anything for you?" He is calculated in every respect to rise in the world, is uncommonly engaging but I think in everything he does has an eye to business.'[33]

Unlike Archibald, the senior partner in Campbell & Co., Colin Campbell himself, was not mentioned in Maclaine's letters during the period that he worked for the McLachlans in their City office. If he was not one of *their* associates, however, he certainly became very close with their partner Donald MacIntyre. Indeed, later in their mutual histories, McIntyre's financial closeness to Colin Campbell almost brought him to grief, when the latter experienced a liquidity crisis from which he was only saved by a massive injection of funds from the Bank of England.[34] The extent of this injection – it amounted to £63,500, for which some of the cream of the City's East Indies business establishment (among others) agreed to stand surety[35] – was not only an indication of the power of Colin Campbell's City connections and of the fact that the Bank's Governor, John Horsley Palmer, was himself closely linked to the City's East India interest.[36] It was also, rather obviously, an index to the scale of his firm's operations.

With associates and friends like this, during the late 1810s the McLachlans were indeed on the way to becoming a significant presence among the City's East India houses. A rather breathless letter from Maclaine to his mother in June 1818 made the point in graphic fashion. He had been delayed in replying to her last letter not only because of the weight of consignments

---

33 GM to MM 24.3.1817. O-M MSS.

34 GM to JG London 8.2.1831. O-M MSS. See also Chapter 4.

35 The minutes of the Bank of England's Court of Directors' meeting 3.2.1831 show that Campbell was lent £55,000 by the bank for a maximum period of two years. Seven days later, on application by Campbell, the sum was increased to £63,500. See Minutes of Court of Directors Meeting 2.2.1831. The individuals named as surety ('... the Parties who are willing to accept the Drafts proposed for the Bank to discount') – a partial roll call of the city's East India establishment – were Sir William Young for £5000; Robert Rickards for £5000; Aneas Mackintosh for £5000; Allan Macdonald of Fullarton & Macdonald for £5000; Rawson Saltmarshe & Co for £2,500; Gregson Melville & Knight for £2,500; James Mackillop for £5000; Sir Charles Forbes for £5000; James Alexander for £5000; John Ward for £5000; Henry Harvey for £5000; Thomas Wilkinson for £5000; E. Fletcher Esq. for £5000 and H.[?] D. Porcher Esq. for £3,500. See The Bank of England's 'Court of Directors Minutes 1830–31 (book 2)', pp. 314–16, 321, http://www.bankofengland.co.uk/archive/Pages/digitalcontent/archivedocs/codm/18311840.aspx (accessed 30/8/2013).

36 John Horsley Palmer, his brother George Palmer and James Mackillop were partners in Palmers, Mackillop and Company (formerly Palmer, Wilson and Company and subsequently Palmers, Mackillop, Dent and Company) of 11 King's Arms Yard, Coleman Street, City. See the entry for James Mackillop (1786–1870), of 4 Montagu Square, in D.R. Fisher (ed.), *The History of Parliament: the House of Commons 1820–1832* (Cambridge, Cambridge University Press, 2009).

from India but also because the McLachlan brothers were moving their premises to an imposing three-storey building in White Lion Court, off Leadenhall (the building – and its attendant lions – was still there at the time of writing). These were premises formerly occupied by one of the City's leading East India houses, Paxton, Cockerill Trail & Co., and (although they would presently only take the ground floor), the McLachlans' move there signified not only a major expansion of their business but also a prestigious shift of their business 'up-market'. Indeed, Maclaine predicted – presumably fed the information by John McLachlan, who had turned positively loquacious about the brothers' plans – that 'if I am not very much mistaken, [the McLachlans] … will in short time astonish most of the dashing East India Houses in the City'.[37]

En Route to an 'Independency'

Ostensibly at least, Gillian Maclaine was motivated primarily by the desire to gain the 'independency' that he so sorely lacked. It was a theme reflected in the mixture of disapprobation and envy with which he reported on his boss's son (and near contemporary), Alexander McLachlan, and on the latter's time as a student at Oxford. From what Alexander had confided in him, he told his mother, the university 'must be a complete hotbed of dissipation … I should sooner see any young friend of mine at Glasgow or Edinburgh'. Inter alia, the young man was 'much gayer [i.e. addicted to pleasure] than his parents are aware of … and affects to be a man of fashion'. However, with a rich father – and here was the nub of the matter – 'young squire McLachlan … knows he is independent …, which is enough to spoil him … He does not want abilities. He is an excellent linguist and I believe not a bad mathematician but knowing that he has a good fortune independent of any profession makes him careless….'[38] Maclaine's own situation of course – with an absent father and (at best) a disputed and meagre inheritance – was very different.

In coming down to London at the close of 1816, the eighteen-year-old had not intended to leave the Highlands permanently. He wanted to return to Scotland but only after he had made enough money to do so – even though in that respect his views were relatively modest. 'I am not ambitious of great wealth', he wrote his mother in 1836, sixteen years and many frustrations later, 'and only prolong my stay abroad to gain an independency.'[39]

37 GM to MM 18.6.1818. O-M MSS.
38 GM to MM 8.1.1818 & GM to MM 15.7.1817. O-M MSS.
39 GM to MM 12.2.1836. Greenfield MSS.

The theme of gaining an 'independency', however, was one that had been broached in his correspondence as early as 1817, when he had scarcely been in business (in the employ of the McLachlan brothers) for six months: mulling over the idea of some kind of mercantile pursuit in Liverpool (a place where trade was currently burgeoning), he observed to his uncle that 'It is true, I would not run the same chance of making a fortune or of accumulating one so rapidly [as by going out to India], but yet think that by industry and frugality I might reckon on a comfortable Independence.'[40] Quite what constituted an 'independency' remained, of course, something that was dependent on the particular aspirations of the individual. One estimate, however, was that in the early decades of the nineteenth century it required, at a minimum, a sum of around £12,000 invested at 4 per cent to produce an annual income sufficient to maintain the position of a modest country gentlemen.[41] Initially at least, a foothold in the McLachlan brothers' London business – however precarious and ambiguous – seemed the most likely first step in this direction.

It was a foothold, moreover, that he was lucky to have. 'I can assure you', wrote one of his Morvern contemporaries on arriving in London a little over year after Maclaine himself, that 'a man requires a great interest before he can get into a good situation in this place, because there are so many out of employment who would give handsome premiums for getting into a good berth.'[42] As Maclaine himself observed, to get a 'situation' in a counting house young men had to accept that they would work unpaid for the first year of their employment and there were plenty of candidates ready to accept these terms.[43] The 'interest' that Gillian Maclaine had with the McLachlan brothers was hence highly advantageous. He thereby established a connection with their business concerns that lasted for a decade and a half – and a connection with 'the East' which was to last his entire lifetime. It also located him along a commodity chain in cotton goods whose key nodal point was unquestionably the City of London, some 5–7,000 miles and a four-to-six-month sea voyage away from the Asian termini of the trade in which the City, and its connections among the cotton manufacturers of Lancashire and the Clyde valley, was so heavily involved.

---

[40] GM to JG 3.7.1817. O-M MSS.

[41] Le Pichon, *China Trade and Empire*, p. 21.

[42] John McMaster to Hugh McMaster, London 11.2.1818. I am grateful to Mr Iain Thornber for providing me with transcriptions of copies of these MSS letters, in his possession (hereafter: McMaster MSS).

[43] GM to MM 6.3.1818. O-M MSS.

Gillian Maclaine's London: 1816–20

By the time of Maclaine's arrival in London in the closing days of 1816, the City (as distinct from the great conurbation of which it was part) was the largest commercial and financial centre in the Western world. It was also already on the way to becoming an area in which 'the better sort' worked rather than slept, and one of offices and warehouses rather than merchant's dwelling houses. By the 1810s, its population of something over 125,000 souls (well under half these people actually lived within the old city walls) was part of a metropolis whose population then numbered well in excess of one million. The senior partner in the McLachlan enterprise lived with his family (as we have seen) outside the city. Young Maclaine was often invited to spend Sunday there, and confessed that 'Mrs. McLachlan's motherly attention makes me feel quite at home.'[44] Maclaine himself also lived outside the City limits – though in his case well within walking distance – in Hatton Garden, an urban district immediately to its north-west, where he lodged in an apartment – 'a house *within itself*' – owned or rented by two the of the McLachlan brothers (subsequently joined by a third), known to their young lodger as 'Mr. Duncan' and 'Mr. Hugh'.[45]

The latter, depicted by Maclaine as a fat, jolly little man, had sufficient social consequence to take his young lodger to a Scots Hospital Dinner, presided over by no less a figure than First Lord of the Admiralty, Viscount Dundas (the Duke of Clarence had originally been billed), for which Maclaine felt properly 'gratified', although the turtle soup and the speeches evidently competed imperfectly for his attention with the Scots music that was played.[46] However, it was Mr Duncan whom the lodger found 'an excellent landlord and a rather amusing companion in evenings [and] by far the most open-minded' of the brothers 'though greatly inferior to them in other respects'.[47] It was evidently to him that Maclaine turned for information: 'Whatever I want to know about the business, I always apply to him for. Indeed, I must say he keeps nothing from my knowledge. Not withstanding this, I think him the worst principled of them.'[48]

Given this degree of censoriousness, it was perhaps as well as that relations in his lodgings were evidently lubricated – literally and metaphorically – by parcels of cheese, ham and whiskey that arrived periodically at the McLachlan's office from Ardtornish ('Mr. Hugh's eyes glistened when

---

44 E.g. GM to MM 31.12.1818 and GM to MM 8.7.1817. O-M MSS.
45 GM to MM 28.12.1816. O-M MSS.
46 GM to MM 4.5.1818. O-M MSS.
47 GM to MM 8.1.1818. O-M MSS.
48 GM to MM 24.3.1817. O-M MSS.

he saw the cheese'). Some of the produce was sent on to the senior partner at Stamford Hill, but enough remained to provide a source of conviviality that clearly encompassed the lodger as well as the brothers: 'the first glass of wine after dinner the day it arrived was tossed off to "those that sent us the cheese etc."'.[49] There were, moreover, other diversions: 'Mr. John [McLachlan] and I walk some evenings out together, and contrive always to go to some place of amusement ere we come in. He blames me always and I with very good nature take it all particularly, as he pays my way.'[50] Some adventures, of course, were of a more formal and less agreeable kind. A visit, in the company of his London-based uncle, Sir Archibald Maclaine,[51] to the celebrated Astley's Amphitheatre Circus was evidently not a success: 'All I <u>gained</u> by it was <u>losing</u> a pocket book containing nothing valuable …', his nephew observed. Worse still, his uncle, whose background was exclusively military, was apparently prone to 'lecture me continually on the advantages of being attentive to business'.[52]

A Haven for Highlanders

Maclaine was not lacking for company, however, among fellow Scots of his own age. 'Scotchmen get on here uncommonly well', he observed to his mother after he had been in London for almost twelve months, and went on to regale her with a 'rags to riches' story of the kind that was common currency among (and about) this particular Diaspora. The McLachlan brothers, of course, were themselves apparently well on their way to achieving this desideratum by the time that Maclaine began to work for them: 'they are worthy and in London, <u>now</u>, respectable men' was how Maclaine expressed the matter to his uncle in distant Ardtornish.[53] Moreover, in their own modest, not to say grudging, way the brothers contributed to the migration of young Scots not only to London but also overseas. In the latter case, in a matter of two or three years towards the end of the 1810s, the brothers dispatched at

---

49 GM to MM 26.4.1819. O-M MSS.
50 GM to MM 19.8.1817. O-M MSS.
51 Archibald Maclaine (1773–1861) had served with distinction (and was badly wounded) in both India and the Peninsula War. He was Lieutenant-Colonel 14th Foot c.1820 and there-after Lieutenant-Colonel 17th Foot (on half pay from 1829). He was knighted in 1831; was subsequently Colonel 47th Foot from 1847; and appears to have been promoted General in 1855. See Frederic Boase, *Modern English Biography* (London: Frank Cass, 6 vols, 1965 [1892–1921]), vol. 2, p. 645.
52 GM to MM 6.6.1817. O-M MSS.
53 GM to JG 12.2.1817. O-M MSS (emphasis in original).

least three young men to Java (and another to Calcutta) on the basis of family and other connections at their Highland base on the Morvern peninsula.[54]

They included the Morvern-born John McMaster,[55] who was subsequently to follow Maclaine to Java and work for him there. Prior to that, however, he had spent some two years employed – and sleeping in the shop – as an assistant in 'a Druggist Wareroom Wholesale and Exportation to the East Indies' in London's Cornhill.[56] The position had been found for him by the McLachlans, after he had arrived in London from Scotland in December 1817, virtually penniless: he had sailed in steerage and found his companions gross – 'a parcel of sailors which had no manner of politeness than your Black Pony', he told his brother, but had been befriended by the steward. Unlike his patrons (and Maclaine), McMaster was not of gentry stock but was (it may be presumed) a promising and literate young man who had somehow been recommended to the McLachlan family. Not only promising, moreover, but also pious, if we can rely on his report from London on a new-found Scots friend (evidently someone other than Maclaine) whom 'I admire … very much. He makes me every night before we go to bed join with him in reading a chapter in the Bible, and in offering up a prayer to the Almighty. He and I attend preaching this day at a Scotch Chapel from 10 o'clock till 1 ….'[57]

Soon after disembarking in the metropolis, McMaster had 'called upon the Glensanda lads and delivered the letter [of recommendation], and indeed they shewed me every kindness'. Maclaine was not so sure. Reporting on Macmaster's arrival in London to his mother, he observed somewhat equivocally that 'the Messrs Mac were very nice (especially Mr. John) in doing for Macmaster … what do you think [John McLachlan] said? "If we get this lad a situation, there will be no end to applications from the country"'. In the event, the job they *had* found him – doing exclusively manual work – was one with which he was very unhappy. Maclaine said he would 'speak with Mr. P[atrick Maclachlan] about him but not to Mr. J'.[58] Meanwhile, he took it on himself to help the young arrival:

---

54 Apart from Maclaine himself, they were John McNeill, a relative through marriage of the McLachlans (see below), who preceded Maclaine to the Indies in 1819 and John McMaster (see below), who followed him late in 1820. A fourth individual, William Menzies (from Perth) had also been 'sent out', this time to Calcutta, by Donald MacIntryre, the McLachlans' business partner.

55 John McMaster, b. Morvern c.1799, d. Java 1825.

56 The firm was Messrs William Brydon & Co., 78 Cornhill. William Brydon and Duncan MacKenzie were still operating as 'druggists' in Cornhill in 1826, in which year they went into bankruptcy (and were still paying their creditors in 1830). See *The Law Advertiser*, vol. 8, 11.2.1830.

57 John McMaster to Hugh McMaster, London 1.8.1818. McMaster MSS.

58 GM to MM 6.3.1818. O-M MSS.

You cannot imagine how glad my dear, dear friend Gillean McLean was as describe upon paper. He instructed me in every way how to behave & told me not to want money for out of his Small sum he would supply me with some.[59]

He found himself in a city in which every sight amazed: 'I am pretending I am not astonished at everything I see or hear', he confided to his brother. Maclaine often saw McMaster once or twice a day – their workplaces were close together – and was even provide him with a suit of clothing when his own became worn out.[60] Evidently, Maclaine was – and remained – a role model for his less socially elevated contemporary, of whom he much approved: 'an excellent young man ... I hope [he] will get on in the world'.[61] Two years later, when they were both in Java, McMaster reiterated his continuing gratitude for being under the guidance of a man 'who has all along supported me through thick and thin and acted toward me more like a brother than one upon which I had no claim ... I must say with Burns that he is beloved at home and revered abroad.'[62]

The City, the Docks – and the Cotton Mills of the North

The office in which Maclaine worked, unlike his lodgings, was located in the very heart of the City, in the web of streets in the proximity of Wren's great baroque church that connected the Bank of England with the East India Company's headquarters in Leadenhall Street. Elaborately reconstructed in the classical style only a decade earlier, it was claimed to be 'the home of the "Grandest Society of Merchants in the Universe"'.[63] The 'Messrs Mac', as Maclaine fondly called them until he got to know them better, were themselves initially installed on the same street, but subsequently moved up the road into Cornhill, where they successively occupied premises just off the main thoroughfare, in White Lion Court and in Sun Court. They were hence situated not only in the City but also near the heart of its long association with the East, in Mincing Lane and the nearby alleys and courts.

In the early years of the nineteenth century, moreover, that long association was further cemented by the opening in 1806 of a dedicated set of East India Docks a few miles downriver on the north bank of the Thames at Blackwall. Some thirty acres (twelve hectares) in extent and connected with the City

59 John McMaster to Hugh McMaster, London 7.12.1817. McMaster MSS.
60 John McMaster to Hugh McMaster, London 1.8.1818. McMaster MSS
61 GM to MM (with postscript to AM) 15.6.1819. O-M MSS.
62 John McMaster to Hugh McMaster, Salatiga (Java), 1.6.1822. McMaster MSS.
63 C.H. Philips, *The East India Company, 1784–1834* (Manchester: Manchester University Press, 1961), p. 1.

of London by the equally new Commercial Road, they were the home base of the East India Company's own shipping, and also the point of departure for the 'private' shipping that cleared out for Asian destinations after the Company lost its monopoly on direct trade with the Indian subcontinent in 1813. Maclaine presumably got to know the East India Docks quite well, because it would have been from Blackwall that the McLachlan's goods were shipped: 'I cannot complain of want of exercise', he wrote to his brother in July 1817, 'I walked about a great deal today, and feel almost as tired as if I had been shooting [on Mull].'[64]The goods themselves, however, did not, for the most part, originate in London. Rather, they came – predominantly it may be supposed – from the cotton mills of Glasgow, in the McLachlan's native Scotland.

Glasgow and neighbouring areas along the Clyde were by then the prime centre of British cotton manufacture outside Lancashire – as well as being one of the three largest ports in the United Kingdom. Manchester and the Lancashire cotton industry in general certainly figured in the McLachlans' business dealings.[65] Nonetheless, their prime connections were with the cotton industry which had grown up along the Clyde, more than 200 miles further north, over the previous fifty years or so. Along with a substantial ship-building industry and docks derived from its position on the Atlantic seaboard of the rapidly industrialising zone of the Scottish Lowlands, Glasgow itself boasted some fifty-two cotton mills fed with raw material from the Americas and operated by a workforce which drew heavily on migrant labour from across the Irish Sea.[66]

By the second decade of the nineteenth century, moreover, some sixteen of these mills were sizeable operations fitted with power looms. Their smoke stacks already made Glasgow, as Maclaine noted soon after his arrival there, a far grimier place than contemporary London[67] and output expanded accordingly. By 1819, with its mills producing around 105 million yards of cloth annually, worth an estimated £5.2 million sterling,[68] Clydeside seriously rivalled its more celebrated Lancashire counterpart. An important difference,

---

[64] GM to Angus Maclaine (hereafter AM) 28.7.1817. Greenfield MSS.

[65] See e.g. 'Evidence McLachlan 1821', p. 277.

[66] See Christopher A. Whatley, 'Labour in the Industrialising City, c. 1660–1830', in T.M. Devine and Gordon Jackson (eds), *Glasgow* (Manchester: Manchester University Press, 2 vols, 1994), vol. 1, p. 367: 'As far as cotton mill workers were concerned ... it seems not unreasonable to suppose that around half of the mill workforce was either Irish or of Irish descent in the early 1800s. By 1841, something like one in three of Glasgow's inhabitants may have come into this category.'

[67] 'I am ... agreeably surprised in finding that the brick houses look so well and that the horizon is so clear. It is much clearer today than I ever saw in Glasgow.' GM to MM, London 28.12.1816. O-M MSS.

[68] Cooke, *Scottish Cotton Industry*, p. 56.

however, was that the Scots industry was very heavily export-oriented and that those exports consisted of 'cheaper, coarser fabrics, plain calicoes and heavier fabrics' that might have been thought particularly suitable for Asian markets.[69]

The McLachlans evidently had close links with these northern manufacturers. Calling through Glasgow in December 1819 in the company of John McLachlan, with whom he had travelled down from the Highlands, Maclaine stayed in his brother's student lodgings ('Angus I found at his studies, with two ponderous volumes before him – Calvin and the Exposition of the Bible', he loyally reported to his mother). The young man also 'accompanied Mr. J [McLachlan] today to several large warehouses to get a knowledge of the different kinds of cotton goods' and 'dined at Mr. McDonalds, a partner in the House of MacDonald and Walker'. With premises next to the city's meat market on Graham Square in the east of the city, James McDonald was one of its leading power-loom cotton manufacturers.[70] 'Mr John' stayed on in Glasgow to attend to the partners' business, while Maclaine himself then continued on to London, via Edinburgh and what sounds like a hair-raising voyage south on board a small coastal vessel or smack.[71]

No Place for an Ambitious Young Man

Maclaine worked in London for the Messrs McLachlan for nearly three and a half years: learning the business; learning French (one of the brothers paid for lessons); learning to modify his 'Scots Twang' and adopt a more 'English tone'; and wondering whether he had a possible future with the firm as a partner.[72] After some fifteen months in the counting house, he reported on a promotion that gave him management of the sales department: 'you may think but lightly of this … but I assure you it flattered my vanity not a little – for it is a task, or rather a charge seldom entrusted to young hands'.[73] In

---

[69] Cooke, *Scottish Cotton Industry*, pp. 57–58.

[70] The reference is presumably to James McDonald, of Graham Square, Glasgow, listed as a 'cotton manufacturer by power loom' and as 'cotton spinner' in *Pigot's New Commercial Directory of Scotland for 1825–6*, pp. 482–83. As such, McDonald would have been among the twenty or so leading cotton manufacturers in the city. It is not clear if this firm was the precursor of McDonald & Co., the later and very large firm of Glasgow manufacturers of 'sewed muslin', with an output valued at £500,000 a year in the 1850s, which subsequently went bankrupt. See Cooke, *Scottish Cotton Industry*, p. 81.

[71] GM to MM, Glasgow 19.12.1819. O-M MSS.

[72] GM to MM 8.1.1818. O-M MSS.

[73] GM to MM 6.3.1818. O-M MSS.

essence, however, he was a supernumerary who worked under the immediate supervision of the newly installed Head Clerk, a Mr Bonhote, a man who had previously worked for eighteen years in 'one of the first Houses in the city'.[74]

The young man initially condescended to find the new arrival 'very obliging ... a very experienced man of business and a perfect gentleman in his manners'.[75] Later, however, he became 'my old friend Bonhote' who was a useful ally in the Counting House (he merited one of the half dozen bottles of whiskey that arrived from Ardtornish in the spring of 1819),[76] and who forwarded Maclaine's letters and newspapers from the Highlands when Maclaine was in Java.[77] The tie was evidently a close one. Indeed, Maclaine subsequently found a place for one of Bonhote's family in his Batavia office, and (as we shall see) the man later became a senior partner in his firm. Other relations in the Counting House were less amicable. His fellow clerk, a Mr Middleton, was and remained, in Maclaine's view, a 'close and obstinate fellow'[78] – perhaps because (quite rightly as it turned out) he saw Maclaine's presence as a threat to his own continued employment. 'Mr. Middleton has got quite jealous', Maclaine reported in October 1817, 'and tells me quite plainly that I wish to supersede him as Bookkeeper ....'[79]

Working conditions were frugal: 'my hands are benumbed with cold', Maclaine lamented to his mother very shortly after he had arrived, and 'I am afraid you will find difficulty in making out my scrawl'.[80] It was a refrain that was to be several times repeated. When business was brisk, he 'seldom left the Counting House before 8.00 in the evening and often remain until 9' and, as he informed his brother Angus, then himself a student at the University of Glasgow:

> I am kept extremely busy and have not one moment to myself. Adding, subtracting, dividing etc. etc. drawing money and paying money etc. etc. takes up all my time, and nothing all days thunders in mine ears but 'a Bill left for acceptance' – 'take a return on this policy' – 'two Indiamen up the river by Lloyd's Books' etc. etc. I some how feel the greatest pleasure amidst this bustle and the more actively I am employed the greater pleasure it yields me. I now have the honour of keeping the Cash Book, which I can assure you is a trust I may plume myself upon, having been so short a time in the Counting House. I am now more interested in the business and go on with double spirit. The

[74] GM to MM 4.10.1817. O-M MSS.
[75] GM to JG 18.7.1818. O-M MSS.
[76] GM to MM 24.4.1819. O-M MSS.
[77] GM to MM 13.6.1824. O-M MSS.
[78] GM to MM 6.3.1818. O-M MSS.
[79] GM to MM (fragment 3.10.1817). O-M MSS.
[80] GM to MM, London 28.12.1816. O-M MSS.

Messrs McLachlan continue to show me every attention and while God grants me health I shall continue to do as much as I can for them in return.[81]

Once he had started to learn the ropes, however, Maclaine quickly grasped that a desk in the Counting House was no place for an ambitious young man. Nor was he sure that there was enough work in the office to ensure him any permanency. Little more than three months after his arrival in London and evidently spurred on by the imminent departure for Calcutta of another young man in the McLachlan's service, he wrote plaintively to his mother, that:

I think it is of the utmost importance to determine soon, indeed immediately, whether I am to go to India or Liverpool. I am now growing old, and unless I go to India it will be necessary for me to remain much longer with the Messrs Mac. Their business is simple and easily managed, and six months in their C [ounting] house does very well to [prepare] a young man for a larger establishment but that is all.[82]

Accordingly, he soon started to press the partners for something more fulfilling and, above all, for some certainty about his future: 'I long much now for some determined arrangement. My patience is almost worn out.'[83] Matters were made worse, moreover, by his suspicion that both the McLachlans *and* his uncle were deliberately keeping him the dark. Indeed, at one point, the young man was sufficiently exasperated to complain directly to the latter 'that you would have settled this without letting me know anything about it, astonishes me a little', and his complaint was softened not at all by his rider that he was 'well aware' that his uncle's action must have had 'better reasons than thinking me yet too much a child to be consulted about matters that regard my welfare'.[84]

Initially, as this rather suggests, the McLachlans were far from forthcoming about his prospects either in India or anywhere else. Presumably, they were more than a little taken aback by the brashness of the young fellow they had taken on board to oblige a neighbour. 'Mr. John gives me no hopes of getting in with themselves, and even feels delicate in keeping me much longer in the House', Maclaine reported to his uncle in July 1817:

He says I discover a talent for business but it would require more care and fostering than they could bestow. Mr. Peter's expressions were that 'from his not having received a mercantile education himself, he could not undertake to make

81 GM to AM 8.1.1819 and 12.3.1817. Greenfield MSS.
82 GM to MM 24.3.1817. O-M MSS.
83 GM to MM 6.3.1818. O-M MSS.
84 GM to JG 12.3.1817. O-M MSS.

a man of business out of me – he might as well offer to make me a politician'. They seem at a loss as to how to advise me …[85]

Nonetheless, and not without much hesitation and a good deal of Scots caution, they eventually obliged. The context was one of new developments in their marketing strategy, developed in tandem with their Calcutta-based associate, Donald MacIntyre.[86] In 1817–18, Duncan McLachlan had voyaged to India, ostensibly (the brothers were much given to secrecy) for reasons of his health but almost certainly to plan a major new venture. While in Calcutta, he sent an 'immense packet of letters' – presumably including pattern samples – back to London, where they were 'immediately locked up' – leaving a curious Maclaine very much in the dark as to what was going on.[87] In the course of time, however, he would find out.

The Cotton Business in the East: Calcutta and Java

Calcutta by the second decade of the nineteenth century was the location of a score of British Agency Houses that performed a variety of commercial and banking functions. The chief commodity in which they traded, however, was cotton piece goods. These had once come from Calcutta's Indian hinterland but now increasingly came from the mills of Lancashire and the Scottish lowlands. Nevertheless, cotton was by no means their only staple. In particular, the production as well as the export of locally manufactured indigo – the dyestuff essential to create 'navy blue' – was also an important item of their business, as was sugar. Capital meanwhile came pre-eminently from the deposited savings of East India Company officials and military men and from Calcutta's large class of wealthy Indian merchants.[88]

Most of Calcutta's British firms had London 'correspondents', but their operations remained substantially autonomous. The doyen of this merchant-banker community – he had been in business there since the 1780s – was John Palmer, the 'Prince of Merchants' and reputedly the settlement's richest British resident. Over several decades, largely on his own initiative, Palmer built up in Calcutta a network of commercial and financial transactions in which patronage and connection played a substantial role. Heavily leveraged as it was, his Indian network relied for a large part of its liquidity on the co-operation and compliance of London associates who, nonetheless, had no

---

[85] GM to JG 6.7.1817. O-M MSS.
[86] 'Evidence McLachlan 1821', pp. 277–78.
[87] GM to MM 6.3.1818. O-M MSS.
[88] For a general account and analysis, see the chapter on 'The Agency House: Trade to India and the Far East' in Chapman, *Merchant Enterprise*, pp. 107–28.

formal role in decision-making. It was a bitter dispute with these associates, some of them previously members of the Calcutta firm, which brought about Palmer's bankruptcy in 1830. Not inconsequentially, the failure of Palmer & Co. was followed over the next few years by the near total collapse of the Agency House system.[89] Nonetheless, during the second decade of the nineteenth century the prospects for the European Agency Houses of Calcutta still appeared alluring, and business was booming and for none more so, it might appear, than Donald MacIntyre, the McLachlan brothers' long-time associate.

MacIntyre is a difficult man to read. According to his own account, he was one of the pioneers of the trade in British cotton goods to the Indian subcontinent. He had started in business in Calcutta in 1810, when he 'went out connected with the [London] house of Duncan & Patrick McLachlan', subsequently setting up his own business there and taking in three Scots-born partners before returning – temporarily as it turned out – to the UK in 1820. As such, MacIntyre was evidently the lynchpin of the entire marketing exercise on which the McLachlans now embarked and into which young Maclaine was drawn. More than that, however, giving evidence to a British Parliamentary Committee in 1821, MacIntyre designated himself as the individual who, having noted what was evidently a growing Indian taste for the design – and above all the price – of imported textiles, had sent examples of the preferred patterns back to Scotland and had them copied in bulk.[90]

How much truth there was in this 'pioneering' story is difficult to determine. Maclaine himself was finally to write off MacIntyre as a deceitful rogue, but that was after a decade of unfaltering trust in him. What is certain, however, is that in 1817, the McLachlan brothers had sent to India, on the board the *Ganges*, a certain Mr Mackenzie from Perth who (according to Maclaine) had 'learned his trade or rather his business in Young, Ross & Co of Perth's house, one of the greatest in the [cotton] printing line in Scotland. It is certainly from his knowledge of printed [cotton] goods that he got his present situation. It is chiefly for the purpose of finding out the taste of the Natives and supplying their wants in goods of this description that he is sent out.' [91] Whatever

---

89 Webster, *The Richest Merchant*, passim; S.B. Singh, *European Agency Houses in Bengal, 1783–1833* (Calcutta: Firma Mukhopadhyay, 1966).

90 Select Committee of the House of Commons on the means of improving and maintaining foreign trade – East Indies and China, *Parliamentary Papers GB* 1821, vol. VI, 'Evidence of Donald MacIntyre' (hereafter 'Evidence MacIntyre 1821'), pp. 294–300. MacIntyre is discussed briefly in Chapman, *Merchant Enterprise*, pp. 109–10 and Webster, *The Twilight*, p. 72.

91 MacIntyre subsequently married Mackenzie's sister, while Mackenzie himself arrived in Java early in the 1820s and in 1822 became (no doubt under MacIntyre's patronage) 'sole partner' in the Singapore branch of the newly founded firm of Gillian Maclaine & Co. See GM to MM 26.3.1817; GM to MM 6.6.1817 and GM to MM, 'On Board the Mary

the veracity of McIntyre's rather grand claims for own initiatives, he was evidently among those who accurately diagnosed and exploited, at a quite early date, the dramatic reversal (taking place over little more than a decade) in a trade that (as we saw in the preceding chapter) had once seen India *export* its cotton goods and which now saw it become a net *importer* of them.[92]

It was, as one of MacIntyre's seasoned contemporaries observed, 'a thing totally unexpected'.[93] Indeed, as MacIntyre himself asserted, 'when I first arrived in India [in 1809], the natives did not use cotton manufactures at all from this country'. Thereafter, however, what started as a modest flow became a flood: 'originally, the trade was almost principally confined to us, but now, I believe, there is not a House in Calcutta who do not receive consignments'.[94] The McLachlans' own consignment business appears to have peaked during the course of 1817. Indeed, Maclaine, evidently somewhat awed by the turn of events, reported to his mother in March of that year that 'their profits from goods sent out to India are truly astonishing and their shipments everyday are becoming more extensive'. Moreover, it was not just a matter of export but also of import: Maclaine cited an example of the sale of a cargo of cassia bark ('a drug not unlike cinnamon') that sold for a profit of £7000.[95] The firm's cash flow around this time appears to have been in the region of £14,000–15,000 a month.[96]

Mid-year 1818, business continued to flourish. The firm had moved into 'a superior' Counting House on whose 'dashing appearance' some £300 had been lavished, and 'had lately extended their concerns in India and are at present on the eve of forming some new establishments'.[97] Inter alia, the Calcutta-based MacIntyre and his partners 'carry on now a very extensive trade with the Interior and have several young men stationed in different parts of India some 5 or 600 miles up the country'.[98] Despite

Ann off Sheerness' 18.4.1820. O-M MSS; GM to MM, Salatiga near Samarang 28.5.1822, Greenfield MSS.

[92] E.g. Farnie, *English Cotton Industry*, pp. 96ff. In 1814 cotton piece goods had accounted for around 6 per cent in volume of British exports to India; in 1820 the figure was 20 per cent; and in 1829 was 50 per cent.

[93] Select Committee of the House of Commons on the Means of Improving and Maintaining Foreign Trade – East Indies and China, *Parliamentary Papers GB* 1821, vol. VI, 'Evidence of John Fairlie', p. 204.

[94] 'Evidence MacIntyre 1821', pp. 294–300.

[95] GM to MM 12.3.1817. O-M MSS.

[96] Maclaine reported that he was now in charge of the Cash Book 'which is a serious charge when the great quantity of money that runs through their hands Is taken into consideration. Their cash account with the Bank [of England?] is generally 14,000 – 15,000 pounds a month.' GM to JG 12.3.1817. O-M MSS.

[97] GM to JG 18.7.1818. O-M MSS.

[98] GM to JG 22.12.1818. O-M MSS; 'Evidence McLachlan 1821', p. 278.

this, it was indigenous Indian merchants who played the vital role in the distribution of British cotton piece goods through the length and breadth of the subcontinent. As Patrick McLachlan himself put on record: '... we sell them at Calcutta to the natives', who took them 'up country' even as far as Naipaul.[99]

In addition to their business in imported cottons, moreover, the McLachlans and their India-based partner appear to have thought (according, at least, to the information that Maclaine had been able to glean, since the brothers were far from forthcoming) that there was also money to made in the subcontinent from non-mercantile ventures: 'I dare say', the young man wrote to his uncle, 'that you will be surprised to learn that we are now indigo planters ...' and proprietors of another 'manufactory' of some kind near Calcutta – and that 'both concerns promise extremely well'. In 1817, moreover, even more ambitious schemes were being mooted, for the McLachlan brothers were 'now thinking of turning their attention to the growing of cotton' in the subcontinent, presumably through the intermediary of MacIntyre's firm in Calcutta.[100] Indeed, late in 1817 Maclaine gained the impression – that 'the greater part of their business is now carried on in India, and they intend daily to diminish their transactions in this country'.[101]

Nonetheless, the longer-term picture was far from rosy. In MacIntyre's phrase, the 'natives are very capricious in their tastes' and, as was also evident from his comments, the cotton goods market ran the constant risk of being oversupplied.[102] Indeed, the immediate post-war boom in exports to India in British cotton goods, in which the McLachlan brothers and Donald MacIntyre had so enthusiastically participated, lasted only until the closing months of 1818.[103] By then, as Maclaine reported:

> A considerable change to worse has taken place of late to the East India market, which prevents the Messrs Mac from increasing their establishment as they at one time expected. Mr. Peter, in a conversation I had not long ago with him, informed me that they were disappointed of late in their expectations abroad and that they would not require so many hands as they formerly imagined.[104]

Among other thing, it appears that one of the problems facing the London partners was a want of remittance cargoes from the subcontinent. Hence Maclaine informed his uncle in April 1819 that:

99 'Evidence McLachlan1821', p. 277.
100 GM to JG 4.10.1817. O-M MSS.
101 GM to MM 4.10 1817. O-M MSS.
102 'Evidence MacIntyre 1821', pp. 294–300.
103 Webster, *The Twilight*, pp. 71–72.
104 GM to JG 2.12.1818. O-M MSS.

The times continue as unfavourable as ever, and the Messrs Mac are much
disturbed by the want of arrivals from India. I cannot describe to you their
state of anxiety for the last month ... Every morning looking out for the arrival
of ships ... the last thing [they did] every night, for weeks back before going
to bed [was] to see from what quarter the wind blows and the first question in
the morning is 'how is the wind today'. I cannot help thinking Mr. MacIntyre
has been very cruel of late and with the most abundant means in his power,
has placed his friends here in a cruel predicament. It is rather a hard case that
people who have the most ample funds should be hard pressed to meet their
engagements .... The Messrs Mac's affairs are prospering in India and they are
extremely fortunate in not having experienced any losses by the late extensive
failures [there] ...[105]

Meanwhile, back in London the McLachlan–MacIntyre partnership appears
to have weathered the downturn ('had reason to congratulate themselves on
escaping so well') better than many of other East India Houses in the City
who, according to Maclaine's information, had sustained 'immense losses ...
by the fall in the price of cotton'. Even so, as Maclaine exclaimed, 'it is really
wonderful how things have changed of late. Produce that could easily be sold
at a profit some months ago, is now fallen 50% and some description 100%.
It is this that has ruined two of the first rate E. India Houses in the City.'[106]

New Directions: The Country Trade and the Lure of 'the Eastern Isles'

Despite this significant downturn in business, however, Patrick McLachlan
told Maclaine 'that by care and attention the market could yet be turned to
very great account'.[107] It appears that what he had in mind was his firm's
entry into the intra-Asian trade from the subcontinent eastward. Hence by
the early months of 1819 Maclaine was confidently reporting to his uncle that
this '... Country Trade ... can still be persecuted to much advantage and the
House [in Calcutta] has embarked of late pretty largely in it'.[108] Evidently,
both the London *and* Calcutta Houses had begun to look to commercial
projects beyond the subcontinent in an effort to sustain their fortunes.

   Although Calcutta was a key nodal point in a global commodity chain
of production, commerce and consumption of cotton cloth that started in
the Americas, it was not its Asian terminus, since the outlet for cotton piece
goods was far from being exhausted even in its huge South Asian hinterland.

[105] GM to MM 11.3.1819. O-M MSS.
[106] GM to JG 26.5.1819. O-M MSS.
[107] GM to JG 22.12.1818. O-M MSS. GM to JG 13.4.1819. O-M MSS.
[108] GM to JG 26.5.1819. O-M MSS. The venture had begun some two years earlier in 1817
    when Maclaine informed his mother that 'the Messrs Mac are now concerned in an indigo
    plantation, which returns them handsomely'. GM to MM 19.8.1817. O-M MSS.

There was still China, and the intermediate region of Southeast Asia. The incomparable benefits of access to the *China* market was one of the classic nostrums of the Imperial age, in the 1820s and 1830s for none more so than the British East India merchants of London and Calcutta, who evidently hoped for a repeat there of what they had so recently achieved in India.[109] For the present, however, participation in the direct trade between the UK and China was precluded by the East India Company's monopoly (and remained so until 1833). The immediate prospect, therefore, was of the extension of trade in cotton piece goods beyond the subcontinent into the 'Eastern Isles' of Southeast Asia.

It was in this context that the McLachlan brothers appear to have grasped that, although the market in the Indian subcontinent for British cotton goods was currently at saturation point, there was still an excellent prospect for sales in the Indonesian archipelago – and particularly in the small but agriculturally rich island of Java, the hub of the Dutch possessions in the 'Indies' with a population that already numbered some six or seven million. In venturing into this potentially lucrative market, the brothers evidently decided to play their cards very close to the chest. 'Secrecy in business up to a certain extent is no doubt prudent, and on some occasions is absolutely necessary', the by now somewhat bewildered Maclaine opined, 'but really I cannot help think that the Messrs Mac carry their <u>closeness</u> to a ridiculous extent.'[110] Be that as it may, the object of their closely guarded attentions was evidently the possibility of a veritable commercial coup.

It seems likely that the McLachlans would have engaged previously with the trade of the archipelago, but largely or exclusively as brokers or commission agents. Webster, in an authoritative recent discussion of the financial arrangements of the London East India houses of the period, describes a system of arrangements which:

> Involved the London houses advancing money to the manufacturers, frequently up to half the value of the commodities to be shipped. The London firms charged interest and commission on these advances. The goods ... would be shipped to India, most often to one of the new houses set up by men who had gone to India since 1813, and from there they were sold on to the Indian market. The results were subsequently repatriated through bills of exchange or

---

[109] See e.g. Select Committee of the House of Commons on the Means of Improving and Maintaining Foreign Trade – East Indies and China, *Parliamentary Papers GB* 1821, vol. VI, 'Evidence of Robert Addison 1821', p. 225: 'Having in view the great consumption [of cotton goods] that has taken place in Calcutta, do you conceive a similar consumption might take place in China? – Most undoubtedly I do.' On the place of British cottons in the nineteenth-century China market in general, see Farnie, *English Cotton Industry*, pp. 120–28.

[110] GM to JG 18.12.1818. O-M MSS (emphasis in original).

by the purchase of return cargoes for the British market, providing the means for the manufacturer to settle his debts to the London house.[111]

Much in line with this, in describing his business affairs to his parliamentary interlocutors in 1821, Patrick McLachlan told them that 'I have latterly acted as agents for constituents … I have left off making consignments for myself.' Nonetheless, he added that he had been engaged over the years in 'shipping the goods and manufactures of this country … on account of private traders … *and on our own account*'[112] and his firm's big shipment of cotton goods to Java in the previous year (despite his earlier testimony) would appear to have fallen into this latter category. If so, given the size of their investment as well as the novelty of what they were doing, their nervousness was understandable. Maclaine called 'this Java speculation … one of the grandest they ever made' and although he did not expand on its full value, a reasonable estimate was that it was worth more than £20,000.[113]

Java and Beyond: Cotton Sales in the Indonesian Archipelago

The Indonesian archipelago was a relatively new and alluring market for the purveyors of British cotton goods. Historically, the island of Java had both manufactured cotton goods of its own and, as far as the 'better sort' of consumer was concerned, also imported substantial quantities of cloth from the subcontinent. As well as 'brilliantly coloured' material, this import also included 'fine white cambrics' which became the basis for the elaborately waxed and dyed batik cloth for which the Javanese were famous. The whole system of cotton trade and textile production on the island existed

---

[111] Webster, *The Twilight*, pp. 72–74. See also Alfons van de Kraan, 'Anglo-Dutch Rivalry in the Java Cotton Trade, 1811–30', *Indonesia Circle*, 68 (1996), pp. 44ff. On the basis of an account by the Dutch Indies official Wappers Mellis, Van de Kraan suggests a very complex dynamic of the cotton trade between the UK and Java c. 1814–1823, characterised by the competing interests and rival activities of manufacturers, brokers and merchants. McLachlan's 1820 cargo may fit into this pattern, but the whole scenario pre-supposes a degree of intimate knowledge on the part of Wappers Mellis that seems inherently improbable. To be sure, Wappers had once worked for the EIC, but during the period concerned – and as an individual of pronounced anti-British sentiments – he seems unlikely to have been in a position to access the relevant 'inside' information. An adventurer seeking to gain and hold a place in the colonial bureaucracy (he finally got an appointment as Director-General of Customs, on the same salary as *Resident*), Wappers had good reason to exaggerate his actual degree of conversancy with the situation he purported to describe. For example, the supposed division between 'brokers' and 'merchants' to which he alludes was nothing like as clear-cut as he implies.

[112] 'Evidence McLachlan 1821', p. 277 (emphasis added).

[113] GM to JG 30.9.1820 and GM to MM 8.10.1820. O-M MSS (emphasis in original).

totally without reference to the manufactures of Europe.[114] Quite suddenly, however, during the second decade of the nineteenth century, the situation changed. Indeed, according to one British trader who had spent three years on the island, when he first went there in 1816 'on the native habiliments you could not perceive one article of British manufacture', whereas some four years later (1820) 'they are very generally clothed with British cottons'.[115]

This was an exaggeration. Indeed, soon after the British occupation of Java in 1811, importations of British cotton goods had already begun, encouraged in part by Thomas Stamford Raffles, the British Lieutenant-Governor, and continued at an increasing pace thereafter. At the same time, the indigenous cotton goods industry was by no means eliminated. Maclaine – who by that stage in his career was certainly in a very good position to know – observed as late as 1830 that in central Java, the most densely populated part of the island, people were clad in cotton clothing that was 'generally the manufacture of the island'.[116] Nonetheless, the broad point remained that from sometime in the second decade in the nineteenth century, cotton goods of British manufacture began to be imported into Java on a considerable scale, either for immediate sale there or for transhipment elsewhere in the Eastern Isles. Piece goods from the UK had gained ground over those from the subcontinent largely because the fall in price in British cottons had enabled them to undercut the Indian product.[117]

Patrick McLachlan and his partners were major participants in this development. Remarking in 1821 to a British Parliamentary Committee that his firm had hitherto traded 'to Bengal chiefly', McLachlan also observed, albeit somewhat cryptically, that 'latterly we have been shipping into the Eastern straits, to Batavia'.[118] His Calcutta partner, Donald MacIntyre, was somewhat more expansive. 'Having an idea that our manufactures would be taken off there, I sent some small consignments, on experiment, to different ports to the eastward', he told the same parliamentary interlocutors in London in 1821. The results were 'better than we expected. We got more for the goods there than we could get at Calcutta', and in consequence, he had set up a branch of his firm in Batavia to handle the new business. Java was not, however, the only destination. MacIntyre was also confident in stating that the cotton goods

[114] Kraan, 'Anglo-Dutch Rivalry', pp. 37–39.

[115] Select Committee of the House of Commons on the Means of Improving and Maintaining Foreign Trade – East Indies and China, *Parliamentary Papers GB* 1821, vol. VI, 'Evidence of John Hare', pp. 266, 270.

[116] Select Committee on China and the Affairs of the East India Company, *Parliamentary Papers GB* 1831–1832, vol. VI, 'Evidence of Gillian Maclaine', p. 92.

[117] Wright, *East Indian Economic Problems*, pp. 226–38; Kraan, 'Anglo-Dutch Rivalry', p. 45.

[118] 'Evidence McLachlan 1821', pp. 277–78.

had also been shipped elsewhere in the archipelago, a point confirmed by another trader contemporary who reckoned that perhaps as much as half the European goods traded to Java subsequently found their way to other parts of the region.[119]

Then there was China. MacIntyre asserted that his firm had 'also consigned some of our British cotton goods ... to China', a point reiterated by McLachlan with the observation that 'some of our own goods, that have been shipped to Batavia ... have gone afterwards to China and met with a beneficial return'. It was in this connection, presumably, that one of the partners in the Calcutta firm had himself been sent to China.[120] If so, transhipment in the ports of maritime Southeast Asia appeared to have been a neat way of side-stepping the EIC monopoly on the direct shipment of British goods from India to China. Nonetheless, it was the Indonesian archipelago and adjacent Malay Peninsula that remained the focus of the firm's attention, and the prime destination for their cargoes.

It was accompanying just such a cargo – indeed, so it would appear, the *first* such cargo of any size dispatched by McLachlans in that direction on their own account – that Maclaine sailed from London in April 1820. Planning (as we have seen) had evidently been going on for some time, perhaps encouraged not only by market reports but also by falling freight rates to Asia, which were said to have dropped by nearly 75 per cent over the period 1817–21.[121] At the very beginning of 1820, Maclaine had alerted his family that he might soon be dispatched on the McLachlans' business to distant Batavia, urging them not to worry – the city's reputation as a graveyard for Europeans appears to have penetrated as far as Morvern and Mull – because he was not slated to stay there any length of time. Instead, it was intended that, having delivered the cargo to his firm's agents on Java, he would proceed rapidly from the Dutch colony back to Calcutta, and become part of the McLachlan–McIntyre establishment in a place sufficiently far 'above the line' to be deemed healthy.[122]

---

119 'Evidence Robert Addison', p. 223. Addison had 'lately returned from Singapore and Java' and was very well versed in the Java trade, having being resident on the island since 1814. See F. de Haan, 'Personalia der Periode van het Engelsch Bestuur over Java, 1811–1816', *Bijdragen tot de Taal-Land-en-Volkenkunde*, 92 (1935), p. 487.

120 'Evidence MacIntyre 1821', pp. 298–99; 'Evidence McLachlan 1821', p. 280. Inter alia, McLachlan remarked that 'It is well-known that there are a great number of our manufactures going in American ships to China.'

121 Select Committee of the House of Commons on the Means of Improving and Maintaining Foreign Trade – East Indies and China', *Parliamentary Papers GB* 1821, vol. VI, 'Evidence of George Larpent', p. 218. Larpent, richly experienced with eighteen years in the East India trade in London, claimed that whereas in 1817 freight rates had been around £20 sterling per ton, by March 1821 they were as low as £5 10s per ton, 'making it a most losing trade as far as the ship-owner is concerned'.

122 GM to MM 4.1.1820. O-M MSS.

The cargo itself, meanwhile, was being assembled in London, presumably from the cotton mills of Glasgow with which the McLachlans were connected. In late January 1820, Maclaine told his mother that there would be some delay since 'much to the annoyance of the Messrs McLachlan, there is not at present any ship loading for that quarter'. Even so, 'the business of the Houses on both sides of the water is rapidly increasing. This very day I am pretty sure we will have transacted more business in the way of Produce than any East India House in the city.'[123] Early in March a deal had evidently been struck and the McLachlans contracted for 100 tons of freight to go on board a ship, the *Mary Anne*, due to clear for Batavia toward the end of the month.[124] According to Maclaine, the firm was the only one to ship goods on her, and her dispatch was 'to be kept secret till the day before she clears …. They got accounts of the market at Batavia from their agent there which induced them at once to enter into this shipment and they wish to keep it as quiet as possible so as to have the start of [*sic*] the other Houses.'[125]

Meanwhile, Maclaine himself was understandably keen to participate in the venture, but he lacked the money to do so. The young man was clearly penniless. Back in the summer of 1817, for example, he wrote thanking his uncle for a subvention, previous to the receipt of which 'Mr. John [McLachlan] was kind enough to supply me with the clothes I needed' and he continued in a similar vein, remarking that 'it grieves me not a little that I should be a burden to my friends…. God knows, I long exceedingly to be in a way of doing for myself and eagerly look forward to the period when I can live by my own exertions.'[126] Until then, however, there was nothing for it but to appeal to his uncle for further financial support, as continued to be the case in 1820 on the eve of his departure for Java.

Gregorson, however, had recently had to raise money to buy the freehold of the Ardtornish property on Morvern where he had previously been a tenant of the Duke of Argyll and was consequently far from being flush with money. Indeed, as Maclaine wrote to him, 'I know … how much your late purchase must press on your funds, and if I did not see very great advantage likely to accrue from laying in a small investment, I would not have troubled you.'[127] As matters stood, moreover, it was unfortunately the case that 'the articles that suit the market best are called cash articles, not sold on credit'. The particular 'cash article' on which Maclaine finally settled was imported into London mainly from Turkey and India and sold in 'Eastern' wholesalers

[123] GM to MM 21.1.1820 and 9.2.1820. O-M MSS.
[124] GM to MM 3.3.1820. O-M MSS.
[125] GM to MM 7.3.1820. O-M MSS.
[126] GM to JG 8.7.1817. O-M MSS.
[127] GM to JG 3.3.1820 and 7.3.1820. O-M MSS.

in and around Mincing Lane, a short walk from D. & P. McLachlan's own premises just off Cornhill. Maclaine called it his 'sleepy commodity' and the captain of the ship on which he sailed likewise made investment in opium.[128] Maclaine used £500, lent somewhat reluctantly by his uncle, to secure a parcel of it.[129]

The *Mary Anne*, under the command of Captain Morgan, a former East India Company captain and a man rich – or creditworthy – enough to also be the owner of the vessel,[130] finally left the port of London early in April. By the eighteenth of the month the ship had cleared the Thames and was off Sheerness, the fortified town and naval dockyard at the end of the Thames–Medway navigation, where the last of its very few passengers came aboard. Maclaine, himself accompanied that far by Duncan and Hugh McLachlan, had already joined the ship at Gravesend, as it made its way down the estuary.[131] After Sheerness, the *Mary Anne*, its crew, passengers and cargo were finally on the open seas. Once through the treacherous waterway under the Downs off the south coast of England, they said farewell to their pilot, something that gave Maclaine the opportunity to write a final shipboard letter to his mother.[132] Crossing the South Atlantic via Rio, they rounded the Cape of Good Hope in late May, and finally arrived off Batavia late in July, after an uneventful voyage of some three and a half months.

In the course of less than four years (December 1816 to April 1820), Gillian Maclaine had made the transition from student in Glasgow to commercial 'apprentice' in London. Now, in the course of less than four *months*, he made an even more dramatic transition from clerk in a Counting House in the City to (de facto) supercargo on a ship bound for Java with a valuable freight of cotton piece goods, and with a placement awaiting him in an Agency House in Calcutta. He had not intended that things would fall out this way. Initially, indeed, he had obviously hoped for employment in the UK, quite possibly in Liverpool, where the direct trade with Asian ports was burgeoning.[133] Patrick

---

[128] GM to MM 29.3.1820 and 18.4.1820. O-M MSS.

[129] GM to MM 7.8.1820. O-M MSS.

[130] GM to MM 29.3.1820. O-M MSS.

[131] GM to MM 18.4.1820. O-M MSS.

[132] GM to MM ('off Beachy Head') 21.4.1820. O-M MSS.

[133] 'Mr. P was lately down in Liverpool for a few days. He thinks the East India Trade [there] will soon equal if not outstrip the London. Clothes, iron, lead glassware etc can be shipped much more cheaply from Liverpool than from here, and by McIntyre's last letters [i.e. from Calcutta] ships from Liverpool disposed of whole cargoes at an advance of 85%. Did I ever engage in the East India trade, it would be from Liverpool.' GM to JG 8.7.1817. O-M MSS. For a broader discussion of Liverpool's role, see Anthony Webster, 'Liverpool and the Asian Trade, 1800–1850. Some Insights into a Provincial Commercial Network', in S. Haggerty, A. Webster and N. White (eds), *Empire in One City: Liverpool's Inconvenient Imperial Past* (Manchester: Manchester University Press, 2008).

McLachlan, however, obviously had other ideas. He deemed his young clerk's prospects in India, rather than in the UK, to be 'fair, very fair', leading Maclaine to conclude that 'it certainly would fully desirable in many respects that I remain in Britain, but by doing so I fear that my chance of securing an independency would not be so good'.[134] McLachlan subsequently followed up with remarks that Maclaine found altogether less agreeable. Not only was he very guarded about the terms on which Maclaine would work in McIntyre's office in Calcutta but also:

> … gave me frequently to understand that they sent me out more for the purpose of making a provision for me <u>than for any occasion they had for my services</u>. He also said several other things with a view to make me of as little consequence as possible, such as that there are numbers of young men at Calcutta at present possessed of <u>double my talents and knowledge of business</u> who cannot find employment. He became latterly more friendly, and said my prospects were by no means bad.[135]

'More friendly' he may have been, but as we shall see his admonitions were not something that Maclaine took lightly, and were to colour the dealings that he had with the McLachlans once he had arrived in Batavia. So too did his misgivings about the whole projected arrangement. As he informed his mother, 'Mr. Peter stated no definite terms, nor would he condescend on any, he said, until I was a year or two in their employ in India … <u>on a good deal of consideration</u>, I am inclined to think it would be imprudent to refuse his present offer.'[136] As Maclaine had earlier remarked to his mother, the pros outweighed the cons, insofar as he had the prospect of 'establishing a connection with a respectable, established house <u>without an advance of capital</u>'.[137] Even so, it was not the best beginning for what turned out to be a stormy – and for Maclaine, nearly disastrous – business relationship.

[134] GM to MM 4.1.1820. O-M MSS.
[135] GM to MM 3.3.1820. O-M MSS (emphasis in original).
[136] GM to MM 4.1.1820 and 21.1.1820. O-M MSS (emphasis in original).
[137] GM to MM 18.6.1818. O-M MSS (emphasis in original).

Three

A 'SCOTCH ADVENTURER': BATAVIA, COFFEE AND COLONIAL WARS, 1820–27

> This is really a strange world and I little thought when I left England of settling in Java, much less of ever being a Coffee Planter or a tenant of the Emperor of Solo. A <u>Scotch Adventurer</u> however must pay his account to many vicissitudes in life.[1]

It is improbable nonetheless that Maclaine could have anticipated what was actually in store for him. Between 1820 and 1827 he first dallied with the idea of setting up as a merchant in Batavia and then established himself as a deeply impecunious coffee-planter in the mountains of central Java. Subsequent to that, his investment there was placed in jeopardy by the hostility of the Indies government and threatened with destruction in a major colonial war. Moreover, as if that were not enough, he had to contend with commercial hazards that had to do, among other things, with a very significant curtailment of the import of British cottons into Java, with the rapacity of his overseas partners and with the spectacular default of a key associate on Java itself.

Maclaine arrived in Batavia in July 1820 aboard the ship *Mary Anne*, together (as we have just seen) with a cargo of cotton piece goods dispatched by the East India house for whom he had been working in London. Founded in its colonial form by the VOC early in the seventeenth century, Batavia was at one time an essentially Chinese city flying a Dutch flag.[2] When Maclaine arrived there, it had long ceased to be that, but was still a city with a large and commercially dominant Indies-Chinese (in modern parlance, Chinese-Indonesian) minority made up both of recent arrivals and of families who had been long settled there. It was merchants from this group of Batavia's

[1]   GM to MM 4.1.1821. O-M MSS (emphasis in original).
[2]   See in particular Leonard Blussé, 'Batavia 1619–1740: The Rise and Fall of a Chinese Colonial Town', in Leonard Blussé, *Strange Company. Chinese Settlers, Mestizo Women and the Dutch in VOC Batavia* (Dordrecht: Foris Publications, 1986), pp. 73–96.

ethnically and culturally very mixed population with whom most of the recently arrived Maclaine's business dealings took place. Maclaine also found himself, however, among a small community of European merchants, the majority of them British – a legacy (as we have seen in an earlier chapter) of the British occupation of the island from 1811 until 1816 by East India Company forces during the later stages of the Napoleonic Wars.

Nonetheless, although Batavia's commercial life was predominantly in the hands of others, the city's rulers were the official representatives of the Kingdom of the Netherlands. It was to them that Java (and the 'Outer Islands' of the Indies) had been restored some four years earlier. The Dutch Governor-General himself had a palace and office in the city, though was more likely to be found at his alternative residence at Buitenzorg (Bogor) in the hills a few hours journey to the south. Indeed, by this date virtually the entire European population had deserted the old parts of the city adjacent to the port and moved inland to the purportedly healthier suburbs around the huge and newly established *Koningsplein* (present-day *Merdeka* square).

Even so, European (and Armenian) merchants – the people with whom Maclaine began to associate immediately after his arrival – retained their offices and warehouses in the commercial quarter of the old city (Maclaine's were to be established first in Malacca Street and later on the canal known as Kali Besar), even though they lived outside it. So too did the officials of the Indies government and well-to-do Indies-Chinese, who a shared a proclivity with their European counterparts for 'country estates' on the outskirts of Batavia. These estates were also the seats of the wealthy members of the city's Indies-Dutch elite, families of often mixed ethnicity who maintained close social ties with more recently arrived 'expatriate' Netherlanders. It was the old city itself, however, together with the surrounding urban kampongs, that was home to the majority of Batavia's population, comprising people styled variously as local Indonesians (or *Batawi*), Malays, Arabs, 'Indos' (poor Eurasians), as well as a variety of immigrants from Java itself and from other parts of the archipelago. In total, by the 1820s Batavia was home to some 50,000 or more people.[3]

Plans in Disarray: Maclaine's First Months in Java

Almost as soon as stepped off the boat, the plans made in London for Maclaine's short-term stay in Batavia were thrown into disarray. He was supposed to liaise with the firm of Menzies and Anderson, who were acting as agents there for Donald MacIntyre's Calcutta partnership, and once he had handed over

---

[3] For a succinct account of nineteenth-century Batavia, see Susan Abeysekere, *Jakarta. A History*, (Singapore: Oxford University Press, 1987), pp. 48–87.

the *Mary Anne*'s cargo, to proceed forthwith to Calcutta. However, William Menzies had (temporarily) left Batavia for Bengal late in the previous month,[4] and within two days of Maclaine's disembarkation, John Anderson broke his arm. All was not lost, however. A couple of fellow Scots came forward to help out and young Maclaine was evidently given a crash course in negotiating the intricate customs regulations at the port of Batavia: 'the difficulties a stranger has to encounter at Batavia [in relation to] transacting business is truly great [he reported to his uncle in September 1820]. The Dutch cramp foreigners with so many arbitrary restrictions that a person, let him be ever so cautious, cannot comply with their vexatious forms in every particular.'[5] Simultaneously, he had to learn to negotiate the equal intricate customs of the Indies-Chinese to whom he hoped to sell the cotton piece goods that had accompanied to the island. In consequence, he was able to write to his mother some ten days after landing that he hoped 'to get a lot of goods disposed of this week'; that he had sold his 'sleepy commodity' (i.e. the Turkish opium that he had brought with him from London) at a 50 per cent profit; and that in consequence she should tell her brother, John Gregorson, 'that I shall lose no time in remitting the 500 pounds' which the latter had lent him for its purchase.

Meanwhile, he was lodged in Anderson's house some three miles outside the city 'in a fine healthy situation', a point which he expanded upon with the further reassurance to his mother that 'the climate is not so bad as it is generally represented. The heat is by no means so great as I was led to expect [and] … the mornings and evenings are very cool.'[6] He thought rather less of the Dutch among whom he found himself, or of most of British who associated with them:

> The society here is not very good, consisting mostly of Dutchmen who are not very agreeable in their manners. They have little refinement or polish and the greater part of the hours that are not employed in business are spent smoking and drinking. The few English here associate largely together – from the want of female society and being mostly young they get greatly into the boorish Dutch fashions. I was a little surprised on my arrival at a dinner party to see many of the young men after the cloth was removed put their feet on the table, at the same time smoking their cigars with the utmost of sang froid. This is making oneself at home with a vengeance.[7]

On this occasion, however, he was not detained at Batavia for long. Business was not so brisk that he could dispose of all – or even the bulk – of the *Mary*

---

4   Menzies had left Batavia for Bengal on 25.6.1820. See *Bataviasche Courant* 1.7.1820/27.
5   GM to JG 30.9.1820. O-M MSS.
6   GM to MM 7.8.1820. O-M MSS.
7   GM to MM 20.10.1820. O-M MSS.

Anne's cargo there, and within a matter of weeks he had sailed with the ship to Semarang, the coastal metropolis of central Java, more than 400 kilometres further east. Semarang in the 1820s, at that time Java's second largest city, was a thriving centre for trade to the mountainous and densely populated interior of the island. In particular, the port was the gateway to the quasi-independent Principalities (*Vorstenlanden* as the Dutch called them) of Yogyakarta and Surakarta, rival mini-states in south central Java that had been formed out of the remnants of a larger kingdom some seventy-five years earlier. Maclaine was to get to know the Principalities very well in the years that followed.

In September 1820, however, he was fully occupied selling his cargo of cotton goods to the Indies-Chinese merchants who dominated the trade of Semarang even more than they did that of Batavia. In the weeks since his arrival in the colony he had already picked up enough Malay – the language of commerce in Java – to enable him, at least so he claimed, 'to drive a bargain in it'. He was evidently a fast learner. 'You would have smiled to see me', he told his mother, 'running about the Bazaars with a large bundle of patterns, selling away to the long que'd Chinamen who were the sole purchasers of our ship[ment].'[8] By the end of the month, the McLachlans' consignment of cottons – 'this Java speculation is one of the grandest they ever made' – was nearly all sold. Maclaine did not expand on the full value of the cargo beyond remarking that he had disposed of around £12,000 worth of it in Semarang alone. As he somewhat ruefully observed to his uncle: 'one half of the profits would content a moderate person like <u>poor</u> me and enable me to return to my country a truly independent man'.[9]

The Lure of Coffee

As we have seen, the issue of being 'truly independent' – of accumulating enough wealth to set up as a landed proprietor among the Highland gentry from whom he stemmed – had been a major concern for Maclaine almost as soon as he had first arrived in London from the Highlands, and it was to remain one for the rest of his life. Already in the closing months of 1820, Maclaine's quest for an independency of this kind led to situation in which he severed relations (temporarily, as it turned out) with the McLachlans and set up as a coffee planter in the mountainous interior of central Java.

Until the 1820s, Java continued, as had been the case since the mid-eighteenth century, to be the largest single producer of coffee for world markets. Coffee cultivation had arrived on the island early in the early 1700s, and by

---

[8]   GM to MM 8.8.1820. O-M MSS.
[9]   GM to JG 30.9.1820 & GM to MM 8.10.1820. O-M MSS (emphasis in original).

the time that Maclaine arrived there in 1820 it was being grown in virtually every part of Java where altitude and climatic conditions were favourable. Moreover, the local market for the commodity was experiencing a period of unprecedented boom, something which tempted Maclaine to throw whatever resources he had – and they were miniscule – into the coffee business. At this point, indeed, cotton and coffee complemented each other. Coffee provided – or was meant to provide – the return cargoes of a trade in cotton goods that otherwise had to be paid for in cash. As we shall see, this apparently neat equation worked far from smoothly. Nonetheless, it points to the way in which two of the commodity chains vital to Maclaine's business were tightly intertwined. Almost contemporaneously, moreover, Maclaine came to participate in the coffee commodity chain both as a merchant who traded in the commodity and as a *producer*. In this latter capacity, he not only had a financial stake in coffee plantations. At various stages in his career during the 1820s, he also directly managed and supervised 'up country' estates on which coffee was grown by a workforce of Javanese peasants.

Coffee had a history on Java that dated back at least a century prior to Maclaine's arrival there.[10] Indeed, it has been calculated that during the 1720s Java had supplied as much as 50 per cent of Europe's requirements of the commodity.[11] In the Preanger Mountains of West Java it formed the basis of a system run by the VOC, whereby Indonesian peasants were compelled to grow the crop, under the supervision of village headmen and local dignitaries. It was a major source of profit for the company. Indeed, it was one of the few commodities that promised to keep afloat an increasingly geriatric enterprise whose best days were far behind it when it was wound up in 1799. Thereafter, however, the Dutch state took over the running of the 'the Indies' and kept the Preanger 'system' firmly in place as one of its anchors of solvency.[12]

Notionally entirely separate from what went on in the Preanger was the widespread peasant cultivation of coffee in the mountainous districts along Java's northeast coast and in the interior of south central Java. Whereas in

10 Robert van Niel, *Java's Northeast Coast 1740–1840* (Leiden: CNWS Publications, 2005), pp. 170–76, 304–07, 339–41; M.R. Fernando, 'Coffee Cultivation in Java, 1830–1917', in Clarence-Smith and Topik, *Global Coffee Economy*, pp. 157–72; William Gervase Clarence-Smith, 'The Impact of Forced Coffee Cultivation on Java, 1805–1917', *Indonesia Circle*, 64 (1994), pp. 214–64.

11 David Bulbeck, Anthony Reid, Lay Cheng Tan and Yiqi Wu, 'Southeast Asian Exports since the 14th Century. Cloves, Pepper, Coffee and Sugar', Data Paper Series, Sources for the Economic History of Southeast Asia, Institute of Southeast Asian Studies, Singapore, 1998, p. 159.

12 The Preanger system and the forced labour that underpinned it is the subject of a recent and authoritative study by the eminent Dutch sociologist Jan Breman (in Dutch): *Koloniaal Profijt van Onvrije Arbeid: Het Preanger Stelsel van Gedwongen Koffieteelt op Java* (Amsterdam: Amsterdam University Press, 2010).

the Preanger, the cultivation of coffee beans was, and continued to be into the twentieth century, a servitude imposed on the peasantry by the Indies government and its agents, in the coastal areas stretching from Cirebon in the west to what the Dutch called Java's *Oosthoek* or East Point across the strait from Bali, villagers were notionally free to grow coffee, without state intervention. In fact, in these directly ruled parts of the colony, what appears to have happened was that European or Indies-Chinese middlemen paid advances to village headmen to ensure cultivation and thereby secured the commodity at spot prices well below the going rate in Batavia.[13] As we shall see, it can safely be assumed that Maclaine and his agents in Semarang and further east in Surabaya would have been alert to these opportunities.

In the Javanese Principalities of Yogyakarta (Yogya) and Surakarta (Solo) in south central Java where Maclaine's coffee operations came to centre, however, the dominant relations of production were different again. The precise political economy of coffee production in this part of Java still awaits its historian. By Maclaine's day, however, a dozen or more European coffee planters were established there. Indeed, this was what excited the young man's interest very soon after landing in the colony in August 1820. Leasing land and (in effect) labour from local dignitaries, the planters set about growing coffee, using locally available workers who were paid a small wage but whose 'feudal' obligations to the proprietors also involved an element of compulsion.

Until the 1830s, the Indies government's authority was much more restricted in the Principalities than elsewhere in Java. Although it posted a Dutch Resident at each of the two main princely courts, the individuals concerned had only limited powers and no brief to control coffee production on the Indies government's behalf. Not that the Residents were indifferent to it, however: indeed, when Maclaine first became interested in coffee growing in the Principalities, by far the most influential Dutch official there, Colonel H.G. Nahuijs, Resident at Yogyakarta from 1816 to 1823 (and of Surakarta 1820–22 and 1827–30), was a keen promoter of 'private' European coffee plantations. Not only did he line his own pockets thereby – he had an extensive plantation in the Yogyakarta Sultanate – but it also fitted with his concept of Europe's civilising mission. Inter alia, that mission was to eradicate 'traditional' society and the constraining servitude associated with it. As Peter Carey, the foremost modern historian of the Principalities in this period remarks, the Resident was, or purported to be, well enough read to be able to cite Adam Smith on the deleterious effects of 'feudal government' on rural welfare.[14] They were sentiments that Maclaine was to echo: 'The good that

---

[13] Van Niel, *Java's Northeast Coast*, pp. 306, 340.

[14] For an extended discussion of Resident Nahuijs and land-lease issue in the Principalities,

European settlers in the Native provinces must do to the country', he assured his uncle, 'is beyond calculation.'[15]

From a merchant's point of view, however, coffee was less about 'civilisation' than return cargoes. It promised to be a staple which would profitably fill the holds of ships that had come to Java laden with bales of cotton cloth, something that was otherwise not easy to achieve. 'I know the great difficulty of the trade between this country and Java to consist in the difficulty of obtaining returns', one of the partners in a large London East India house asserted in evidence to a British parliamentary committee in 1821.[16] For Maclaine and the people with whom he associated in Batavia, coffee seemed the ideal commodity to plug the gap, the more so since it held out the promise of being a commodity produced with a minimal financial outlay on the part of European planters. As a result, colonial merchant circles in Batavia were evidently in the grip of a coffee-mania when Maclaine arrived there. It proved one from which the young man was far from immune.

During the Napoleonic Wars, with little shipping available, coffee beans had changed hands there for very low prices. Toward the Wars' end, however, the price began to rise sharply, and continued to do so for some years thereafter. In 1817 beans fetched a little over thirty-five guilders per quintal (100 kg) at Batavia, and by 1822 had reached what proved to be the peak price of eighty-eight guilders. Around this time, according to one enthusiast, anyone with capital was investing in coffee and shipping it to Europe.[17] Maclaine did not have the money for that, but he could hope to join in the boom by becoming involved in the *production* of the commodity at source. Coffee was one of the 'easiest, safest ... and most rapid modes of realising a fortune that possibly exists', he wrote to his uncle at the end of September 1820:

> In the Planting line there is a fine opening at present even for young men without much capital. When up the country I visited some very extensive Coffee Plantations held in lease by Europeans from the Emperor or Sultan of Soloo [*sic*]. I was so much delighted with the salubrity [*sic*] of the climate and the beauty of the country and ... struck by the amazingly moderate rate at which the lands are leased from his majesty that I almost determined on becoming coffee planter. I am not joking – had I not been under engagements

see Peter Carey, *The Power of Prophecy: Prince Dipanagara and the End of an Old Order in Java, 1785–1855* (Leiden: KITLV Press, 2007), pp. 454–64.

[15] GM to JG 21.7.1821. O-M MSS.

[16] 'Select Committee of the House of Commons on the Means of Improving and Maintaining Foreign Trade – East Indies and China', *Parliamentary Papers GB* 1821, vol. VI; 'Evidence George Larpent', p. 221. Larpent was a long-time member of the firm of Paxton, Cockerill Trail & Co, inter alia the London correspondents of the Calcutta House of John Palmer & Co.

[17] William Cotes to Willem van Hogendorp 11.9.1826. NA Collectie Van Hogendorp, 189.

to the Messrs Mac and had I your authority to keep the 500 pounds for three years, I would without hesitation have accepted an offer of ½ of the lease of an extensive piece of ground made me by a Mr. Cotes here. The expense of labour is so trifling and the advance of capital so little, there being no Sink of money for an Estate, slaves etc. as in the West Indies, that coffee can actually be raised for 8 or 10 shillings per cwt. Mr. Cotes has got a lease of 13 years from the Sultan of a piece of land of sufficient extent to hold 400,000 coffee trees at a rent of 300 dollars per annum (75 pounds sterling). From the above number of trees we can calculate on a return of 4000 cwt. of coffee annually.[18]

The prospect was evidently just too alluring. Long before John Gregorson would have received this excited outpouring – let alone had any chance of responding to it – Maclaine committed himself to a partnership to establish a coffee plantation on land in south central Java, leased (so he reported) from the ruler of Surakarta. He readily conceded that he did not have Gregorson's 'authority to keep the 500 pounds' lent him earlier that year, and admitted that 'I cannot pretend to say when I shall be able to repay you.' Nonetheless, he reported that he had committed the money to an arrangement with four other young men to set themselves up as planters. Menzies (who had meanwhile returned to Java from Calcutta) and Anderson had an eighth share, Maclaine had a quarter share, his new friend William Cotes (see below) had an eighth and a young man from the southern Netherlands, Medard Louis,[19] had a half share in the enterprise 'in consideration of his having secured the lease from the Sultan [*sic*] and his remaining on the plantation as manager or rather overseer'. The plantation, known as Melambong, lay on the north-eastern slopes of *Gunung* Merbabu volcano, in the mountains between Surakarta and the north coast. Maclaine was to be based there along with Louis.

What the partnership was aiming for, however, was not simply a plantation venture. Indeed, the initial object was to establish a base in the Principalities from which to purchase at source coffee already being grown in south central

---

[18] GM to JG 30.9.1820. O-M MSS.

[19] Medard Joseph Louis, b. [date unknown] in the rural town of Jodoigne, South (i.e. Walloon) Brabant (Netherlands/Belgium), d. Java 1835 (see *Javasche Courant* 63/1835). Until 1820, Louis was a First Lieutenant in the Dutch army in Java, and head of the garrison at the Dutch fort which dated from c.1806 at Klaten (Klathen) in central Java, mid-way between Surakarta and Yogyakarta (Carey, *Power of Prophecy*, p. 184 fn. 78). In 1820, he left the army, moved into the coffee planting business and married Louisa de la Brethoniere, the Java-born sister of a fellow planter (whose father had arrived in Java in 1782). He made a short return journey to the Netherlands in 1823–24, probably in connection with disputes with the Indies government over the 'coffee' leases in the Principalities (see below). He arrived back in Java in May 1825. For biographical information about Louis, see 'Petition of M.J. Louis to the King of the Netherlands', 10.3.1824, NA Collectie Van Hogendorp 150, lett. G; MK 3106 & 3138 (i.e. lists of Europeans in Java); *Regeerings Almanac* 1821; *Bataviasche Courant*, 26.7.1823/30 & 25.5.1825/21.

Java. Though data are scant, it looks as if coffee had been grown from the late eighteenth century onward in the area in which Maclaine was proposing to set up operations, initially perhaps under the auspices of the VOC who had a string of forts along the road linking Semarang to the Principalities. These included Salatiga, only a few kilometres from Maclaine's new base at Melambong, where the Dutch stronghold, *De Hersteller*, dated from the time of VOC Governor-General Baron van Imhoff (1753–1750).[20] As he explained to Gregorson: 'The principal object however we have had in view in entering into this speculation is to gain a footing up the country in a good Coffee district. I intend settling at Melambong … chiefly for the purpose of collecting coffee.' Even so, for the next three years he 'expected to be able to do little more than be able to keep myself in <u>Curry and Rice</u>.'[21] Maclaine was to retain an association with Melambong for the rest of his life: that association, however, was shortly to become much more problematic than he might have anticipated.

Maclaine and the McLachlans at Loggerheads

In the meantime, however, there was the matter of how Maclaine's decision to become a coffee planter impacted on his relations with the McLachlans, under whose aegis he had sailed to the East not much more than six months earlier. To say that the brothers were put out by Maclaine's decision (when they finally heard about it around April 1821) would be a gross understatement: 'They seem to take tremendous umbrage', Maclaine reported to his mother and no doubt (though direct evidence is lacking) communicated their fury to Gregorson at Ardtornish.[22] Maclaine, however, held firm in the face of this disapproval. He had heard enough from Menzies and Anderson about the situation of the McLachlans' and Macintyre's junior partners in Bengal ('the accounts received are by no means encouraging … they have only 1/8th each, which they say scarcely pays their expenses') to make him reluctant to enter into a mere clerkship in Calcutta in the hope of eventual 'better' things.

Java seemed to offer altogether more attractive prospects. Not least, his potential business partners there were fellow Scots and evidently much to his liking. The thirty-year-old Menzies,[23] he assured his mother, was 'a complete

---

20 Van Niel, *Java's North Coast*, p. 172: Carey, *Power of Prophecy*, p. 287 fn. 103.

21 GM to JG 3.1.1821. O-M MSS (emphasis in original).

22 GM to MM 4.1.1822. O-M MSS.

23 William Menzies b. Scotland 1791, d. Batavia 1855. He was a merchant in Buitenzorg [Bogor] and Batavia from 1816 onward (firm of Menzies and Anderson dissolved 16.8.1822 – see *Bataviasche Courant* 31.8.1822/34), and subsequently part-owner of the Koeripan estate in West Java (e.g. NA MK 2815 GG in Rade 13.5.1828/32). He was unmarried.

Highlander in appearance and manners. Perthshire gave him birth. He is a warm-hearted fellow with a lot of common sense. I never knew a person give a more regular Highland Shake ....' The Glasgow-born Anderson he recommended for her approval as a 'young man of excellent abilities' and who 'not withstanding the ridicule of several of his acquaintances ... maintains his strict Presbyterian principles'. Both men had been in the East for about five years at the time that Maclaine met them in Batavia: Menzies, it would seem, initially as a saddler in Calcutta (whence he had been sent by Donald MacIntyre) and Anderson initially as a clerk in the major Calcutta house of Fairlie Fergusson & Co. For the newly arrived Maclaine, they were evidently an important source of advice and inspiration – role models, even.[24] Pondering his future, Maclaine first thought to engage with them in a joint business venture with the McLachlans and MacIntyre, but when the latter's terms proved unacceptable, coffee planting became the only real alternative:

> By the *Wellington* Messrs M & A have received letter from McLachlans offering terms of partnership which are by no means so liberal as I should have expected. M & A have been under the necessity of refusing them and I cannot but think they have acted prudently in doing so. This interferes greatly with the prospects I had of associating in business with my friends here. Honest Anderson was desirous the moment Menzies arrived of giving me a full share. It was however thought best to wait the Messrs Mac's proposals. They have been made and have now been refused. So I must content myself for the present with the partnership in the Coffee Plantation.[25]

Underlying all this, moreover, was the fact that Patrick McLachlan's parting shot – in his last talk with Maclaine prior to the latter's departure for Java he had been at some pains to underline the young man's superfluity to the McLachlans' enterprise – continued to rankle. The senior partner's remarks were reiterated more than once by Maclaine as he sought to justify to his family his 'desertion' of the McLachlan interest. Nor was he shy of reminding the brothers of what had been said to him before he left London. In his eyes, it offered a complete justification for his striking out on his own. Well might Patrick McLachlan write to him that:

> I own I am a good deal surprised about the crude notions you let out about stopping & settling in Java etc. etc. You surely cannot have forgotten the understanding on which you left us, that your destination was Bengal, that you went out in our employ and were to undergo a probation of three years on a salary before you could expect any share in our concerns. Now this understanding seems quite irreconcilable with the notions you entertain of settling in Java,

[24] GM to MM 20.10.1820 and 4.1.1821. O-M MSS.
[25] GM to MM 7.1.1821. O-M MSS.

charting a distinct path and proposing an immediate junction with Messrs Menzies & Anderson, and that too at a time when our connection with them was only pending and contingent. Such views would almost imply that you had lost sight of your destination and <u>our</u> views in sending you to Bengal but also that you consider your dependence on us for your future prospects so loose as to be at liberty to act as your own views of your interest suggest. Now though we don't wish to tie any of our friends down to our Service against their own inclinations, yet surely with such an understanding and in such circumstances, some regard was likewise due to our views and interests, but I will think no more of this matter, confident a little reflection will convince you that such sentiments are premature and not very becoming, and that perhaps they convey more than you ever meant, for we all think so favourably of your principles, disposition, zeal and fidelity, and have so much confidence in you that appearances alone will not prejudice you in our esteem. Meanwhile, you will consider yourself as on the footing upon which you set out.[26]

Maclaine, however, remained unmoved, and scarcely even conciliatory:

On my arrival in Batavia I was led to understand by Messrs Menzies and Anderson that Mr. McIntyre had made arrangements prior to his leaving Bengal that gave me reason to dread I might be considered as a <u>supernumerary</u> there – an idea by no means agreeable to my feelings. Bearing also in recollection my dear Sir a remark of your own 'that it was to make a provision for me and not from any occasion you had for my services that you sent me to India', you will not be surprised that I was anxious to look out for a station where any little assistance I could render would be most required and where I had no reason to consider myself in any way burdensome to you. From the success of your first speculation to Java, I conceived you might soon view it as a place of great commercial importance, and in the course of time direct your attention fully as much to this quarter as to Bengal.

Nor was this all he had to say: indeed, the necessity to justify himself not only to the McLachlans but also – and even more importantly – to his uncle and his mother made him positively loquacious:

These considerations made me anxious to remain on the Island and almost determined me previous to Mr. Menzies arrival from Calcutta, to settle here. When I first however entertained such ideas, I had no intention of engaging in the interior business, under the impression of finding ample employment in another department. In this opinion I was mistaken, M & A having no occasion for my services. Viewing an establishment in the interior for the purpose of purchasing Coffee, as I still do, of great moment as a means of facilitating remittances, I conceived I could not be more usefully employed for the time than Collecting Produce for you up the Country, and I feel confident if you

---

[26] 'Extract from a letter received from P. McLachlan Esq., dated London 5 May 1821', in GM to MM 4.1.1822. O-M MSS.

continue your shipments you will perceive the necessity of having more than one person stationed in several of the coffee districts for the same purpose. With regard to the Plantation business, I embarked in it entirely at my own risk, regarding it as a promising speculation, and at all events calculated to gain me some weight and influence among the Natives in the Neighbourhood. Had I even been on a salary (which would have been more profitable to me than any trifling commissions last season) I suppose you would not have objected to my laying out the little funds I possessed on Coffee Planting. .... The truth is having abandoned the idea of going to Bengal for the reasons previously mentioned, and disappointed in my expectations here, I was obliged to do the best for myself, having never touched a *pice* of salary since my arrival in the Country.[27]

By the beginning of 1822, therefore, and in consequence of what seemed to be a complete break with the McLachlans, Maclaine had been thrown almost entirely on his own resources. Indeed, the business of coffee growing, and coffee purchase, at Melambong had already become a prime theme of his letters home during the course of the previous year.

'Greatly Pleased by the Praises Bestowed': The Novice Coffee Planter

Our plantation looks extremely well [Maclaine reported to his mother in mid-1821]. I was greatly pleased by the praises bestowed on it some few days ago by some very respectable persons who visited us. Louis and I get on famously together, and understand each other perfectly now, which by the way is more than we did some months ago. I am much pleased with the country and climate and may safely say I enjoy better health than I did while a Cockney. I take a great deal of exercise – sometimes tire out two Java ponies a day, and to prevent me forgetting my former Counting House acquirements, I have an hours writing or so each day, keeping up the Plantation books and accounts, which are under my charge.[28]

Melambong, high in the mountains of south central Java was the place, then, where a young man well versed (presumably) in the husbandry of sheep and in the sailing of boats but not at all in the peculiarities of tropical agriculture, set out to make his fortune. A few decades later, his cousin Donald Maclaine of Lochbuie, similarly situated as an (absentee) coffee planter in much the same part of the world as Gillian Maclaine had earlier been, had an Indies-Chinese overseer – identified simply as Babie – who was evidently fully conversant with the locality and with the crop they were growing. The reports sent to Scotland (by this time Donald Maclaine has retired to the

---

[27] 'Extracts from a letter dated 1st January 1822 to P. McLachlan Esq., London', in GM to MM 4.1.1822. O-M MSS. A *Pice* is an Indian monetary unit, equivalent to a *Rupee*.
[28] GM to MM 27.5.1821. O-M MSS.

family's remote mansion on Mull) by his plantation manager are instructive on a number of counts. Not least, they detail the problems of cultivation ('I am sorry to say that a great deal of the beans have got black on the trees and many empty pods …'); the need to manure the 'gardens' ('I have two large gardens that have been planted three years and before I manured them you would think the trees only a year old'); coffee's propensity to be attacked by vermin – including rats – and the difficulties of supervision ('Old Babie's son is a good and honest man but neither a person to be trusted to give orders among the natives here, the people don't care much for Chinamen').[29] In short, coffee was very far from being a failsafe venture, something not always apparent from the ebullience of Gillian Maclaine's early communications to Scotland at the outset of his career as a planter.

On his 'estate', Maclaine told John Gregorson in 1822, there were some thirteen villages: 'the management of the police of which and letting out land to new settlers etc. comes under my department. You would laugh [his uncle was himself a local magistrate] were you to see how <u>sheriff</u> like I sit in my great elbow chair & decide on the several cases that come before me.' What he was also at pains to explain, however, was the system 'free' labour under which the land was worked, and in so doing could not resist a Tory jibe at the corrupt parliamentary power-base of the celebrated British emancipationist:

> We had 400–500 men employed during the planting season – at present only about 200 – each labourers receives 13 Doits per day (about three pence). He supplies himself with food and the necessary implements for cultivating the ground. Wilberforce himself would have no scruple of conscience against being Planter in this country. It would be I rather think agreeable to the Hon. Member for Bramber's feelings[30] to see 4 @ 500 Javanese contented and happy under the mild sway of a mild employer, free to leave him whenever they felt the least displeased with his conduct.[31]

Though Maclaine may not have been aware of it (only having been in the locality for a few months) this was not an entirely accurate account of the prevailing relations of production on his plantation. His villagers turned out for work partly for the cash that he offered and partly because of the requirement on them, common throughout the Principalities, to provide labour services to the leaseholder (nominally for two days a week) in line with what had formerly been required of them by the court aristocrats who had

---

[29] For this (and much more) see the small collection of letters from A.R. Soesman to Donald Maclaine, 1857–1861, National Archives of Scotland, Edinburgh, GD 174/2351/1-10.

[30] William Wilberforce (1759–1833) was MP for the notorious 'rotten' borough of Bramber in Sussex from 1812 to 1825. The constituency, which had at most two score of eligible voters, was one of those abolished by the Reform Act of 1832.

[31] GM to JG 21.7.1821. O-M MSS.

leased their 'estates' to Europeans. In short, what Maclaine and other lease-holders like him had actually taken over was not simply the land but also a (limited) obligation laid on the locally settled peasantry to work it.[32]

An almost contemporary account of another, nearby coffee plantation tells us rather more about the work involved and who performed it. Women were much to the fore in the workforce. After planting, it was women rather than men who kept the coffee 'gardens' free of weeds, and it was likewise women – and children – who picked, dried and husked the beans 'by pounding ... in wooden mortars or troughs with long wooden poles'. (The men meanwhile would most likely be preparing rice fields, carting goods on their backs, performing labour-service for the state or otherwise employed.) Each person was reckoned to clean around thirty kilo of beans ('half a *picul*') a day, for which on this particular plantation, they were paid '20 doits or about four-pence'.[33] Again, the labourers on his plantation would most likely have been working under the supervision of *mandur* or foremen, who would have taken a percentage of whatever Maclaine paid his people.[34] This probably held, too, for the workers who transported the prepared beans (in bag weighing about sixty-three kilos each) down to the coast at Semarang on packhorses, there to be warehoused prior to sale and shipment overseas. It may well be that Maclaine, in his early days as a planter, was unaware of these niceties.[35] Speaking (broken) Malay rather than Javanese, of course, he would have had no direct verbal contact with his workers. He might just as well have spoken Gaelic – which indeed, is precisely what he did, though not to his tenants.

The Europeans involved in some way or other in the Melambong venture now included two other Highlanders from Mull or Morvern, John McMaster

---

[32]   Carey, *Power of Prophecy*, pp. 462–63, especially fn. 74.

[33]   [J.D.P], 'Journal of an excursion to the Native Provinces on Java in the year 1828, during the war with Dipo Negoro', *Journal of the Indian Archipelago and Eastern Asia*, 8 (1854), pp. 159–60. The author, simply identified as 'J.D.P.', may have been John Pitcairn, a Scot living in Batavia 1826–1828 and 1830–1836, and partner in the Batavia firm of Pitcairn, Syme and Co.

[34]   Carey, *Power of Prophecy*, pp. 462–63, especially fn. 74.

[35]   A subsequent letter to his mother, some six years later, concerning a new – and neighbouring – plantation that he was on the point of leasing from the Yogyakarta court, suggests that by that time Maclaine may have become a little more au fait with the situation: 'On the 1st of last month I took a lease with the sanction of his Excellency the Commissioner General of a pretty extensive piece of land situated close to Melambong and belonging to the Sultan of Djogjo-carta. This new acquisition is secured to me for thirteen years by a lease signed by the Sultan and ratified by the Government, or at least to be ratified as soon as the necessary forms are gone through. I have entered in this speculation and hope in a few years to derive some benefit from it. I exact no rent from the people, in return for which they give me a day's work once every ten days gratis. By this means I expect to get a good many coffee trees planted at little or no expense.' GM to MM 12.3.1827. O-M MSS.

(see Chapter 2) and John Maxwell, as well as the Sassenach William Cotes and (as Maclaine styled him) the *Chevalier* Louis. McMaster, like Maclaine himself, had been sent out from London by the McLachlans:

> I have hinted at you different times about my intention of going to India [he wrote to his brother in December 1820] but ... I was quite surprised when Mr. Peter McLachlan called upon me this morning & told me I had to prepare immediately for to go to the East Indies. After some explanation about my prospects, I of course consented. Messrs McLachlan ... are to fit me out and pay for my passage. I expect to sail in 10 days if not sooner. They have got an establishment in Batavia where I am to go for some time but how long I may be required to stay is as yet uncertain. Mr. Gillean McLaine lives on this establishment and this of itself is a great encouragement to me. Even the very idea of going to live in the same house with such an amiable young gentleman is enough to cheer me up. I have no doubt he will be glad to see me, and it is needless of me to tell you how happy I shall be to see one whom I so much esteemed, especially in a foreign clime .... I go with the full view (if it please God to spare my life and under whose divine protection I always place myself) of doing myself some good and of getting a little forward in the world, and perhaps be of some service to you and the rest of my relations ....[36]

John Maxwell,[37] the other Highlander with whom Maclaine was closely associated, was his senior by some eight years and had arrived in Java some eight months after Maclaine.[38] Unlike McMaster, as the son of Highland *taksman* or bailiff, he was Maclaine's social equal, and his father was well known to the Gregorsons at Ardtornish. Maclaine judged him to be 'a young man of most superior information and most agreeable manners' (a verdict he later had cause to revise). 'Up country' in 1822, to Maclaine's evident relief, Maxwell was also somebody with whom it was possible to talk in English or Gaelic, after months of conversing in 'nothing but Malay and French [to his partner Medard Louis] or French and Malay, from Sunday to Monday and Monday to Sunday'.[39] (The refrain was to be repeated a couple of years later, apropos his relations with McMaster: 'The most enjoyable moments I have enjoyed for many months were those I passed with honest John in my Bungaloe

---

36 John McMaster to Hugh McMaster, London, [?].12.1820. McMaster MSS.

37 John Argyll Maxwell (1790–1857). His father, James Maxwell (c.1757–1829), had been the Duke of Argyll's 'chamberlain or taksman' on Mull. From 1791, the family had lived on the island of Aros, in the channel between Mull and Morvern. See Currie, *Mull*, pp. 188–89. This was a similar position, that of rent collector and administrator, to that held (prior to 1819) by John Gregorson.

38 Maxwell had arrived at Batavia from the UK on 5.2.1821. See *Bataviasche Courant*, 10.2.1821/6.

39 GM to JG 2.7.1821. O-M MSS.

at Salatiga, talking Gaelic together and recalling to mind many anecdotes of the happy days we spent together in the "Land of the Heather".')[40]

At this stage in his career (he subsequently relocated to Singapore) John Maxwell had 'determined on joining the number of Scotch Coffee Planters',[41] and along with Maclaine and several others was involved in a scheme hatched during the course of 1821 to rent a further and very large tract of land for coffee growing from the ruler of Surakarta. For the Dutch colonial government, however, this was going too far. On the grounds that the proposed plantation bordered on teak forests that were subject to state monopoly and that a new 'estate' might become a centre for timber smuggling, they forced the scheme's abandonment:

> Government on the plea of having previously demanded a lease on the same ground from the Emperor and on the ground of its vicinity to one of their large teak forests, have deprived us of the land. By this arbitrary act we shall lose no money, as we are to be repaid for all the expenses incurred, and it affords us a salutary lesson in how cautiously speculations of such a nature are to be engaged in under a government never the most famed for the liberality of its measures.[42]

It was a portent of things to come. Most immediately, however, Maclaine was short of cash. As early as July 1821 (he had been on Java almost exactly a year), he was already confessing to his uncle that:

> The great difficulty I have to combat at present is to muster funds to meet my share of the plantation expenses. I am however in hopes through the assistance of Messrs M[enzies] & A[nderson] ... to be able to weather it out for two years, by which time we now expect to be repaid for all our outlays. It is unnecessary for me to say that the debt I owe you will be punctually paid, as soon as I possess funds to enable me to do so. On this subject I shall not touch again in any of my future letters until such time as I am able to make you a remittance. It only vexes me and I am sure affords you no pleasure to be constantly repeating that I am still unable to pay you.[43]

40 GM to MM 13.6.1824. O-M MSS.
41 GM to JG 21.7.1821. O-M MSS.
42 GM to MM 4.1.1822. O-M MSS: 'Mr Cotes – Menzies – a Mr. Chasteau and Mr. John Maxwell secured a beautiful piece of ground of great extent (about forty miles in circumference) from the Emperor of Solo, which from the rice alone the ground produced would have yielded us about $20,000 (twenty thousand dollars) per annum without laying out a single stuiver. We obtained a lease of it for thirty (30) years on condition of paying $5000 a year, three years rent in advance, say $15,000. My share (one fourth) was advanced by Mr. Chasteau ....'
43 GM to JG 21.7.1821. O-M MSS.

Reconciliation at a Price: The Establishment of Gillian Maclaine & Co.

Indeed, even reduced to a diet of 'rice and curry' (presumably not the staple dishes of his youth at Ardtornish), by this date Maclaine was in serious difficulties financially. The McLachlans' displeasure with his independent course of action in Java meant that he was cut off from any (further) credit from that quarter. Worse still from Maclaine's point of view, they had applied to his uncle for funds to cover a bill that he had had the 'temerity' to draw upon them. Duncan McLachlan wrote Gregorson, somewhat caustically, in October 1821 that:

> I do not know if he has written to you on the subject of his money wants to enable him to go on with his coffee estate, but in his letter to us he says he has to draw upon us for 500 pounds and hoped that we would honour his draft, one of which has made its appearance for 250 pounds, but we declined accepting it until we should hear from you. Of course we shall do the needful to it if you put us in funds to meet it at maturity and on that of the other 250 pounds under the same conditions. We are not a little surprised on his drawing upon us in the face of the course he determined on following so shortly on his arrival in Java & so contrary to our just expectations. I shall say nothing of the time he was here, or that of his passage out being paid by us, but I will say that carrying in his pocket an open letter from us to the House in Calcutta, a copy of which I subjoin, we had the most unquestionable right to expect a very different result to that which has taken place. However, I most sincerely hope that he will succeed in his speculation, indeed, I have no doubt he will provided he has the means of bringing the place to give a return, which by the by takes a long time before he can have any. At same time, I am surprised at his having agreed to advance one half of the expenses of cultivation and holding only a quarter of the land.[44]

By the middle of 1822 his paucity of resources, so dryly forecast by 'Mr. Duncan', forced Maclaine into a new strategy. He had arrived in Java (as we have already seen) in the service of the McLachlans and the Calcutta-based Donald MacIntyre, and subsequently broken with them in acrimonious circumstances and struck out on his own. Now, a visit to Java by McIntyre himself during the middle months of 1822 became the occasion for reconciliation. Maclaine, together with John Maxwell, entered into an agreement with MacIntyre and his London associates for the establishment in Batavia of a mercantile house, to be known as Gillian Maclaine & Co. Ostensibly, it took the form of a partnership between principals in several different parts of the world.[45] Nonetheless, the interests of the colonial partners were clearly

---

44 'Copy of letter from D. McLachlan Esq. to John Gregorson Esq., London 6th October 1821'. O-M MSS.
45 The notices of the firm's establishment in the *Bataviasche Courant* (21.9.1822/23) read: 'Messrs Gillian Maclaine and John Argyll Maxwell have the established themselves as

subordinated to those of the metropole. In this sense, as we shall see, Gillian Maclaine & Co. differed markedly from the form taken by the Maclaine Watson enterprise established some five years later.

The situation in which Maclaine found himself, however, appeared to preclude other options. Java's coffee trade (see below) was not growing at the rate that Maclaine had perhaps anticipated and, as he was acutely aware, the Indies government were becoming increasingly hostile to the planter interest in the Principalities. It was also abundantly clear that, back in Scotland, John Gregorson was not only *not* going to advance his nephew any more capital (despite the latter's broad hints) but was also demanding repayment of the amount he had already lent and (presumably, since his side of the correspondence has not survived) some explanation of bills drawn on the McLachlans which the latter were expecting him to cover. Consequently, when Donald McIntyre himself paid him a visit, Maclaine was in a vulnerable position.

Piecing together the details from several of Maclaine's letters from the middle months of 1822,[46] it is evident that McIntyre made him an offer – 'to use his own expression, "opened the door for my return to the House"' – which the younger man 'deemed it prudent to accept'. The arrangement was that Maclaine would relocate to Batavia from south central Java, while Maxwell, moving to Singapore, would open an associated business there, together with McIntyre's brother-in-law, Graham McKenzie.[47] The other partners would be MacIntyre himself and (in London) the Messrs McLachlan. In the process, McIntyre took the opportunity to terminate connections with Maclaine's Batavia-based friends Menzies, Anderson & Co. and to direct his and the McLachlans' cotton consignments exclusively to Maclaine and Maxwell.

In a sense, Maclaine had reason for congratulation. Within less than two years of arriving in Java, he had his 'own' house of business and, in shifting from Melambong to Batavia was relieved of 'a quiet retired life to which, candidly speaking, I was never very partial [and which] … I do not think … the best calculated for a young man'. It also left him in a position to pay off his debts, and repay his uncle as soon as the opportunity to make a remittance arrived. In short, as he explained it to his mother, he hoped that his return

Agents and Merchants under the firm of Gillian Maclaine and Co' and 'We beg leave to intimate that we have appointed Messrs Gillian Maclaine and Co our agents for the general management of our affairs on the Island of Java for D. and P. Maclachlan of London and self D. MacIntyre.'

46 The information in this and the following two paragraphs (together with the quotations therein) derives from: GM to MM 28.5.1822; 29.5.1822; 21.9.1822; 29.11.1822 and 28.12.1822. O-M MSS.

47 The firm of Graham MacKenzie & Co. was extant in Singapore in 1830, two years after Maxwell had left the colony. See e.g. Jardine Matheson Archive, Cambridge University Library, Manuscripts/MS JM/A8/13/Bills of Lading/23.8.1830.

to the McLachlan fold would be both personally gratifying to his family and literally recompense his uncle for having 'occasioned him so much anxiety & been the means of adding ... to his embarrassments'.

The downside of the new arrangement, however, was considerable. Almost from the start, there were difficulties. Among other things, Maclaine was forced to subsume his hard-won share in Melambong into the assets of the partnership as a whole ('several of my friends blame me for not having kept it entirely to my own account') and McIntyre had obliged him – with what turned out to be dire consequences – to take on a relative stranger as his agent in the crucial position of Gillian Maclaine & Co.'s agent at Semarang. The fundamental problem, however, related to the terms (binding for four years) on which he and Maxwell were admitted to the partnership. Maclaine never divulged them to either his mother or uncle, beyond claiming that they were better than those previously offered to Menzies and Anderson, his erstwhile business associates on Java (terms which they had refused). Nonetheless, the general drift of his comments indicated that he knew he had got a poor bargain even from the very beginning. He had an apparently unalloyed regard for McIntyre himself: 'he really is as kind clever and determined a little fellow as I ever met with ... [and] of his liberality I have the highest opinion'. Nonetheless, he confidentially warned his mother ('I intend this letter should be confined to you and my brother's perusal') at the close of 1822 that 'unless my share in the House is increased, I fear that twenty years of good business will not put me in possession of a comfortable independence'. There was to be more – much more – in the same vein.

Maclaine and his Associates in the New Firm

Business, meanwhile, was evidently brisk. Indeed, it was at this point in 1822 (and not earlier, as some older accounts mistakenly assumed)[48] that Maclaine's eventual chief business partner and 'spouse commercial' for the next decade and a half entered the story. Edward Watson[49] did so initially as an 'assistant'

---

48 The story, sanctified in the firm's 'centenary history' of 1927 (*One Hundred Years*, p. 3), that the firm was established by Gillian Maclaine and 'his friend' Edward Watson, who had previously worked together in London and sank their modest joint capital into the new colonial venture, can safely be consigned to the realm of 'foundation myths' that say more about the ethos in which the firm's twentieth-century managers saw themselves operating than about a significantly different – and altogether more fraught – historical reality.

49 Edward Watson (b. London c.1800, d. London [?] sometime after 1867). He was said to have attended Christ's Hospital School, London (vide: GM to Mrs Gregorson, 12.4.1831. Greenfield MSS) He arrived in Java (presumably sent out by the McLachans) in 1822, returned temporarily to the UK in c.1834–35, and left the colony permanently early in

in Maclaine's office in Malacca Street in the old town of Batavia, and as somebody with whom he shared his living accommodation, as did other of his bachelor clerks, further inland in the newly established European quarter of the city at *Tanah Abang*, immediately to the west of the *Koningsplein*.[50] The new arrival was evidently a complete stranger to Maclaine, who, in introducing him to his mother, referred to him as 'a Mr. Watson' (rather than the more familiar 'Watson').[51] He was, Maclaine felt it necessary to tell her, a Londoner: 'Watson being a Cockney by birth and considerably tinged with the Epicureanism of the great city, I have handed over to him the charge of the table or (as we in India term it) Bazaar expenses.'[52] Much as he may have deferred to Watson's skills when they messed together, however, and much as he evidently had a very high regard for his business acumen (Watson became a partner in 1827), the two were hardly close friends. Maclaine's crisp comment on Watson's retirement to London in 1837 speaks volumes: 'Watson sails for England on the 15th next month, and by his departure Batavia loses a very respectable member of its English society, but as he never went out or paid visits, his absence will not be missed.'[53]

John McMaster, meanwhile, took over from Maclaine at the coffee-buying and coffee-growing end of the business in central Java, at Salatiga (where the firm had a warehouse) and at the Melambong plantation itself. 'I write this in my Coffee store', Maclaine wrote to his mother from Salatiga at the end of May 1822, shortly before relocating to Batavia, 'where John MacMaster is busy talking to the people in Malay and asking me questions in Gaelic. John has been sent here to assist me by McIntyre, to gain a knowledge of the Coffee business.'[54] Both there and subsequently at Semarang, where he became Maclaine's agent at the close of 1823, McMaster's admiration for his boss remained unabated:

> Mr. G. McLaine has been with me here for the last three weeks [he wrote to his brother Hugh in May 1824], and has only left for Batavia a few days hence.

1837. Subsequently he lived in London, first in Islington and then (c.1845 onward), in Hampstead (Frognal). Watson signed an affidavit in 1867 relating to the circumstances of the death of his former business partner, a copy of which exists in the South Australian Archives.

[50] 'Our establishment here musters strong. I have lately got out two fine young men as assistants, a Mr Frazer and a Mr Baird [*sic?*], both Scotchmen, to whom I have given a room each at my house, which makes our society un peu mieux.' GM to MM 10.9.1823. O-M MSS.

[51] Maclaine remarked in a letter to his mother dated Batavia, 29 November 1822 (O-M MSS), that 'Since my arrival here [from central Java], I have had, as you may easily conceive, an immense deal to do, and though I have two assistants, a Mr. Watson and Mr. Scott, yet scarcely have a moment's leisure.'

[52] GM to MM 31.12.1822. O-M MSS.

[53] GM to MM 16.12.1836. Greenfield MSS.

[54] GM to MM 28.5.1830. O-M MSS.

He is in good health and looks better than ever he did in the Highlands. I need scarcely tell you that I am proud of his good conduct and upright principles. He is universally respected here, and God grant him long life to return home in comfort to his nearest and dearest Relations. His unceasing kindness to me I can never sufficiently acknowledge.[55]

Maxwell and McMaster were not, however, the only Scots involved in the new enterprise. Maclaine was also joined by John McNeill, the 'son of a small Argyllshire Laird' from the island of Islay, off the west coast of Scotland. 'An excellent, gentlemanly fellow', who was related through marriage to the McLachlans (which may explain how he came to be in the East), he had been in the Indies since 1819 and now took up residence in Surabaya to manage Gillian Maclaine & Co.'s affairs in the major port of East Java.[56] Two years later, in 1825, he moved to Semarang, initially as Maclaine's agent. He was subsequently founder there of McNeill & Co., one of firms that came to comprise (as we shall see) the group of Asia-based enterprises that formed the core of the Maclaine Watson network.

'The Sight of the Old British Flag': Singapore and Imperial Rivalries in Maritime Southeast Asia

At the time of the establishment of Gillian Maclaine & Co. in 1822, Singapore was a very recent European settlement indeed, having been founded as such only three years earlier by Sir Stamford Raffles. As the former Thomas Raffles ('I see', wrote John Palmer from Calcutta on hearing the news of his knighthood, 'that poor humble Thomas is now quite sunk'),

55 John McMaster to Hugh MacMaster, Semarang 30.5.1824. McMaster MSS.
56 John McNeill b. Ellister, Isle of Islay, Argyll, Scotland, 1800, d. Scotland 1857. McNeill was active in the Indies as trader 1819 onward (initially in Surabaya) and, as founding partner of McNeill & Co. of Semarang, was closely associated from 1827 onward with Maclaine Watson & Co. in Batavia and Fraser Eaton & Co. in Surabaya. While on a return visit to the UK in the late 1830s, he married Catherine Campbell, b. Kilmelford, Scotland [date unknown], d. Campbelltown, Scotland, 1847. McNeill subsequently was remarried in 1855, two years before his death, to Agnes Loudon (b. [date unknown], d. 1906), daughter of Captain William Loudon of the Royal Navy and Elizabeth Webster (information kindly supplied by Peter Christiaans, Centraal Bureau voor Genealogie, Den Haag) and see GM to Hector Maclaine, Batavia 8.2.1837 (Greenfield MSS). For McNeill's family connection to the McLachlans, see: 'By the bye you can inform Mrs. McLachlan Salachan that her nephew McNeill is well' (GM to MM 31.12.1822. O-M MSS) and 'There is also a nephew of Mrs. McLachlan Salachen of the name of McNeill residing at Semarang here with whom I am intimately acquainted and you may inform his Aunt that he is quite hearty' (John MacMaster to Hugh MacMaster, Semarang 2.11.1822. MacMaster MSS). Donald McLachlan (d.1816) had been, inter alia, *taksman* of Sallachan, on the sound of Mull.

he had been the Lieutenant-Governor of Java from 1811 to 1815, during the British occupation of the island. Raffles's action, taken on his own initiative, since his superiors, given the delicate state of their relations with the Dutch, could scarcely officially sanction it, was the most momentous of his career. As Webster remarks, 'the foundation of Singapore in 1819 represented a major extension of British imperial power in Southeast Asia' and paved the way for a greatly enhanced British presence in the region as well as securing the route from India through to China.[57] Bitterly disappointed by Java's return to the Dutch in 1816, Raffles had cast about for other means to frustrate what he saw as the latter's attempts to re-assert their commercial hegemony in the Indonesian-Malay world – and to re-assert his own importance in the imperial scheme of things.

More than coincidently, the occupation-era official turned Batavia businessman, Thomas MacQuoid, a partner in the substantial mercantile Java firm of MacQuoid Davidson & Co., was a close associate.[58] Indeed, it was to MacQuoid and his friends that Raffles, while Lieutenant Governor, had sold off a huge estate, carved out of Government-land, in West Java – a deal in which he was suspected of himself having an interest. There was also an important and enabling context. By the second decade of the nineteenth century, a great deal of Anglo-Indian capital, based in Calcutta, was invested in the trade to Southeast Asia and beyond, and the firms concerned were vital to the EIC's own commercial strategy and financial good health. Accordingly, high officials in Bengal were more than prepared, however tacitly, to let their subordinates do whatever was necessary to frustrate the Dutch.[59] Matters relating to Singapore were finally resolved (as we saw earlier in the book) by the Anglo-Dutch Treaty of 1824 which (inter alia) delineated the two imperial power's zones in maritime Southeast Asia. As Webster observes, however, the fact was that the treaty 'contained rather than ended Anglo-Dutch conflict'.[60]

Unsurprisingly, in the wake of the contested establishment of Singapore, Raffles became the bête noir of the Dutch authorities, and in 1823, when a ship carrying him called at Batavia for repairs, he was famously refused permission to land, though Sophia Raffles, his heavily pregnant wife, was

---

[57] Webster, *Gentlemen Capitalists*, p. 83.

[58] Rebecca Lamb, *Macquoid of Waniassa* (Canberra, Australian Capital Territory: Waniassa Publications, 2006), pp. 23–67; Van Enk, *Britse Koopleiden*, pp. 187–22.

[59] Webster, *Gentlemen Capitalists*, p. 84. For a detailed statement of this argument, see Anthony Webster, 'British Export Interests in Bengal and Imperial Expansion in Southeast Asia, 1780 to 1824. The Origins of the Straits Settlements', pp. 138–74 in Deborah Ingham and Colin Simmons (eds), *Development Studies and Colonial Policy* (London: Frank Cass, 1987).

[60] Webster, *Gentlemen Capitalists*, p. 104. For a detailed and authoritative reconstruction of the actual negotiations, see Tarling, *Anglo-Dutch Rivalry*, pp. 81–178.

allowed ashore – and lodged chez MacQuoid. This display of Dutch 'bad manners' did not prevent, however, a bevy of expatriate British residents from calling on her husband to pay their respects as the ship rode at anchor (which it did for a full week, much to the increasing vexation of the Netherlands Indies' aristocratic Governor-General, G.A.G.P. Baron Van der Capellen). Maclaine, already a keen reader of Sir Stamford's literary output ('I wish you could get a reading of Raffles *History of Java*', he wrote to his mother) was among them.[61]

Singapore itself in the early 1820s was a place rather devoid of such dramas and still something of a backwater. 'He likes Singapore very much as far as regards the climate, but does not think very highly of its commercial advantages', Maclaine reported of John Maxwell, installed in the new settlement for but a matter of months.[62] Visiting it himself two years later, Maclaine observed to his brother that there was 'nothing particularly striking in the appearance of this far famed infant settlement when viewed from the Roads. The great part of the European houses are concealed from view, and were it not for the ships in the harbour, I could not have distinguished it from any of the adjoining Malay villages.' Even so, what Singapore signified in imperial terms was not lost on him: 'the sight of the old British flag displayed on Government Hill refreshed me not a little', he reported, 'having never seen it, at least flying, on terra firma since I left home'.[63]

It was precisely this, of course, that so annoyed and alarmed the Dutch, not least because the new settlement, for all its modest beginnings, was singularly well placed for the trade to southern China, a voyage of some ten days away when the monsoon was favourable.[64] The port was not simply astride the East–West trade route between the Indian subcontinent and southern China (and much better situated in this respect than the older EIC settlement of Penang further up the Malacca Strait): it was also located on the important north–south commercial axis that linked Bangkok and its hinterlands with Batavia and the rest of Java. Along this axis, moreover, were a constantly expanding number of Chinese settlements producing a wide variety of commodities ranging from tin, pepper and gold to sugar, birds' nests and forest products that were largely destined for the Chinese metropolitan market. These scattered 'kongsi' settlements, places to which indentured labourers were brought by Chinese mercantile consortiums, were

[61] C.E. Wurtzburg, *Raffles of the Eastern Isles* (London: Hodder and Stoughton, 1954), pp. 658–61; GM to MM 7.1.1821 and 10.9.1823. Greenfield MSS.
[62] GM to MM 31.12.1822. O-M MSS.
[63] GM to AM 27.12.1824. O-M MSS.
[64] 'I intend going to Singapore in the course of the next month, and will probably proceed from there, in a ship belonging to the House, to China. The voyage to the Celestial Empire can be performed in ten days at present.' GM to AM 27.7.1824. O-M MSS.

far from self-supporting, and needed provisioning not only with foodstuffs but also with cotton goods and (as we shall see) opium.[65] As one leading student of Singapore's nineteenth-century trade has argued recently, 'the expansion of Southeast Asian trade in the first half of the nineteenth century was based partly on the growth of intra-regional trade' and in this wider context Singapore 'played a significant role as a British free port in the connection between Western long-distance trade and intra-regional trade: it was trade, furthermore, that during the first half of the nineteenth century increasingly shifted its focus from Java to Singapore'.[66]

In short, under the notional sway of a handful of European mercantile houses and officials, but with its commerce largely in the hands of Chinese traders, it was through a rapidly evolving Singapore that commodities from the Indian subcontinent and the UK reached markets elsewhere in the surrounding region, as well as the Chinese mainland to the port's north-east. Among these commodities were guns: indeed, the Lion City soon came to play an important role in the Southeast Asian arms trade and continued to do so for many decades to come. Maxwell and Gillian Maclaine & Co. were early participants: in July 1824, for example, they were the recipients at Singapore of a consignment of firearms from London.[67]

Nonetheless, the great bulk of Gillian Maclaine & Co.'s commerce at Singapore in the mid-1820s was probably in things other than guns. It comprised not only cottons but also woollen goods, from Hamburg as well as from the UK, which were dispatched to Canton largely on Chinese junks and sold or bartered for tea which, Maxwell asserted, went to the German market (since until 1833 its sale in the UK market was monopolised by the EIC). There can be little doubt that Maxwell was also involved in the opium trade, which revolved around the purchase of the drug from its source in British India and its export both to Southeast Asia and to southern China. We shall return to this aspect of Maclaine Watson's business in a subsequent chapter. On occasion, moreover, the trade to China also included cargoes of rice (presumably from Siam or Java) which were shipped to Canton in response to temporary shortages in its hinterland.

---

[65] See Carl A. Trocki, 'Opium as a Commodity in the Chinese Nanyang Trade', in Eric Tagliacozzo and Wen-Chin Chang (eds), *Chinese Circulations. Capital, Commodities and Networks in Southeast Asia* (Durham, NC: London, Duke University Press, 2011), pp. 92–95; Carl A. Trocki, *Singapore. Wealth, Power and Culture* (London and New York: Routledge, 2006), pp. 15–21; Carl A. Trocki, 'Chinese Pioneering in Eighteenth Century Southeast Asia', pp. 83–102 in Anthony Reid (ed.), *The Last Stand of Asian Autonomies* (Basingstoke: Macmillan Press, 1997).

[66] Atsushi Kobayashi, 'The Role of Singapore in the Growth of Intra-Southeast Asian Trade, c.1820s–1852', *Southeast Asian Studies* [Kyoto], 2, 3 (December 2013), p. 443.

[67] GG in Rade 13.7.1824/46 NA MK 2783.

It was one such Singapore cargo that took Gillian Maclaine himself on his only voyage to China late in 1824.[68] He had first sailed from Java to Banka island – where the Dutch Resident proved 'a polite, soldierly looking man in place of a rough, pot bellied Dutch burgher as I expected', and then on to Singapore[69] to embark on a journey across the South China Sea that ought to have taken an uneventful ten days or so.[70] In fact, it almost cost him his life when the ship on which he was travelling was struck by a typhoon off the Philippines: 'It is only waste of time [he told his brother] to describe how the gale commenced, but it blew a gale and such a gale for six days that I more than once wished myself plodding at my desk in Malacca St [in Batavia] or quietly pacing the verandah at the Bungaloe at Tanah Abang.'[71] Once arrived in Canton (having landed initially at the Portuguese settlement of Macao) Maclaine was evidently somewhat taken aback by the 'despotic manner' in which the inhabitants of Canton 'lorded it over' Europeans:

> You are aware that no Fan Quoy or White Devil as they call us is allowed to go into the city, but if even a person moves at any distance from the Factories [i.e. the European settlement] he is generally pelted with mud or stones. A party of six, of which I formed one, made a circuit of the city walls a few days ago. We went completely round in about two hours and a half, and … [were] obliged to run for a good part of that time in order to avoid the crowd that chased us.[72]

Even so, Maclaine evidently found some solace in the fact that, it being winter:

> The weather is extremely cold, but not that bracing pleasant kind of cold you have about this season of the year at home. The thermometer stands generally at 45 [Fahrenheit] in the morning, which is about 40 degrees lower than we have it at Batavia, and I have daily the pleasure of seeing blazing coal fires in every house – comfortable carpets in every room – of wearing woolen clothes from top to toe – and of sitting down to and partaking with an English appetite of dinners served up in good English style – and to crown all of sleeping every night under <u>three</u> blankets.[73]

---

[68] 'Evidence Maxwell 1830', p. 248; GM to AM, Canton 27.12.1824. O-M MSS.

[69] He left Batavia on 8 September 1824, bound for Muntok, Riouw and Singapore, aboard the *Sourabaya*, Captain J. Farrett. See *Bataviasche Courant*, 11.9.1824/37.

[70] GM to AM, Canton 17.12.1824. O-M MSS.

[71] GM to AM, Canton 17.12.1824. O-M MSS.

[72] GM to AM, Canton 17.12.1824. O-M MSS.

[73] GM to AM, Canton 17.12.1824. O-M MSS.

'An Unlooked for Misfortune': Louis Chasteau and the Semarang Agency, 1823

The Canton venture (though he told his brother nothing whatsoever about the sale of his rice or any other business conducted in Canton) was perhaps designed to enable Maclaine to recoup some of the very substantial losses that he had made in Java during the previous year. The arrangements for the setting up of Gillian Maclaine & Co. in 1822 had removed Maclaine himself from central Java to Batavia and left the important agency in Semarang to a relative stranger to the Scots who otherwise ran the firm. This was the twenty-five-year-old Louis Chasteau, a Frenchman from Mauritius (he claimed to have been born in Paris), who Maclaine had earlier met and liked. The choice turned out to be disastrous. Chasteau had been doing business of some kind between Mauritius and Batavia a couple of years before Maclaine arrived in the Dutch colony, and had settled there in 1819.[74]

Subsequently, Chasteau became involved with Maclaine in an abortive land-leasing scheme in the Principalities in 1821. Indeed, 'as a young man from whom I have experienced on many occasions much kindness', he had been one the scheme's putative financial backers.[75] In fact, his proffered support was probably illusory, as was the reputation he appears to have established not only with Maclaine but also with Maxwell, at whose urging (so Maclaine told his mother), MacIntyre had installed him at Semarang. It was news from that quarter that had send Maclaine hurrying there in September 1823:

> My last letter was dated in September and if I remember well written in high spirits. A few days after its dispatch I was suddenly called down to Samarang in consequence of the unexpected failure of Mr. Chasteau, our agent there, by whose villainy, I regret to state, the House will suffer an immense loss. The unprincipled scoundrel contrived to conceal from us and the rest of his creditors his heavy embarrassments, but finding concealment no longer possible, he confessed he had made away with our Property and instead of attempting to alleviate the evil endeavoured to heighten it by every means in his power. It is impossible for me to describe my mental suffering for the last three months, particularly during my stay at Samarang. My mind is now however tranquil, though I cannot help occasionally reflecting with agitated feeling on the treachery and ingratitude of a person with whom I was once on intimate terms of friendship. I shall not enter into detail of the measures I adopted to recover our Property or to get the author of our misfortune punished. Suffice to say there is little chance of getting back any of our money, and that the

---

74 See e.g. *Bataviasche Courant*, 7.2.1818/6 and 25.5.1818/21.

75 'Extracts from a letter dated 1. January 1822 to P. Maclachlan Esq., London.' In GM to MM 4.1.1822. O-M MSS.

infatuated Chasteau has, it is supposed, committed suicide. He has been missing for several days back, and as letters have been found, from which his intention to commit the rash act can be gathered, I fear the reports in circulation may prove too true.[76]

In fact, Chasteau had chosen not suicide but Timor, and had been able to smuggle himself on a ship to that island, well over 2,000 kilometres to the south-east, early in 1824. Not that this fact was of any use to Maclaine, since the Portuguese part of that divided island was beyond the reach of the Dutch colonial authorities, even had they been motivated to pursue him for the monies he presumably owed them as well as Maclaine.[77] 'Heavy as our loss is', Maclaine concluded, 'I do not despair with the blessing of God soon to retrieve it … [The affair] has made me, I hope both a better and a wiser man.' Even so, there were the longer-term and 'global' consequences to be considered:

> As we correspond with three or four Houses in Glasgow, our loss of 1823 would of course be known to them. Losses as well as profits are generally exaggerated. I am sorry to say this was not the case with ours. This is however necessarily a subject which almost makes me nervous when I think of it, I shall therefore pass on to something more agreeable.[78]

Coffee: A Question of Loyalties

'Something more agreeable' included a degree of apparent relief from the vicissitudes that his investments in coffee production were undergoing. The immediate problem related to the leaseholds on which Maclaine and his fellow planters held land in the Principalities. Maclaine's reportage on the development of his plantation interests in Yogyakarta and Surakarta had always betrayed an unease about the attitude of the Dutch colonial authorities to the whole venture. Colonial officialdom was divided on the score. As we have seen, the Anglophile Colonel Nahuijs, the Dutch Resident (for a time)

---

[76] GM to MM 29.12.1823. O-M MSS.

[77] Chasteau had fled Semarang for Surabaya and from there secretly took passage to Timor at the beginning of 1824 on board the ship *Recovery*. See GG in Rade 7.9.1824/28 and GG in Rade 23.5.1826/11, NA MK 2784 & 2793. A Louis Chasteau (presumably the same) appears again to have been operating as a merchant in Semarang in 1828/29, and in the latter year one Israel David was a member of the Semarang firm of Chasteau & Co., as he had indeed been prior to his withdrawal from the (earlier) firm in October 1823. See GG in Rade 7.7.1829/17 and 8.12.1829/10 NA MK 2827 and 2832; *Bataviasche Courant*, 11.10.1823/41.

[78] GM to MM 24.5.1825. O-M MSS.

at both the princely courts, had done much to promote the leasing of land to European planters, many of them British, but there were those in Batavia who were strongly opposed to it. They came to include the Governor General, Baron Van der Capellen and his principal advisor, H.J. van de Graaff. Their opposition stemmed from a mixture of concerns.

One key point was that the Indies government feared that competition from private planters might undercut their own lucrative monopoly on coffee produced in the Preanger area of West Java by depressing prices on the Batavia market. In 1818, some 50 per cent of the government's total revenues came from its sales of coffee, and although this figure had fallen to around 33 per cent by 1823, it still represented (as it was to do until late in the century) a very high proportion of colonial revenues.[79] Opponents of land-lease within the administration seized on a wild guesstimate by Nahuijs, that the plantations he was promoting in south central Java would soon be producing more than 12,000 metric tons (MT) of coffee annually, roughly equivalent to the colony's total exports in 1820, to demand action.[80] Yet again, however, tensions of empire came to the fore, since the 'threat' of a massively increased coffee output in the Principalities was exacerbated by the fact that many of the planters were of British nationality and therefore of purportedly doubtful loyalty to the Dutch crown. Hence coffee came within the purview of imperial rivalries and, more specifically, of the Dutch fear that the growth of British interests in the very 'heartlands' of Java boded ill for their long-term control of the island.

It was also feared, moreover, that presence of European planters – of whatever nationality – would upset the existing relations of production among the peasantry and between peasants and supra-village elites to an extent that might undermine the social fabric of the countryside, give rise to 'oppression' and possibly provoke rural revolt. More significantly, perhaps, influential people within the Indies government were also concerned that the activities of the planters might add to the volatility of the political situation at the courts of Yogyakarta and Surakarta, while, more or less simultaneously, elements in the colonial administration were concerned that the leasing of land would frustrate their own plans to extend control over the Principalities. What appears to have been envisaged in some quarters in Batavia was that the Indies state, using a similar device to that of the planters, would, in effect,

---

[79] Figures for the period 1818–1823 from W.Ph. Coolhaas, *Het regeerings reglement van 1827 : het werk van 1818 aan de ervaring getoetst* (Utrecht: Oosthoek, 1936), pp. 18–22.

[80] See P.H. van der Kemp, 'Rapport van de Waarnemend Hoofdinspecteur van Financien, H.J. van de Graaff, dd. Batavia, 23 Maart 1822 aan Gouverneur Generaal Van der Capellen, over de Landverhuringen aan Europeanen in de Vorstenlanden', *Tijdschrift voor Nijverheid en Landbouw in Nederlandsch-Indie*, 41 (1890), pp. 143–95.

take over large tracts of territory as leasehold estates, in what amounted to annexation by stealth.[81]

For a variety of reasons, therefore, the colonial government became increasingly opposed to Nahuijs' rival vision for the Principalities and to the existence there of a substantial European 'planter class'. In October 1821, they decreed that no further leases be granted (a prohibition which Nahuijs ignored), and in May 1823 they decided to revoke existing leases, and put arrangements in place for compensation of the planters that, however inadvertently, struck hard at the interests of the Court aristocracies. It looked like a formula for trouble – and it was. Meanwhile, the man who might have massaged the situation, Resident Nahuijs himself, famous for his apparent ability, in colonial parlance, to 'get on with the natives', had already left Yogyakarta, and gone on leave to the Netherlands, there to lick his wounds and drum up support against his opponents in Batavia.[82]

The immediate impact of the revocation of the leases was on the planters themselves. For some of Maclaine's contemporaries and associates, indeed, the turn of events was disastrous. One of the biggest coffee speculators, the Northumbrian parson's son William Cotes (a man whom Maclaine had encountered very early after his own arrival in the colony), was utterly ruined.[83] Cotes had arrived in Java in a military capacity at the beginning of the British occupation in 1811; had been taken up by Raffles and given a number of civilian postings; and had stayed on in the colony (as did a number of his contemporaries) when the island was returned to the Dutch in 1816. Subsequently based in Salatiga and Surakarta, he had carried on considerable business in coffee and had himself become a planter, with a stake in several plantations, including Maclaine's Melambong and J.A. Dezentje's Ampel (see below). In the changed circumstances of the mid-1820s, his speculations quickly unravelled.

---

[81] See in particular G.G. Van der Capellen to [Colonial Minister] Falck, 4.6.1823, MK 27.11.1826/56. NA MK 531.

[82] Carey, *Power of Prophecy*, pp. 519, 526–36, 559–61. For an extended survey of European plantations (including coffee) in the Principalities, c.1816 onwards (mostly with reference to post-1830 developments), see Vincent J.H. Houben, *Kraton and Kumpeni. Surakarta and Yogyakarta 1830–1870* (Leiden: KITLV Press, 1994), pp. 257–304.

[83] William Cotes, b. Bedlington, Northumberland, c.1791, d. Buitenzorg (Bogor), Java, 7.10.1826. Presumably he was a son of the Rev. Henry Cotes, Rector of Bedlington, who died 'at an advanced age' in 1835, having been presented to the living by the Dean and Chapter of Durham Cathedral in 1788 (*The Gentleman's Magazine*, vol. 157 (online) notice under 7.2.1835). The Rector was co-author of a famous book on *British Water Birds* by Thomas Bewick (1805). Wiiliam Cotes was not the only one of his family to make a career in the East: his brother, Henry Cotes, was living at Bangalore in India in 1826 (see John Palmer to Henry Cotes 16.9.1826, Letter Books of John Palmer, Bodleian Library, Oxford, Eng. Lett. c. 104, pp. 42–43). For William Cotes's career in Java, see below.

By September 1823, already in deep trouble, Cotes petitioned the Indies government for letters of *Atterminatie* (i.e. an officially promulgated 'stay of execution') on account of his inability to fulfil his contracts with a number of large mercantile houses.[84] Subsequently, he visited Calcutta, probably in the hope of raising funds and staving off his creditors, but apparently to no avail.[85] He had been financed, among others by the great Calcutta merchant John Palmer and by the latter's Bengal business associate Roggorram Gosain,[86] and had been consigning coffee to the London East India house of Cockerill Trail & Co. (Palmer's long-standing business correspondents in the UK).[87] Some hundred thousand guilders (*eenige honderd duizend gulden*) or more was reputedly involved. It was the end for Cotes. In the following year, 1826 he died at Buitenzorg, in West Java, having, it was said, lost not only his money but also his mind. He left behind a wife, an Indies-born woman whom he married in south central Java almost a decade earlier, and five children.[88]

Maclaine's own experience of this evolving situation, however, was altogether different and revealed something of the complexity and possible confusion of contemporary developments in Dutch colonial circles. His version of events was that by the end of 1823, Governor-General Van der Capellen, faced with the repercussions of his revocation of the leases, '... has of late repented of the severe and unjust Regulation promulgated in May last, and seems anxious to make amends for his former misdeeds. I lately had the honour of having several private audiences with his Excellency, and found him very polite, indeed friendly.'[89] Maclaine was alluding to the ramifications of a system of compensation devised by the Indies government to placate the

---

[84] GG in Rade 9.9.1823/43 NA MK 2779. The background to this appears to have been what Cotes described as the '*onwettig arrest*' [unlawful distraint] of his person and goods by order of the High Court of Semarang in August 1823. In order to escape imprisonment for debt, he claimed that he had been obliged to raise money by selling his claims to various plantations in the Principalities. See GG in Rade 8.2.1825/41 NA MK 2787.

[85] In July 1825 he was staying with John Palmer in Calcutta. See Palmer to Davidson 12.7.1825, Eng. Lett c.102, p. 229.

[86] See Webster, *The Richest Merchant*, p. 80, 'A key figure in the firm [of John Palmer & Co] was undoubtedly the *banian* [an established Indian merchant who looked after the business's relations with his fellow countrymen] Roggorram Gosain. [Palmer's one-time partner William] Prinsip commented upon the high regard in which Roggorram Gosian was held generally, and his very close friendship with John Palmer.'

[87] Palmer to Deans 24.11.1826 and 11.6.1827, Eng. Lett., c.104, p. 223 and c.106, p. 146. These were, of course, far from Cotes's only business connections. In the early 1820s, for example, he had been involved in court proceedings over *sugar* purchases with several Indies-Chinese traders in Semarang. See GG in Rade 30.11.1822/4 MK 2467.

[88] Willem van Hogendorp to G.K. van Hogendorp 20.10.1826, NA Collectie Van Hogendorp 91.

[89] GM to MM 29.12.1823. O-M MSS. Carey points out that a number of the Solo land-leasers got together and petitioned the colonial government for redress (Carey, *Power of Prophecy*,

planters and, altogether more importantly, to placate the Javanese aristocrats who stood to lose heavily from the revocation of the leases. In the case of lands leased from the Surakarta court – which was what concerned Maclaine – the government arranged for the planters to be compensated for their losses by being allowed to take delivery of all the coffee grown on their former properties until an agreed sum in compensation had been recovered. The rationale was to ensure that the Surakarta court was not ruined by having to find huge sums of cash to 'recompense' the erstwhile leaseholders.[90]

Maclaine and MacMaster had travelled to Surakarta together to finalise arrangements with the government's Commissioners appointed to adjudicate matters, and were evidently well pleased with the settlement they had been able to secure. The agreed compensation awarded to Gillian Maclaine & Co. in respect to Melambong amounted to the equivalent (in coffee) of some £20,000 sterling.[91] It was this tidy sum, and the fact that it implied that his firm would have access to Melambong's output for the foreseeable future, evidently buoyed Maclaine's spirits at the close of 1823. As he reiterated the situation to his brother in the middle of the following year:

> You would be happy to learn by my late letters that I succeeded in effecting an excellent arrangement with the Government respecting our Coffee Plantation. The settlement is in fact so very advantageous as far as we are concerned that I really think we are in a better situation than we were previous to the celebrated Decree of 6th May last. We receive the Coffee as usual and have every reason to hope that the speculation is now placed on a firmer basis than ever. Vivre Melambong et les arbres de café![92]

The Java War 1825–30 and Its Impact on the Coffee Industry

Jubilation, as it turned out, was a tad premature. Within less than eighteen months, hostilities had broken out in south central Java between the Dutch and elements of the aristocracy of the princely courts, led by the Yogyakarta aristocrat, *Pangeran* Dipanagara. The resultant Java War (1825–30) impacted directly and immediately on Gillian Maclaine & Co. in so far as John MacMaster, Maclaine's old acquaintance from Mull and by then the firm's agent in Semarang, was killed in a skirmish with insurgents in the early months of the war, when hostilities spilled over the mountains into the adjoining

---

p. 532, fn. 54). As Maclaine's remark's reveal, however, their lobbying evidently went significantly further than that.

[90] Carey, *Power of Prophecy*, pp. 531–34.

[91] I.e. 'We now have Government security for an indemnification of 20,000 pounds ....' GM to MM 13.6.1824. O-M MSS.

[92] GM to AM 27.7.1824. O-M MSS.

districts of Java's north coast. What appears to have happened is that the young man was part of twenty-strong contingent of Semarang merchants and associated British, Dutch and Armenians who had formed themselves into a 'volunteer cavalry' in the city soon after the commencement of the war. Early in September 1825, in company with sixty sailors from the port, some 'native' troops and a handful of European officers, they constituted a small force of around 100 men who advanced eastward from Semarang to confront what they perhaps fondly supposed was no more than a 'rabble' of insurgents.

Instead, they found themselves opposed by a well-organised force of 500 or so troops (one European eye-witness put the number at 5,000), under the command of Raden Ayu Serang, the young wife of *Pangeran* Serang, a Yogyakarta aristocrat who held territory in the area, and one of his sons. Forced into flight, only eight of the twenty volunteer cavalry got back to Semarang. Their companions, MacMaster among them, met their deaths (it would appear) either in the ditch that separated the road from the adjoining rice-fields (*sawah*), or in the fields themselves, where their horses could make no progress against their pursuers.[93]

Maclaine was understandably anxious to reassure his mother about his own personal safety and to counteract the 'exaggerated accounts' that he feared would appear in the British newspapers. He was also keen to let her know that 'poor MacMaster's balance of salary will be remitted home next month, and I now hope by a favourable exchange to make it amount to 220–250 pounds sterling. His relations may depend on my doing the best for them.' Somewhat prematurely, he predicted that the war would terminate as soon as the wet monsoon lifted (and troop movements thereby facilitated), remarking – fairly enough – that 'there is now not the slightest danger of the Subversion of Dutch power in this part of the world'. Even so, he readily conceded that 'had the Solo [i.e. Surakarta] Princes not espoused the cause of the Government, matters might have terminated very differently, in fact we should all have been driven off the island before now'.[94]

The 'Old Prince', Maclaine and Melambong

Among those 'Solo Princes' was his own landlord, *Pangeran* Buminata, to whose relations with Maclaine we shall return shortly. Meanwhile, the war threatened both to engulf the entire plantation network that had been built

---

[93] See Carey, *Power of Prophecy*, pp. 613–14; Joseph Bremner to [?], Semarang 4.9.1825 – enclosure in J. McLachlan to [Hugh MacMaster] London 16.2.1826 and GM to MM 8.10.1825 [copy]. MacMaster MSS.

[94] GM to MM 28.12.1825. O-M MSS.

up in south central Java over the previous decade and to cut off such supplies of coffee as still emanated from that quarter. When, in August 1826, Maclaine determined on a visit to the Principalities (the occasion was to obtain a new lease on his plantations, which had now been fully restored by the Batavia authorities), he was only able to reach Surakarta – 'what a marked change in the appearance of the place. The European part of the town nearly deserted, the <u>Burghers</u> in arms and their *vrouws* [wives] and children in the fort' – because he could make the journey in the company of a contingent of colonial soldiers:

> I left this [Batavia] for the East about the middle of August and on reaching Samarang was sorry to learn that the insurgents had advanced within a few miles of Melambong and had completely cut off the communication between the Sea coast and Solo. A large body of European troops and some Madurese were fortunately sent up the country to clear the road, and under their protection I reached Solo in safety [and subsequently] ... I returned to Salatiga with General de Kock and his troops....[95]

Nonetheless, the disruption caused by the Java War to the coffee industry in the Principalities was far from total. Coffee continued to be harvested there during the course of the Java War and continued to reach the coast. For example, a traveller proceeding on the mountainous route westward from Salatiga toward Magelan in September 1828 found 'the road nearly covered with packhorses and oxen conveying coffee ... from the interior to Semarang'.[96] Moreover, Maclaine's own plantations, as well as those of some of his neighbours, were largely or totally unscathed by the war. Toward the end of 1826 he was assuring his mother that he now had 'an excellent manager on the estate, a Mr. Cushney all the way from Aberdeen,[97] a fine spirited fellow with a great store of the prudence which his townsmen are reputed to possess', and 'the people are attached to us and Boeminoto [aka Buminata] will do all he can to protect our property'.[98]

'The old Prince', as Maclaine dubbed him, was perhaps an even more useful ally than Maclaine realised. He was a key figure among the aristocratic elite of Surakarta, and a major leaser of land to European planters. At Melambong, as did some of his contemporaries, Maclaine raised a small contingent of guards, but appears to have place more faith in Buminata's protection and in the Netherlands Indies Army:

---

95 GM to MM 6.10.1826. O-M MSS.
96 JDP, 'Native Provinces', p. 163.
97 William Cushnie, b. Scotland [Aberdeen], c.1796. Listed as 'Opziener [overseers] te Melambong, Solo', in 1826. See 'Registers Europeesche Bevolking', NA MK 3130.
98 GM to MM 6.10.1826. O-M MSS.

> I was several times at Solo and was always well received by my good friend the Prince Boeminotto. In these troublesome times he proves really a good friend. The insurgents have frequently been within four or five miles of Melambong, but our Plantation has not been once molested by them. We have now a small armed force of our own, and are surrounded by Government Forts which leaves me under no apprehension for the security of the place, especially as the Government expect next month a reinforcement of three or four thousand troops from Holland.[99]

Not surprisingly perhaps, Buminata was reckoned to be friend of Nahuijs, the former Resident, and was one of the Surakarta aristocrats who had protested against the revocation of the leases by the Indies government in 1823.[100] He was also a devout Muslim, known as the patron of religious communities. In circumstances where the Islamic cause was one of the insurgent's rallying cries, this may have added to his influence in ensuring that Maclaine's plantations remained safe.[101] He was reputedly well disposed toward Maclaine who was, of course a (potential) source of much-needed cash for the *Pangeran*. Late in 1825, when the Java War had already started, Maclaine recorded that Buminata had 'honoured me … with a call and we talked of old times' during an official visit to Batavia.[102] In the following year, when Maclaine himself visited Surakarta, Buminata 'was quite delighted to see me, and embraced me several times with a cordiality I was not prepared for. Never have I met on Java with so friendly a reception. There was nothing Javanese in it – it was perfectly <u>Highland</u>.'[103]

Retrospect: Maclaine's Early Years in Java, 1820–27

As we have seen, Maclaine's activities as a coffee grower in the Principalities were not curtailed to any significant degree by the Java War. Moreover, as the head of a mercantile house based in Batavia that was heavily engaged in the purchase of coffee for export, the impact of the war was likewise marginal. Much of Java's coffee came from parts of the island that remained unaffected

---

[99] GM to MM 12.3.1827. O-M MSS.

[100] Carey, *Power of Prophecy*, p. 436 fn. 5 and p. 531.

[101] Carey, *Power of Prophecy*, pp. 93 and 630: '… *Pangeran* Buminata, the pious Surakarta grandee, [was] renowned as the patron of religious teachers in the *Sunan*'s capital'. Specifically, as Carey points out, he was the patron of Kyai Maja, a religious teacher who acquired a 'favoured position … amongst the ranks of Dipanagara's religious supporters'. The supposition that this Islamic connection had anything to do with the fact that Maclaine's plantations came unscathed through the Java War, however, is mine rather than Dr Carey's.

[102] GM to MM 28.12.1825. O-M MSS.

[103] GM to MM 6.10.1826. O-M MSS.

by the ongoing hostilities in south central Java – indeed, most of it came from the Preanger Mountains and adjacent areas of West Java, and from the directly ruled territories along the island's north-east coast.[104] To that extent, Maclaine's early ventures in Java had evidently met with some degree of success. His operations in south central Java had weathered the attempts by the Indies government to rein in the activities of the European coffee planters *and* the subsequent threat to their existence posed by the outbreak of the Java War. On the commercial front, meanwhile, he had survived an acrimonious break with his erstwhile employers and patrons in London; established his own mercantile house in Batavia (Gillian Maclaine & Co.); and managed to stay in business despite the massive default of his agent at Semarang, the port at which much of that business was done. These were no mean achievement for a tyro trader, who had also enmeshed himself in the production as well as the export of coffee.

Nonetheless, on a number of fronts, the future looked bleak. Maclaine remained in thrall to overseas partners whose conduct he regarded as far from 'liberal' and which led to a final break with them in 1827. The underlying problem, however, related to the two commodities that were the staples of his business: cotton goods and coffee. As we shall see, developments took place in the cotton goods trade to Java during the course of the 1820s that – ostensibly at least – impacted detrimentally on the fortunes of the British traders in Java for whom it was a commercial mainstay. Above all else, however, was the effect the collapse of the bull market in coffee on which Maclaine and those like him had pinned their hopes.

In this context the emerging problem for Maclaine and other coffee traders was not the *supply* of the commodity. Rather, it was the *price* that they obtained for it. By the mid-1820s, far less was being paid for coffee on world markets than had been the case in the heady days at the beginning of the decade. The prime difficulty faced by Java's traders and growers in their attempts to integrate the island into the coffee commodity chain stemmed, that is to say, from global rather than local factors. Combined with a number of other factors, this brought Maclaine near to ruin, at the very time that he was in the process of restructuring his business interests and redefining his relations with London and Calcutta. It is to these several developments that we can now turn.

---

[104] Van Niel, *Java's Northeast Coast*, p. 307 quotes an official estimate from 1829 that of a total Java coffee production of 256,000 *picul* (1 *picul* = 63 kg approx.), some 120,000 came from the Preanger, 76,000 from the Residencies along the north-east coast and 60,000 from the Principalities. He also remarks, however, that 'little can be said about these figures, except that they should be treated with suspicion'.

Four

THE PIVOTAL YEARS: 'MACLAINE WATSON', TREACHEROUS CHAINS, SICKNESS AND DEBT, 1827–32

> Do not be under any apprehensions that we acted rashly or, as the homely proverb has it, 'quarreled with our bread an butter'. On mature reflection I see no cause to regret the step we have taken, though I do not know whether McIntyre will receive our intimation to quit in the spirit of kindness. I hope he may, because it is not my wish that our departure should give rise to any angry feeling or disagreeable bickering.[1]

The story so far has concerned a young 'Scotch adventurer', as he styled himself, arriving first in London and subsequently in Dutch-controlled Java in search of a financial 'independency' that would compensate for the lack of material resources of the Highland gentry family into which he was born. In London, he had been no more than a clerk (albeit it a privileged one, since his employers were also closely connected socially with his own kith and kin) in an East India house in the City. Java, where he had arrived in that house's employ in 1820, seemed to offer altogether better possibilities. Breaking with the London house and the trajectory of subordinate employment that they had envisaged for him, he set up as a coffee-planter in the island's interior, using a minute amount of capital provided (however unwittingly) by his maternal uncle.

Within less than two years of his arriving in Batavia, however, Maclaine's plantation, and the commercial ventures associated with it, had already reached a sufficiently parlous state to force him to re-connect with his erstwhile London employers and their Calcutta associates on terms that they dictated. Meanwhile, in Java itself, and as we saw in the previous chapter, his stake in the coffee 'industry' was threatened on a number of fronts by the Dutch colonial government's suppression of the lease-hold system on the basis

---

[1]   GM to MM, Melambong 18.5 1826. Greenfield MSS.

of which his plantations had been established, and by the outbreak two years later in 1825 of a major insurrection against the Dutch in the area of south central Java where his operations were located.

Even so, it appeared to Maclaine that the chief obstacle to his hopes of gaining an 'independency' lay in the poor share in the profits that he was getting from his London and Calcutta partners for his role in the sale and purchase (respectively) of the cotton goods and the coffee which constituted at this time the two major staples of the bilateral trade between Java and Europe. Nevertheless, underlying this particular aspect of the tensions inherent in the colonial–metropolitan nexus (as we shall see) were global and local upheavals in the two commodity chains – coffee and cotton goods – in which both London and Batavia were tightly bound.

To add to his woes, during the course of 1829 Maclaine became so seriously ill that he felt forced to take ship back to the UK. Nonetheless, this had the advantage at least that by the middle of 1830 he was living in London and in a position to extricate himself from the morass of his former partner's affairs, albeit at considerable expense. While they were forced into bankruptcy, he was not. In the event, he was able to repair both his health and his fortunes and, early in 1832, after a sojourn of more than eighteen months in Europe, took a ship back to the Indies to rejoin his firm.

The Break with London and Calcutta: The Establishment of Maclaine Watson in 1827

Maclaine's split with his London and Calcutta business associates in April 1827 had a long gestation. As early as 1818, when he had known them for just over a year, he had remarked to his mother that 'Notwithstanding all the Messrs Mac's good qualities, I often see a meanness in their character that surprises me – a kind of lowness which lurks concealed in them, but sometimes as it were peeps out unawares ...'[2] Now his disgruntlement gained a quite specific edge. What he saw as the harsh terms his London partners had extracted in 1822 from him and his Singapore associate, John Argyll Maxwell, had been apparent from the very beginning of an arrangement that they had only accepted for want of anything better. 'The terms of partnership of which I have accepted are ... probably as fair as Mr. Mac[Intyre] could venture to give', Maclaine had written his mother at the time, 'but in justice to myself I deem it necessary to inform you that unless my share in the House is increased, I fear that <u>twenty years of good business</u> will not put

2   GM to MM 6.3.1818. O-M MSS.

me in possession of a comfortable independence.'[3] Two years later, in 1824, the situation was little altered. Without any significant capital of their own, Maclaine and Maxwell were still far from being on an equal footing with their metropolitan associates:

> I look forward with confidence, if my health is spared, to the acquirement of a competency, but unless some new arrangements are contemplated by the House at home, I fear that even a <u>competency</u> must be the work of time .... Our friends have taken the Lion's Share and we must remain contented with a very moderate portion of the hard earned gains of the Batavia firm. In Mr. McIntyre's liberality I am inclined to place reliance and I hope the Messrs Mac will soon discover the policy of exercising a little more of it toward their poor partners abroad.[4]

It was against this background that Maclaine and Maxwell – evidently supported by the still-junior Edward Watson – finally determined to sever the link with the McLachlan brothers and to set up in business in Batavia on their own. 'Their conduct toward me', he wrote in forewarning to his uncle in February 1826, '...has been far from liberal, and I earnestly beg of you never to come under any obligation to them on my account. You must not be surprised if you hear shortly of my having separated from them, for I cannot really afford to toil longer in this climate without a sufficient recompense for my labour ....'[5] Scarcely three months later, telling his mother to treat what he wrote in the strictest confidence ('In any conversations that you and my uncle have with Mr. John McLachlan Glensanda, I hope you will be particularly guarded in saying nothing of my proposed separation or of my views or intentions'), Maclaine let her know that: 'Maxwell, Watson and I were unanimous in dissolving our connections with the House in London. Indeed, nothing would induce me to remain under the thralldom [in which] our friends wished to place us and, what is more displeasing, to keep us.'[6] He was evidently determined to keep to his resolve: 'our letters from the Messrs Mac & McIntyre are very sweet of late', he told his mother, 'but I must have something sweeter than letters 'ere I deviate from my former intention of closing our mercantile connection'.[7]

The formal break – announced in Batavia's only newspaper, a government gazette that also carried commercial notices – took place in April 1827, at which point the firm of Gillian Maclaine & Co. was closed down, and the

3   GM to MM 28.12.1822. O-M MSS (emphasis in original).
4   GM to MM, Canton 16.12.1824. O-M MSS (emphasis in original).
5   GM to JG 5.2.1826. Greenfield MSS.
6   GM to MM 18.5.1826. Greenfield MSS.
7   GM to MM 6.10.1826. O-M MSS.

new firm of Maclaine Watson, independent of its erstwhile London connections, began business at Batavia. 'All claims', the notice of dissolution of G. Maclaine & Co. said, 'may be presented … to the undersigned partners of the said firm … [signed] G. Maclaine, E. Watson.'[8] It had all the signs of the standard formula for winding up a business. In fact, it was to have ramifications that had a potential to bring the newly established Maclaine Watson to a premature end.

Paying off the White Lions: Maclaine Watson and the 'Old Concern'

The point was that the termination of the partnership did not mean that Gillian Maclaine and his associates in Java and Singapore were rid of the 'White Lions', as Maclaine caustically termed the McLachlan brothers in presumed reference not only to their original address off Cornhill in the City of London but also to their propensity to consume his substance. Far from it: as Maclaine and his partners in Batavia and Singapore discovered, severing ties was one thing but it was quite another to be rid of their financial obligations to the 'Old Concern' – the McLachlan–MacIntyre partnership – in London and Calcutta with which they had been associated since 1822. Matters are rather murky, but it rather looks as if, perhaps unbeknown to Maclaine, the 'Old Concern' was already in serious financial difficulties by the mid-1820s, and possibly even earlier, and that it had incurred substantial debts prior to Maclaine's separation in 1827.

Moreover, it would appear that a sharp fall in the value of coffee (see below), the commodity that formed the bulk of Maclaine's remittances to London, meant that his balance with his metropolitan partners was far less favourable than he seems to have assumed. Indeed, if the accounts drawn up in relation to the McLachlan–MacIntyre bankruptcy proceedings in 1831 (see below) are to be taken at face value, by 1825 Gillian Maclaine & Co. had an unfavourable balance with the Old Concern amounting to the considerable sum of £14,000.[9] Given the amounts which he had subsequently to remit to London to cover his debts to the Old Concern, the figure appears to be entirely conceivable. The upshot was that, for the first five years of its existence, the bulk of the profits made by the newly founded Maclaine Watson

---

8   *Bataviasche Courant* 21.4.1827/22.

9   McLachlan/MacIntyre Bankruptcy 1831. B3/3613: 'Lett C …. Debts due to the Bankrupt's Estate/Old Concern ending 30th June 1825' records Gillian Maclaine (Batavia) as owing over £14,000 to the McLachlan/MacIntyre partnership, but it is not clear to what extent this sum takes Maclaine's ongoing remittances into account (i.e. consignments to London received after the books had been balanced as of 30.6.1825). Even so, it suggests – at the very least – that by mid-1825 he had a significant adverse balance with his London partners.

– and certainly Maclaine's own share of them – were siphoned off to London to repay what he was adduced to owe, first to the McLachlans and MacIntyre, and subsequently (after their bankruptcy) to their assignees.

One dimension of the situation in which Maclaine found himself had to do directly with the people with whom he was associated in business. In June 1825, Patrick McLachlan, senior partner in the London house, had died suddenly at his home in Stamford Hill, thereby removing from the firm the person whom Maclaine, at least, regarded as the leading light in the enterprise – not only its founder but also a man possessed of a far greater degree of business acumen than his surviving brothers. Maclaine came to harbour grave doubts about the latter's competence and, indeed, probity. At the same time, he maintained considerable confidence in Donald McIntyre, the McLachlan's close associate. 'I do not hear now from the Messrs McLachlan but hope they are well', he wrote to his brother in June 1828, whereas 'Mr. McIntyre is now connected with our [new] establishment in Java and at Singapore, and we continue on the same friendly terms and I hope are likely to remain so now that we have come to a clear understanding.'[10]

Maclaine's erstwhile business partner in Singapore, John Maxwell, evidently saw matters differently, at least in relation to the ongoing imbroglio over the affairs of the Old Concern. It was reported that he 'lays the blame entirely on Mr. McIntyre, who I infer from what he says has been using the Firm and the House in very unjustifiable speculations on his own account and consequently putting the credit of the whole Partnership both at home and abroad in manifest hazard'.[11] For Maclaine himself, the moment of truth (if such it indeed was) came somewhat later. He appears to have retained his confidence in McIntyre until shortly after he returned to Batavia from London in the middle of 1832, at which point he discovered that his erstwhile friend and colleague was attempting to ruin him by spreading rumours in Calcutta (whence McIntyre had returned earlier that year) about financial difficulties that Maclaine was purportedly experiencing. Even so, at least as Maclaine reported the matter to his mother, 'His shaft fell harmless and I never considered him worthy of attention. Our firm is now, I rejoice to say,

---

10 Angus appears to have passed on some potentially disquieting information, presumably with reference to McIntyre, which Maclaine was at pains to rebut: 'With reference to the report of which you take notice, and the person with whom it originated, I find it easier to take the saddle of the wrong than get it on the right horse ['to put the saddle on the wrong horse', i.e. accuse an innocent person] …. If I thought there was the slightest truth in the report I never would have offered [him] … an interest in our House or continued his acquaintance.' GM to AM, Semarang 14.6.1828. Greenfield MSS.

11 J. Maxwell (Senior) to John Gregorson, Aros, 31 October 1826, Enclosed with GM to MM, Batavia 6.10.1826. O-M MSS.

in every respect beyond the reach of his malice.'[12] Meanwhile, the severing of ties with the Old Concern and associated recriminations extended to Maxwell himself:

> A year has now nearly elapsed since my gloomy communication was made to you [he informed his mother in October 1828], and a pretty successful year in a business point of view it has proved to our new firm. Our earnings however alas! go only a small way to pay up the losses of the old concern and I fear another eighteen months gains will not satisfy the White Lions. My partnership with the Messrs Mac, and John Maxwell, has not only involved me in tremendous losses but given me of late more vexation and annoyance than I can express. Were I to put on paper a few instances only of Maxwell's rancour displayed toward me as opportunities opened since my last visit to Singapore, you would I think form the same opinion of him as I now hold, which he is either of unsound mind or an unprincipled villain. His conduct since our truly lucky separation has been extra-ordinary in the extreme, sometimes evincing apprehensions of being cheated by his former partners, with accounts before his eyes proving of course to the contrary, and that he was deeply in our debt. At other times disputing on the veriest trifles and giving source of the very finest specimens of a litigious spirit ever witnessed. He would have made an excellent Lawyer.[13]

Yet there was more to the situation in which Maclaine found himself than the animosity and deviousness of business associates. Most immediately, he and his (erstwhile) partners in London were struggling to survive what the historian David Kynaston has described as 'as arguably the most severe financial crisis of the [nineteenth] century' effecting the City.[14] With its 'ensuing atmosphere of uncertainty and recrimination',[15] the crisis had both a global reach and global causes. Inter alia, in common with Maclaine in Batavia, his partners in London and Calcutta were caught in adverse developments in worldwide commodity chains over which they had little or no control. Consequent on a variety of factors – the catalyst (at the very least) was the collapse of a veritable 'South Sea Bubble' of speculative investment in the newly independent states of Latin America – the crisis began in the closing months of 1825 and showed few signs of letting up a year later.[16] Matters were so bad that at one stage it looked as if the Bank of England itself might have to close its doors.

For the City's mercantile community in general, the crisis meant a drying up of credit and resultant liquidity problems and for the East India houses like the McLachlan–MacIntyre partnership was all the more severe because of its impact on the import–export trade that was at the core of their operations. As

---

12 GM to MM 9.7.1834. Greenfield MSS.
13 GM to MM, Balliedono near Melambong 16.10.1828. O-M MSS.
14 Kynaston, *City of London*, p. 65.
15 Kynaston, *City of London*, p. 83.
16 Kynaston, *City of London*, pp. 69–72.

one contemporary London house explained to their correspondents in distant Canton in April 1826, 'the stagnation in general business is fully as great at the present moment as it has been at any time since the commencement five months ago of the extraordinary panic'. In consequence, they could scarcely quote more than nominal prices for Asian commodities, 'it being impracticable to effect sales to any extent'.[17] In particular, it has to be assumed that many of the difficulties in which the Old Concern found itself resulted from the falling price of coffee on Western markets, together with a much-reduced volume of British cotton goods sold in Java coinciding with a market glut in India.

'The Game is Over': The Java Trade in the Late 1820s

On a fundamental level the problems facing the new firm and its business associates in London and Calcutta stemmed from their continuing involvement in the two commodity chains that had brought Maclaine to Java in the first place, and subsequently kept him there. In this context, the second half of the 1820s was hardly a propitious time to start up a new business heavily dependent on cotton goods and coffee. One of Maclaine's contemporaries – and a good friend – remarked of his own fortunes at this time that 'I find that moderate as my expectations have always been, I am yet far short of the mark, and, what is worse, now have little chance of ever accomplishing it *as the game is over in Java*, the place of all my experience.'[18] To be sure, this was an excessively gloomy picture, and both McLean and Maclaine survived better than they might have dared hope. Ostensibly, however, McLean's prognostication was reasonably accurate.

Cotton Goods, Imperial Rivalries and Global Trends

We can begin with cotton goods. To be sure, the manufacturing side of the cotton commodity chain continued to be dominated by Lancashire and Glasgow, whose producers remained the world leaders for the rest of the century. Nonetheless, they were far from being the only ones, as cotton piece goods began to be manufactured industrially in various other places in

---

17 Fairlie Bonham & Co. to unnamed constituents in Canton, as quoted in Kynaston, *City of London*, p. 73.

18 Colin Maclean to [?], undated c.1826–27, MacLean MSS (a small collection of letters to and from Colin Maclean 1822–c.1858 in the possession of Nicholas Crickhowell, who kindly provided me with copies in London in 2011). Emphasis added.

Western Europe. These included the Kingdom of the Netherlands, newly created at the end of the Napoleonic Wars, and with major manufacturing centres in its southern 'Belgian' provinces, most notably in and around the Flemish city of Ghent. In promoting the growth of this cotton industry, the Dutch King Willem I – very much the CEO of the Netherlands Inc. – sought to appease his new southern subjects, modernise his country's economy and increase Dutch shipping's hold on a colonial trade to the Indies that showed every sign of being overrun by British interests.[19]

Faced with a 'flood' of British manufactures, the Dutch colonial regime, solidly backed by the metropolitan government, determined to privilege Netherlands suppliers over those from the UK (with whom Maclaine and his associates dealt) by imposing a hefty tariff on cotton piece goods brought to Java in foreign ships. It was a reminder that states – even minor ones – could be at times as potent as 'the market' in the evolution of commodity chains. Though aware of the dangers of alienating the British (by then the world's maritime superpower), Willem I and his advisors opted in 1824 to challenge the British hegemony in the Java trade – as we saw in an earlier chapter – by founding the NHM (Nederlandsche Handel-Maatschappij or Netherlands Trading Society). The new company was a state-backed enterprise, in which Willem I was the largest single shareholder, and which was to be accorded preferential treatment in all matters relating to the commerce of Java.[20] It was in conjunction with the founding of the NHM that the king agreed to a scheme designed to break the domination of the Java market by British cotton manufacturers.

As Maclaine explained, from mid-1824 onward, the new tariff regime meant increasing 'the duties on all British cotton and woolen manufactures to about 50 percent ....' In reporting on this, the young man was inclined to play down the impact on his own business: 'Notwithstanding the bad times', he assured his brother, 'we are doing pretty well'[21] and in the same vein there were subsequent references to the continuance of large consignments. Despite Maclaine's protestations, however, the fact was that the new level of duties resulted in a huge reduction in the quantities of British cotton goods imported into Java. Though the Java War might also be thought to have had a significant impact on local consumption, this appears not to have been the case. The absolute quantity of cotton goods landed in the colony showed no diminution in the second half of the 1820s: on the contrary, they continued to

[19] For the information about Dutch policies and cotton goods imports into Java in the 1820s, I am drawing gratefully in this and the following two paragraphs on Kraan, 'Anglo-Dutch Rivalry', pp. 35–64.

[20] De Graaf, *Voor Handel en Maatschappij*, pp. 39–45.

[21] GM to AM 27.7.1824. O-M MSS.

grow, albeit somewhat erratically. What fell dramatically, on the other hand, was the percentage coming from the UK, as cotton goods of Dutch origin began to replace them, consequent on the favourable new tariff regime.

The change was not absolute and there were ways of circumventing the new tariff. One contemporary of Maclaine's, apparently well-informed, casually observed at the end of the 1820s that 'It is generally known that large quantities of English cottons do find their way into Java, without passing through the customs house.'[22] A more legitimate way of circumventing the tariff was by shipping British goods in non-British bottoms. In 1827, for example, Maclaine told his mother – without further comment (since the post was not always secure) that 'we have at present a good many ships consigned to us, which keeps us very busy. Among others, two Swedish vessels which is rather a novelty.'[23] Even so, the fall off in direct trade with the UK was considerable. Although at the end of the 1820s, cotton goods of UK origin still amounted to around 30 per cent (in value) of the total imports into Java, earlier in the decade they had amounted to more than 96 per cent. Moreover, in Java itself, imported cotton goods had to compete with a resilient indigenous artisan manufacture of cloth.[24]

Even so, adverse developments in the commodity chain in cotton goods were by no means particular to Java. Indeed, Maclaine and other members of the British mercantile community on Java were caught up in developments that reached far beyond the attempts of the Dutch government to curb their 'stranglehold' on the trade in piece goods. On the Asian 'periphery', as elsewhere, markets for cotton piece goods were inherently unstable, and much prone to glut and undersupply. It was a case, among other things, of long chains and slow communications. Towards the close of the 1820s, for example, John Palmer was writing to Maclaine from his Calcutta base advising him that his (Palmer's) London correspondents had apparently escaped 'without a scratch from the numerous failures at Glasgow', but that 'there is a glut of British piece goods all over India' and London had largely 'suspended operations' in cotton.[25] As reported at the time by another substantial East India house there was 'no disposition shewn by dealers to become purchasers except at very low rates'.[26]

---

22 [J.D.P.], 'Native Provinces', p. 81.
23 GM to MM Batavia 12.3.1827. O-M MSS.
24 See e.g. Peter Boomgaard, 'The Non-Agricultural Side of an Agricultural Economy: Java, 1500–1900', pp. 20–24 in Paul Alexander, Peter Boomgaard and Ben White (eds), *In the Shadow of Agriculture. Non-Farm Activities in the Javanese Economy, Past and Present* (Amsterdam: Royal Tropical Institute, 1991).
25 John Palmer to Gillian Maclaine 14.7.1829, Palmer Eng. Lett. c. 110.
26 Inglis Forbes and Co.'s Circular 16.4.1827, as quoted in Kynaston, *City of London*, p. 77.

New World Production and the End of the Bull Market in Coffee

Maclaine's difficulties with cotton goods might have been resolved by his simultaneous role as a coffee planter and trader. As luck would have it, however, this secondary commodity chain in which he was involved was contemporaneously experiencing developments that worked to his disadvantage. As we have already seen in the previous chapter, events on Java itself impacted adversely on the coffee growing and purchasing ventures of Maclaine and his contemporaries. In the first place, the Dutch authorities in Batavia forced the curtailment of the system of leasehold that formed the basis of coffee planting in south central Java, and second, the entire plantation network in which Maclaine was involved was threatened by the outbreak of a major colonial war. Nonetheless, the key to the situation in which he found himself related less to local circumstances than to the global impact of burgeoning New World production on the coffee commodity chain as a whole.

Although one authority has aptly remarked of coffee production worldwide that 'statistics for the early nineteenth century are rare and unreliable', it seems likely that around 1830 Asian and African suppliers (with Java well to the fore) still accounted for around one-third of the world's coffee exports.[27] Indeed, a likewise somewhat speculative estimate was that in the mid-1820s, Java alone provided more than one-fifth of the world's total recorded exports.[28] At the same time, however, a significantly greater amount of coffee was coming onto the world market, mostly from South America, so that although Java retained (however tenuously) a significant market share, it did so in rapidly changing market conditions that put downward pressure on prices.

In particular, during the 1820s a flood of coffee from Brazil and other American producers underlay a sharp fall in the commodity's world price.[29] In consequence, traders (and growers) based in the periphery lost the big profit margins that they had enjoyed at the beginning of the decade, as the core-based distributors forced down the price they paid to their suppliers. By the middle of the decade, the latter's position had deteriorated sharply. Java was no exception. Indeed, writing (in May 1825) from his vantage point in the Indian subcontinent, the great Calcutta merchant John Palmer had cautioned one major speculator that, 'I fear ... that you must abandon all idea of a high price for coffee in the present condition of the world, for our present accounts show miserable results upon large consignments from Java in

---

[27] William Gervase Clarence-Smith, 'The Coffee Crisis in Asia Africa and the Pacific, 1870–1914', in Clarence-Smith and Topik, *The Global Coffee Economy*, p. 100.

[28] Bulbeck et al., *Southeast Asian Exports*, Table 5:4, p. 152.

[29] Clarence-Smith and Topik, *The Global Coffee Economy*, pp. 412, 432, Tables A.1, A.14.

1824 .... Neither are we encouraged to expect a rise.'[30] The slump in coffee prices meant that by 1825 coffee was selling at Batavia for almost 50 per cent less than had been the case only four years earlier, reflecting the fact that in Rotterdam, the main market for Java coffee at this time, the price had fallen by 60 per cent or more over roughly the same period, thereby more than halving the notional profit margin previously enjoyed by those in Java who had been in a position to dispatch it to Europe. In short, coffee planting on the island ceased to be the sure-fire route to making a fortune that Maclaine and his equally enthusiastic contemporaries had fondly supposed at the beginning of the decade. Trying to put a brave face on the situation, Maclaine remarked to his brother in June 1828:

> Money is becoming scarce in consequence of the heavy outlays for the War. The staple produce of the island, coffee, is at a very low price, which is against me as a planter but in my favour as a merchant. The Government makes unlikely professions of both assistance and encouragement to both planters and merchants, and at the same time throws numerous obstacles in the way of both one and the other prospering.[31]

Nonetheless, as the gist of Maclaine's letter conveyed, the whole mercantile plantation enterprise in Java was imperilled. The falling price of coffee cut deeply into whatever expectations he and his friends had entertained of the commodity as a sure and swift route to 'independency'. Indeed, Maclaine claimed in 1828 that he was more than 200,000 guilders in debt at his Melambong plantation alone.[32] Low prices also meant, of course, a steep decline in the value of return cargoes from Java. Between 1822 (when statistics begin) and 1828, the *value* of Java's coffee exports fell by more than 50 per cent, while over the same period the volume of exports actually *rose*.[33] In turn, this fall in value of the returns with which Maclaine supplied them was undoubtedly one of the key underlying factors contributing to the breakdown of his relations with his London partners.

The joint impact of the adverse developments in the coffee and cotton commodity chain impacted significantly on Java's European mercantile houses, the majority of which were at this time British. The major Batavia house of MacQuoid Davidson – the firm had connections in both Bengal and London

---

30 John Palmer to William Cotes 18.5.1825, Palmer Eng. Lett. c. 102.
31 GM to AM 14.6.1828, Greenfield MSS.
32 GM to Willem van Hogendorp 12.1.1828. NA Collectie Van Hogendorp 190.
33 W.L. Korthals-Altes, *Changing Economy in Indonesia: General Trade Statistics, 1822–1940 v.12A: Selection of Statistical Source Material from the Early 19th Century Up to 1940* (Amsterdam: KIT, 1992), p. 13, Table 6A, p. 136; Peter Creutzberg, *Changing Economy in Indonesia; A Selection of Statistical Source Material from the Early 19th Century up to 1940; vol 1: Indonesia's Export Crops 1816–1940* (The Hague: Nijhoff, 1975), Table 12 pt 2, p.105.

– failed in 1826, and in the following year another big operator, Deans Scott and Co. of Semarang closed down. Even so, this adverse development was not perhaps quite as bad as it looked. The leading partner in the latter firm, John Deans (Campbell), returned to Scotland a rich man (presumably having got out in time), and the reasons for MacQuoid Davidson's collapse, which certainly bankrupted MacQuoid himself and very probably contributed to the ruin of his old associate Sir Stamford Raffles, by then back in the UK, were not to be found exclusively in their involvement in the cotton trade.

It rather looks for example, as if MacQuoid Davidson's investments in sugar in a very large estate that they part-owned in West Java proved very disappointing.[34] Other singular factors may well have been involved: one contemporary report had it that having bought coffee on their own account, rather than on the more usual commission basis, when the price was still fairly high, MacQuoid Davidson were then caught by a subsequent sharp fall in the commodity's value.[35] Moreover, for the remaining British firms, there was business to be picked up. Maclaine, whose closeness to Deans was to be a major factor in the revival of his business fortunes in the following decade, was able to gain from Deans Scott the Java agency for the great Calcutta house of John Palmer & Co., presumably on the recommendation of his friend. 'The respectable Mr Palmer of Calcutta, who has appointed our House his agents in Java, spent some days with me lately here [Maclaine recorded in July 1828] accompanied by one of his friends. We made some very pleasant excursions in the neighbourhood, and performed feats on horseback that would have astonished the fox hunters in England.'[36] He also obtained the Java agency for one of the major maritime insurance firms operating in the East, the Calcutta Insurance Company.[37] Accordingly, during the course of 1828 he was able to write home 'I have now much pleasure in acquainting you with the fact that my prospects have become considerably brighter.'[38] Even so, in explaining to a very senior Dutch functionary why he was unable to become a subscriber to the newly formed Javasche Bank (DJB) – an independent financial institution that nonetheless enjoyed a modicum of backing from the Indies government

[34] See G. Roger Knight, 'From Plantation to Padi-Field: The Origins of the Nineteenth Century Transformation of Java's Sugar Industry', *Modern Asian Studies*, 14, 2 (1980), pp. 177–204.

[35] Some such sequence of events is implied in Mansvelt's account (W.F.M. Mansvelt, *Geschiedenis van de Nederlandsche Handel-Maatschappij*, 2 vols, Haarlem [1924, 1926]), 1, p. 153) of the 'commercial crisis' in Java in 1825–26, a narrative that takes into account vital short-term fluctuations in price that are obscured by 'global' annual averages.

[36] GM to MM 22.7.1828. O-M MSS; Palmer to Princip, Batavia 21.1827, Palmer Eng. Lett. c. 127: 'I have requested Maclaine, Watson & Co to accept our agency during the absence of Deans from Java.'

[37] Mansvelt, *NHM*, 1, p. 193.

[38] GM to [??] Undated fragment [1828?] O-M MSS.

– Maclaine may not have strayed too far from the truth when he claimed that 'the greater part of all the little capital I had at my disposal when I settled in Java, having unfortunately been sunk in agricultural speculations, I am now left absolutely with scarcely more than sufficient funds to carry on respectably the commercial operations of my firm'.[39]

Sickness and Recovery 1829–31

The unravelling affairs of 'the Old Concern', the vicissitudes of the trade in cotton goods and coffee, and the opportunities for making new business were not the only things on Maclaine's mind at the close of the 1820s. During the course of 1829 he was struck down by an illness debilitating enough to make him feel that he needed better medical attention than was available in Batavia. Writing from his plantation in the 'Highlands' of central Java, he wrote to his mother in July 1829 that:

> On my arrival here about the middle of May, I was attacked with a severe inflammation of the Liver which soon made itself known by the usual symptoms of a pain in the right shoulder all too well known to almost every resident in a hot climate, symptoms which soon hurried me to Samarang for medical attention. I was fortunate in finding a very able Doctor at the latter place, who through copious bleeding and low diet, though he reduced me a near skeleton, affected a complete cure and that in the short space of three weeks. He sent me back here as soon as I could bear the fatigue of the journey, and never have I so much enjoyed the comparatively cool climate of the place so much as during my convalescence. I purposely deferred writing until I could state with a clear conscience what I can now most positively do, which is that I never felt stronger, eat with a keener appetite, slept better nor took my usual exercise on horseback with more enjoyment than I do at present. With such symptoms I trust I am warranted in concluding that all is sound again in the interior, and if temperate living can prevent a recurrence of the complaint.[40]

Maclaine's optimism proved premature. Despite assurances to his mother a month later that 'I now live much more quietly than I used to' and protestations that 'I now content myself with the plainest of fare, and though my food

---

[39] GM to Willem van Hogendorp 12.1.1828. NA Collectie Van Hogendorp 190.
[40] GM to MM, Ballie Dono 4.7.1829. Greenfield MSS: '… I do not know to what to attribute my late attack, unless it may have been caused by hard riding and exposure to the sun when inspecting a large Estate near Batavia which we purchased a short time ago for Mr. Palmer. I frequently rode thirty, forty and fifty miles in the course of a day without feeling any inconvenience from so doing, but after nine years continuous residence in a hot climate such hard exercise I find does not answer. I shall be more cautious in future in exposing myself to the sun but shall continue my rides on horseback, though of course in a moderate way.'

is not exactly fruit, my drink is chiefly from "the crystal well"', toward the end of the year he had a recurrence of what was most probably viral hepatitis (or possibly gall stones).[41] It was evidently severe enough to convince him that he needed better medical attention (though he expressed the point somewhat differently) than that reckoned to be available in the colony. He informed his mother that:

> I have been sadly reduced, and lost the greater part of the little flesh I had on my bones. I should be sorry … if you saw me in my present emaciated condition. [Nonetheless] though I would cut a laughable figure in the Highland dress at this moment, yet I feel there is some Highland stamina yet left, and the Doctors assure me that a very short residence in a cold climate would restore my constitution to its former strength.[42]

Accordingly, leaving his two chief Java associates, Edward Watson and John MacNeill, in charge of Maclaine Watson's operations in the Indies, Maclaine departed as quickly as possible for the UK. 'I learn with sorrow', wrote John Palmer from Calcutta to Edward Watson, 'that a relapse of his complaint has driven him from you, for besides my own unfeigned concern on his own account, the juncture is particularly inauspicious in relation to our affairs in Java.'[43] Indeed, evidently in too much of a hurry to wait for a berth at Batavia, Maclaine had taken passage early in February 1831 at Anjer (Anyer), the Dutch signal station on Java's westernmost tip where European ships passing through the Sunda Strait between that island and Sumatra had perforce to call. The vessel on which he found a berth, the HCS *Waterloo* – an East India Company ship returning from the China run with tea and porcelain aboard – got him to London in mid-July of that year.[44] He was not to see Java again for another eighteen months.

Back in London: Maclaine and the 'Old Concern'

> Once more in old England! I arrived here late last night in much better health, thank God, than when I left Batavia. I have very little flesh on my bones and I am not a Hercules in point of strength, but my spirits are good and I have every hope of soon being as strong as ever I was in my life.[45]

---

[41] I am grateful for this cautious analysis of Maclaine's ill heath to the modern-day London-based practitioners, Dr Colin Brewer and Dr Adam Bakker.

[42] GM to MM, Batavia 8.12.1829. Greenfield MSS.

[43] John Palmer to Edward Watson 5.2.1830, Palmer Eng. Lett. c. 113, pp. 115–19.

[44] GM told his mother that he proposed sailing from Anjer in January 1830 on the HCS *Waterloo*. The vessel appears to have been regularly on the China run.

[45] GM to MM, London 15.7.1830. Greenfield MSS.

Arriving in London in mid-summer 1830, Maclaine set about repairing both his health and his fortunes. Good medical advice, a change of climate and, perhaps most important of all, a break in the round of 'boisterous' (his word) bachelor parties among his fellow Scots expatriates in Batavia, saw him returned, albeit over a period of almost a year, to rude health. Although warning his uncle and brother in the Highlands to prepare his mother for his changed appearance – he reckoned that he had lost some 40 pounds in weight over the preceding twelve months and 'to state the truth I look a wreck of what I was on Java'[46] – Maclaine appeared in general sanguine about the state of his liver and his general well-being. The medical men whom he consulted in London immediately on his arrival – they included a Dr Arnott, erstwhile practitioner in India – assured him, he reported to his uncle, that 'the inflammation has completely left my Liver and that there is nothing dangerous or serious the matter with me'.[47] A month later indeed, he felt confident enough to assure his mother that 'I am not only going on as well as could be, but better than I expected …. I look pale yellow and am as thin as a starved chimney sweeper or thread paper, but begin to relish my food, walk a few miles every day without difficulty and sleep well, all you will allow unquestionable symptoms of convalescence.' Even so, it was not until September 1830, almost three months after his arrival in the United Kingdom, that he was able to embark on a journey north to be reunited with his family at Ardtornish.

It was less health issues that had delayed him, however, so much as the need to grapple with the financial problems that he faced in London as a result of the imminent collapse of the partnership between the McLachlan brothers and Donald MacIntyre that had formed the core of the 'Old Concern' in which Maclaine himself had been associated prior to the dissolution of his partnership with them in 1827. By the time he arrived in London from Java in July 1830, Patrick McLachlan himself had been dead for five years, and the remaining brothers – in tandem with Donald McIntyre – were in deep financial trouble. On first arriving in London, Maclaine's letters to his mother reflected a degree of optimism:

> You will rejoice to hear that I find matters here, I mean as regards my business arrangements, better than I expected. The McLachlans I have not seen, but McIntyre is as kind and friendly as any of my nearest and dearest relations

---

[46] GM to JG, London 4.9.1830. Greenfield MSS: 'My health is improving, but not quite so rapidly as I expected. The society of my relations and my native air will, I hope, soon bring me round. My personal appearance does not, I am sorry to say, indicate strength or health as yet, and as I may not write again ere we meet, I may as well prepare my Mother and those relations who remember me for a slight shock.'

[47] GM to JG, London 23.7.1830. Greenfield MSS.

could possibly be. One of my wealthiest Correspondents here has also given me a warmer reception than I could have looked for. In short, I feel now on many accounts pleased at making up my mind to come home. It will prove as beneficial in matters of business as gratifying in other respects.[48]

Maclaine's optimism was soon tempered, however, by his perception that 'the provoking dilatoriness of the Messrs. McLachlan retards everything … and that a system of recrimination has been pursued by the partners on this side highly disreputable and unworthy of British merchants'.[49] Whatever the actual rights and wrongs of the situation – and we only have Maclaine's version of events, compelling as that appears to be in many respects – his conviction that he held the ethical high ground, and was determined to remain there, was to be a recurring theme in his subsequent correspondence.

In May 1831, Donald McIntyre and John McLachlan – by this date the senior of the Morvern brothers involved in the enterprise – went into bankruptcy. The repercussions for Maclaine, who had been their business partner until April 1827 were considerable, since many of the creditors' claims dated from a period prior to that date. The immediate background to the bankruptcy, however, appears to have been the inability of John McLachlan (and his surviving brothers) to reach any agreement with their erstwhile partner Donald McIntyre that would have satisfied their creditors. The convoluted commercial affairs of the McLachlan–McIntyre partnership were to dog Maclaine for the better part of a year. In the middle months of 1831 (as we shall see) he had paid a visit to the Continent, amongst other things taking the opportunity to renew his contacts in the Low Countries. Returning from Paris to London in June of that year, the detritus of his former partners' affairs proved inescapable. His separation, however, was neither cheap nor easy. On Maclaine's own reckoning, at least, the 'White Lions' had cheated him. Their bankruptcy in the middle months of 1831 left Maclaine to make what settlement he could with the assignees. Even so, it could have been worse:

> Since my arrival here [he told his mother] I have been sadly tormented by the lawyers and assignees of Mc L and McIntyre & Co, now <u>bankrupt</u>. I cannot describe to you the ordeal I have gone and have, alas, yet to go through. God knows what the result may be, but I shall endeavour to prepare myself for the worst. Never was a poor mortal placed in such difficulties …. I shall not conceal from you my very dear Mother that my spirits have given way a little and that my heart is very, very sick, but in a day or two I shall recover my tranquility.

---

[48] GM to MM, London 15.7.1830. Greenfield MSS.
[49] GM to JG, London 23.7.1830. Greenfield MSS.

The more I pay off, the heavier are the sums brought against me – it is truly disheartening. Keep all this to yourself.[50]

There followed several months of continuous to-ing and fro-ing between the parties, carried out by a solicitor (or possibly law clerk), whose daily accounts have survived to demonstrate what a tedious and contentious process it was. Not until early August 1831 were matters resolved as far as Maclaine was concerned, culminating in an agreement with the assignees, Colin Campbell and James MacKillop, both of whom were major figures in East India business circles in the City:

> [2/8/1831] Attending Mr. Maclaine on the state of this business and on claim on him & his anxiety to have it settled and conferring with him on the necessity for a meeting with the assignees to finally agree the terms when he promised to see them on the subject. [3/8/1831] … attending Mr. Maclaine in long conference on the claim on him and on the result of his communication with Mr. Mackillop and Mr. Campbell and afterwards attending Mr. Campbell and Mr. Maclaine in long conference on the business and the mode of settling it when meeting agreed to be fixed with Mr. Mackillop engaged considerable time … Writing to Mr. Mackillop accordingly for an appointment with Mr Campbell to arrange about Mr. Maclaine's affairs. [4/8/1831] Writing Mr Campbell to apprise him Mr. Mackillop has appointed 11.00 tomorrow for a meeting on this subject and to request his attendance. [5/8/1831] Attending Mr. Mackillop and Mr. Campbell by appointment on Mr. Maclaine's debt and discussing the same when they agreed upon the terms upon which they would arrange that claim …[51]

As this indicates, one of the advantages John McLachlan and MacIntyre having gone into bankruptcy was that Maclaine could now deal with his erstwhile partner's assignees rather than with his erstwhile – and obdurate – partners in the Old Concern itself. As luck would have it, moreover, at least one of the former was evidently well disposed toward him. As a result, he was able to inform his mother that:

> By my late letter to Ardtornish you would have learnt that I have at last come to a settlement with the Assignees and am now out of the clutches of Messrs McLachlan MacIntyre and all their concerns on better terms than I had

---

50 GM to MM, London 17.6.1831. Greenfield MSS.

51 Extracted from the (voluminous) account rendered by the solicitors Oliverson Denby & Laire (of Fredericks Place, City) for 'The costs incurred in and about the liquidation of the affairs on Messrs Maclachlan Macintyre & Co. previous and subsequent to the Deed of Arrangement … 6th July 1833.' See Files of the Office of the Commissioners of Bankrupts and Court of Bankruptcy, National Archives UK, Kew, B3/3613. Papers relating to the bankruptcy of John McLachlan and Donald MacIntyre Sun Court, Cornhill, London, merchants, bankrupts. 1831.

expected – through the kindness of my worthy friend [James] Mackillop [of the East India House of Palmers, MacKillop] .... I have made a more favourable arrangement than the [one] communicated to my Uncle, indeed feel perfectly satisfied with the settlement.[52]

Indeed, as he reported to his mother immediately after his return to Batavia in 1832:

Our business goes on as prosperously as I could wish & and much more comfortably than it used to be when connected with the White Lions – I send them home my last installment of 934 pounds by this ship and now that I am in possession of a full and ample release from their assignees feel lighter and more [...] than I have done for years. Watson, who fortunately for him was not a partner in the bad years of the old concern I find now actually rich – while I, who made him a partner from being my clerk, am obliged to begin the work again – even the *Bodachan* [Maclaine's invariable reference to the diminutive James Fraser] at Singapore had a round sum at his credit – They had nothing to pay the Messrs Mac – not being partners. I had to pay up for claims brought against me about 10,000 pounds]!! I shall not give it a thought – it is now over & I hope soon to forget all my annoyances and profit by past experience.[53]

Most immediately, the settlement with the assignees had finally freed him from all commercial encumbrances stemming from association with his erstwhile partners, and freed him to build new connections for the his business in Batavia. As he pointedly informed his mother, 'I have been complimented in a manner flattering to my feelings, for doing only what any honest man would have done, and I actually find, paradoxical as it may appear, that my misfortunes have raised my credit. I really now feel comfortable and breathe in a different atmosphere, being forever out of the dirty grasping clutches of the MacL's.'[54]

Glasgow's Premier Cotton Baron: Kirkman Finlay

The most important of Maclaine's new connections was that forged with the Finlay family and the manufacturing and commercial businesses that

[52] GM to MM, London 10.8.1831. O-M MSS.

[53] GM to MM, Batavia 2.7.1832. Greenfield MSS (emphasis in original). Bodachen Sabhaill (Little Old Man of the Barn) (pronounced 'botuchan so-will'), Ireland, Isle of Man, Hebrides. Brownie who lives in farm buildings and does threshing for aging farmers who are tired. Can appear as an old woman, man or pony and guides lost travellers back onto the road. See http://www.tartanplace.com/faery/hobg2.html (accessed 29/7/2013).

[54] GM to MM, London 10.8.1831. Greenfield MSS (emphasis in original).

they ran in Glasgow and London. 'My dear Uncle', Maclaine informed John Gregorson early in September 1830, when he had been scarcely three months in the UK, 'you will I know be happy to learn that one of the foremost Houses in the East India line [now] act as agents in London for my Establishments in Batavia and Singapore on very favourable terms....'[55] The family patriarch, Kirkman Finlay (1772–1843), was reportedly the biggest cotton goods manufacturer on Clydeside (where he had inherited a business started by his father) and a man of considerable substance and influence not only in Scotland but also in London. He was many times Chairman of Glasgow's Chamber of Commerce, Lord Provost of the city and rich enough both to engage heavily (as we shall see) in London politics to promote his overseas commercial agendas, and to build himself a magnificent mansion further up the west coast, well away from the smoke, grime and stench of the city where he made his money.[56]

Quite how Maclaine came to know the Finlays is unclear. What is certain, however, is that by the closing months of 1830 he was already on excellent terms with them. Indeed, in Glasgow in September of that year, and on his way to Ardtornish to be reunited with his family, he delayed his return home because 'I am obliged to start out for Castle Toward to see Mr. Kirkman Finlay. I spend tonight and all tomorrow at Castle Toward and return here on Monday.'[57] The visit was evidently a productive one. Maclaine was subsequently to declare that with 'the Finlays and their English partners I am on the best of terms and consult them now as my most confidential friends'. He appears to have forged particularly close ties with Alec Finlay, one of Kirkman's sons, who was slated to join a Finlay-connected business in Bombay and presumably found Maclaine, only eight years his senior, a convivial source of information about the East.[58] The younger Finlay travelled north with Maclaine in August 1831 'and will perhaps go with me to the Highlands' (earlier in the year a plan had been mooted for him to join Maclaine on his trip to the Continent). In London, he told his mother, 'Hodgeson's and Finlay's houses are a home to me', while in the north 'I find my Glasgow friends very kind, but none nearly so much as the worthy Laird of Toward from whom I have just parted [after spending a further week at his

55 GM to JG, London 4.9.1831. Greenfield MSS.
56 On Finlay, see R.H. Campbell, 'The Making of the Industrial City', in Devine and Jackson *Glasgow*, vol. 1, p. 202; 'Finlay, Kirkman (1773–1842)', in *The History of Parliament*, accessed online at: www.historyofparliamentonline.org › Research › Members › 1790–1820; Webster, *The Twilight*, pp. 58, 72, 96–99; [Colm Brogan], *James Finlay and Company Limited. Manufacturers and East India Merchants* (Glasgow: Jackson Son and Company, 1951), pp. 6–13.
57 GM to MM, Glasgow 18.9.1830. O-M MSS.
58 Alexander Struthers Finlay (1806–86).

country house]. He backs his professions of kindness with consignments to us at Batavia and Singapore.'[59]

Maclaine had already been active in drumming up business for his partners back in Java: 'The length of my stay here I cannot yet determine', he reported to John Gregorson in November 1830. 'I suspect however I shall be obliged to take a short trip to Manchester ere I return to the Highlands. There are numerous competitors at present in the field, and unless I show myself as active as my neighbours, my Indian associates in business, Watson and Fraser, may probably be seized with the prevailing spirit of insurrection and meditate treason contre leur chef.'[60]

It was links with the Finlays that had become the key to his strategy, to the extent indeed of replacing arrangements that he had earlier made with one of the partners in the major London East India house of Palmers, McKillop:

> ... Not from unwillingness on the part of Mr. McKillop – far from it – but solely on account of the Finlays desire to keep me to themselves. They have positively pressed me into their service, and believe me I have entered it with heart and hand – and lament I did not fall into their hands years ago. Amidst all my distresses and difficulties it is most gratifying to my feelings to be thus clung to by people of first-rate respectability and wealth.[61]

In return for his 'professions of kindness', moreover, the Laird of Toward also recruited Maclaine for his political ventures in the British capital. Maclaine was early aware of Kirkman Finlay's proclivities in this respect. Writing from Glasgow late in November 1830, he told his uncle that:

> Mr. Kirkman Finlay has gone to London to attend his election business which comes before the house on the 2nd next. His partner Buchanan appears afraid of a Dissolution of Parliament which will render Mr. Finlay's journey to London 'vera useless'. The Glasgow Reformers are quite Cock-a-Hoop about the new [Gray] Ministry – and many sage predications are afloat respecting its probable durability.[62]

Maclaine can hardly have been surprised therefore, though perhaps slightly alarmed, at being pressed into service early in 1831 in the interests of Finlay's longstanding campaign against the East India Company's monopoly of

---

[59] GM to AM, Glasgow 25.8.1831 and GM to Marie Maclaine, Ardtornish 19.9.1831. O-M MSS. Gillian's paternal grandmother, the formidable Marie Maclaine née MacQuarie (1748–1846) had left Mull to live in Edinburgh, at 12 Warriston Crescent, with her two unmarried daughters, Mary and Margaret Ann (both d. 1855). See Curry, *Mull*, pp. 288–90.

[60] GM to JG, Glasgow 25.11.1830. Greenfield MSS.

[61] GM to MM, London 12.3.1831. Greenfield MSS (emphasis in original).

[62] GM to JG, Glasgow 25.11.1830. Greenfield MSS. The 'election business' to which Maclaine refers is detailed in the entry for Finlay in *The History of Parliament* (see above).

British trade between the Indian subcontinent and Canton. The company's erstwhile monopoly on the shipping of goods from Britain to India had been abolished almost two decades earlier in 1813. Now the 'Reformers' were determined to extend their triumph to the China trade.

It was in this connection that, in February 1831, Maclaine had written to his uncle at Ardtornish, urgently requesting a pamphlet that he had left there, dealing with what he termed 'the liberality of Mynheer [i.e. the Dutch] in his system of colonisation in Java'. He wanted it, he told his uncle, because 'I have recently noticed that I am to be examined before the Committee of the House of Commons on the E[ast] I[ndia] Question' – something that had almost certainly happened at Kirkman Finlay's behest (though Maclaine did not say so). Just over a month later, he reported back (from the house of Finlay's English partners, the Hodgesons, in London's West End):

> On Thursday last I was examined before the Select Committee of the House of Commons – and got through the ordeal better than I expected. My evidence took up the Committee during the whole time of their sitting on Thursday and though I was before them three hours I fancied the duration of the examination but three quarters of an hour. A director of the East India Company, Col. [Hugh Duncan] Baillie MP, attempted to cross examine me but made nothing of it for I confined myself to what I knew – and to facts that came under my own eye. Before going in to the Committee Room I reasoned with myself that as a merchant I ought to be better informed on the subject of investigation than my examinators, though MPs – and this I believe made me so collected and feel less awe, wonderfully little I assure you, for the grave and potent Senators around me. Seeing a shorthand writer (the celebrated Mr. Gurney) taking down every word I spoke and the idea that all was to be published – was rather staggering and made my tongue in its movements slower than I wished – especially when called upon to explain anything at length to the Committee. Mr. J. Wood – Sir Henry Parnell – Col. Baillie – [Sir] R. C. Fergusson – were my principal examiners – also young Marshall, a stupid fellow – and Mr. Whitmore, a clever fellow. If you feel anxious, I shall send you a copy of the Evidence when printed.[63]

Re-financing the Business: John Deans Campbell

The Finlays, however important to the immediate revival of Maclaine's fortunes at the beginning of the 1830s, were not alone in this respect. Despite the McLachlans' best efforts to take him with them into bankruptcy, Maclaine had survived the financial storms of 1831 with his credit intact, but with

[63] GM to JG 12.3.1831. Greenfield MSS. Maclaine was examined on 10 March 1831. See Select Committee on China and the Affairs of the East India Company, *Parliamentary Papers GB*. Session 1831–1832, vol. VI, pp. 81–96.

virtually no capital at his disposal. Help was at hand, however, in the shape of a fellow Scot, although in this instance, in contrast to the Highlanders who formed the great bulk of Maclaine's British acquaintance, a Lowlander from Ayrshire. Later known, following a presumably lucrative marriage, as Deans-Campbell,[64] John Deans was a connection whom Maclaine had acquired while both men were in Java during the previous decade. Twelve years older than Maclaine, he first arrived in Java with the British occupation force that had seized the island from the Dutch in 1811, during the later stages of the Napoleonic Wars. After the return of Java to its former masters in 1816, he had stayed on, becoming a partner in the Semarang mercantile firm of Deans Scott & Co. and agent on Java for the great Calcutta house of John Palmer & Co (see Chapter 3), a long-established commercial and financial business that was closely associated with leading figures among the East India merchants of the City of London.

Deans had repatriated in 1828, a rich man, so it would seem, with capital invested in East India Company stock,[65] and on the lookout for a chance to place other of his funds. In short, he was a man of some substance, found in the company of such East India luminaries as Sir Charles Forbes and Charles Grant among the signatories in 1836 to a protest against a proposed equalisation of the duties on West Indian and East India sugar.[66] He proved very useful to Maclaine both in terms of his contacts and the considerable sum of money that he was prepared to invest with him. To be sure, back in 1820, Maclaine's initial reference to Deans in his letters home (when he had scarcely been in Java for six months) was a slighting one: his firm were 'worse than nothing. I refused to take their bills while at Semarang.'[67] Subsequently, however, the younger man evidently came to see matters very differently. It was Deans who, as we have seen, was presumably responsible in 1828 for getting Palmer's agency for the newly established firm of Maclaine Watson, and there are plentiful indications of the pair's closeness during Maclaine's

---

[64] John Deans [Campbell], b. Scotland 1786, d. [Scotland] sometime after 1868. On Deans's career in Asia prior to the 1820s, see the brief account in G. Roger Knight, 'John Palmer and Plantation Development in Western Java during the Earlier Nineteenth Century', *Bijdragen tot de Taal-, Land- en Volkenkunde*, 31, 2 & 3 (1975), p. 315. Deans returned to the UK from Java c.1828 and lived initially at Ardeer (Ardier) House, near Stevenston in Ayrshire. Subsequently, as John Deans Campbell ('I shall write my friend Deans or rather now Deans Campbell of Curreath.' See GM to MM 16.3.1835. Greenfield MSS), he lived at Curreath House – 'a gentleman's seat' – near Troon in Ayrshire, Scotland, where he was still in residence in 1868. See *Pigots Ayrshire Directory* 1837 and *The County Directory of Scotland* 1868.

[65] GM to MM 24.8.1835: 'Deans' ... capital is locked up in India Govt. Paper until August 1836.' Greenfield MSS.

[66] See *The Asiatic Journal and Monthly Miscellany*, Vol. 20, online at archive.org › eBooks and Texts › American Libraries (accessed 5/3/2014).

[67] GM to MM, Batavia 4.1.1821. O-M MSS.

UK sojourn in 1830–32. Indeed, less than a month after he had arrived in London he informed his mother that:

> I now hope to get away from this [i.e. London] in about a week or perhaps sooner and can do so without sacrifice of my interests. I shall have to spend some time at Manchester and a day or two perhaps at Birmingham and Liverpool – four days at Glasgow where our correspondents are numerous – a day at Ardier House, Ayrshire, with my friend Mr. Deans who has come up purposely to London to see me on business matters and who is living at the same quarters with me here.

A year later, in August 1831, he had again 'spent a few agreeable days with Deans in Ayrshire',[68] and departing from the Highlands in November of that year on a journey that was eventually to take him back to Java, it was 'my little kind friend Deans' who accompanied him to London, 'and I dare say will see me off from Holland, should I embark there. Angus will tell you what a nice set of kind little people they are at Ardier House.'[69] The vital point about the friendship, however, was that it enabled Maclaine to re-capitalise a business that was drastically short of funds after the large payments he had made to the McLachlan and MacIntyre assignees. His needs were pressing. Indeed, as early as August 1830, his London-based uncle, the semi-retired Lieutenant-Colonel Archibald Maclaine (a knighthood came in the following year) had evidently suggested that he and his rich wife should use their excellent connections among the city's social elite to 'aid in securing a fair partner for me, one too who would bring money into the concern'.[70] In the end, however, it was Deans who provided the wherewithal:

> Deans, my kind, noble little friend, has actually placed 15,000 pounds of his capital at the disposal of my Firm, on my simple letter to employ this sum as advantageously as I can for himself and my House of Business – This confidence, of which I feel proud, has made others come forward with offers of assistance, but I never shall forget the kind generous friend who first helped me out of my difficulties. As the old song goes, "When I have a sixpence under my thumb, I have credit in any old town".[71] This I find literally to be the case. Say nothing of this credit given me by Deans ... to strangers who may talk of it, to my uncle of course I wish you to communicate it for I know the pleasure it will give him.[72]

68 GM to AM, Glasgow 25.8.1831. O-M MSS.
69 GM to MM, Glasgow 2.11.1831. O-M MSS.
70 GM to MM, London 15.8.1830. O-M MSS.
71 'When I have a sixpence all under my thumb, then I can get credit in any old town. But aye, when I'm poor, they bid me pass by.' The song appears, inter alia, to have a setting by Haydn.
72 GM to MM, London 6.1.1832. In 1834, Deans placed a further £20,000 sterling at Maclaine Watson's disposal. See GM to AM 19.9.1834. Greenfield MSS.

Insurrection: The Belgian Secession and the Cotton Trade

In writing to his relatives in the Highlands during his sojourn in London, Maclaine had several times made reference to the 'disturbed' state of continental Europe, even joking, as we have seen, that the prevailing 'spirit of insurrection' might spread to his business partners in distant Batavia. In the middle months of 1831, however, he was able to experience insurrection at first hand, though a good deal nearer home.

Maclaine spend the bulk of the period between July 1830 and February 1832 in London and Scotland. That was where the centre of his business interests lay. Nonetheless, he did not neglect Holland, where he had a number of well-placed contacts in official circles dating from his Java years. He was twice there, on journeys that also enabled him to see at first hand the disintegration of the Kingdom of the Netherlands that had been formed from the erstwhile Dutch Republic and the former Austrian (once Spanish) Netherlands at the end of the Napoleonic Wars. During his visit in May 1831, Maclaine professed to find the Belgian 'rebels' entertaining and even endearing, and on the Dutch side met up with military officers whom he had known from the Java War.[73]

Yet there was rather more to his 'jaunt' than that. His journeys not only gave Maclaine a chance to network (as it would now be described) with significant figures in Dutch colonial circles. They also enabled him to connect at first hand in the Low Countries (and further afield in Germany) with the people with whom he and McIntyre – at this date still a trusted associate – had ongoing commercial dealings. Coming down the Rhine to Rotterdam in the middle of May 1831, he stayed 'with my kind friends Mr. and Mrs. MacPherson, whose kindness, as well as that of Mr. Young and his family, I shall not forget in a hurry'.[74] Both family heads were well established in business in the Low Countries by the time of Maclaine's visit. The elder of the two, James Young, one-time Provost of Aberdeen (where he had been born in 1776), had relocated to the Low Countries as a merchant in 1814 and died in Rotterdam in 1840. The twice-married James MacPherson (d. 1839) – subsequently Young's son-in-law – was at this juncture the Netherlands-based partner of the great London and Glasgow mercantile house of Colin Campbell & Co., with whom (as we saw in an earlier chapter) Donald McIntyre had close ties.[75] Maclaine's familiarity with these people,

---

73 GM to MM, Paris [?].6.1831. O-M MSS.
74 GM to MM, Paris [?].6.1831. O-M MSS.
75 James McPherson had married Young's eldest daughter Jessy in London in 1838. The couple perished, together with their newly born offspring, in a shipwreck in the South China Sea in the following year (McPherson had been travelling to Canton to set up in business there).

and with Campbell and Co.'s Rotterdam and Antwerp offshoots, was yet further evidence of the degree to which he and his (erstwhile) partners in the Old Concern were, and continued to be, embedded with major mercantile interests both in the City of London and on the Continent.

It was to Antwerp, a major centre of the Belgian insurrection against the Dutch monarchy, that Maclaine proceeded after his stay in Rotterdam with the McPhersons. Armed with a passport from the British ambassador in The Hague, Sir Charles Bagot, he crossed successfully through the Dutch and Belgian lines. Adopting a jocular tone, presumably to avoid alarming his mother, he reported that:

> About a mile from the last Dutch post, I observed trees of liberty stuck in the middle of the road which announced my proximity to a Belgian outpost and sure enough twenty or thirty ragamuffins, liberty boys dressed in blue frocks, soon made their appearance and though liker to Brigands than Soldiers treated me with the politeness of Courtiers. Having got an officer to sign my passport, I met with the same civility at the other Belgian posts and got in comfortably to Antwerp before the gates were shut.

> The evening I arrived the inhabitants were in some fear of a second bombardment, in consequence of some skirmishing that took place near the Citadel, and business entirely at a stand. The town as you are aware is in possession of the Belgians and the Citadel of the Dutch and not the slightest communication allowed between either. If an unfortunate Dutchman puts his nose out of the fort, he is immediately fired upon and no person from the town dare approach the outworks of the Citadel.[76]

As a merchant, Maclaine presumably grasped the broader commercial significance of what he was seeing. The Dutch loss of their southern 'Belgian' provinces, already confirmed de facto by 1831–32, took away the source of the cotton goods whose rivalry with British manufactures on the Indies market the Dutch had been actively promoting. It would take Dutch capitalists and the NHM (the Netherlands Trading Society, founded under royal patronage, as we have seen, during the previous decade) more than a decade to replace the cotton mills that they 'lost' in Flanders, and the opportunity afforded thereby for the sale of *British* cottons in Java can scarcely have been lost on Maclaine. Indeed, it was an 'opportunity' that he continued actively to exploit in the metropolis on the very eve of his departure back to Java early in 1832:

See 'A Short Memoir of James Young, Merchant Burgess', online at archive.org/stream/.../ ashortmemoirjam00youngoog_djvu.txt (accessed 4/01/2014).

76 GM to MM, Paris [?].6.1831. O-M MSS. For the full ramifications of the Dutch occupation of the Antwerp Citadel in 1831–32, see Chapter 5.

> ... Since my arrival here [he assured his mother] I have not been idly employed, and you will be happy to hear that I have lately succeeded in making some business arrangements which are likely to be productive of considerable benefit to myself and partners ... the longer I remain here the more new business springs up, and I regret much leaving a field here by no means occupied.[77]

Back in Java, these arrangements were initially to pay handsome dividends. Even so, the fact that he elected to sail back to the Indies on a Dutch ship from Rotterdam (rather than on a British one from London) brought an even greater reward. Maclaine found a wife, one singularly well connected in the official world of Batavia. His return to Batavia, moreover, proved to be the prelude to important new directions in the evolution of his business network which had little to do with his (erstwhile) ties to the UK and Europe.

[77] GM to MM 6.1.1832. Greenfield MSS.

Five

THE NETWORK TAKES SHAPE: CONNECTIONS, BUSINESS AND ASSOCIATES, 1832–40

> You must prepare yourself, my dear Angus, for a piece of intelligence which I am sure will surprise you – I am to be married in August to one of my fellow passengers in the Anthony! It is needless to state how the attachment began or give an account of its rise and progress, the upshot of the matter is that the sweetness and modesty (I shall say nothing of beauty) of Katherine van Beusechem completely captivated me – I fancy she possesses all the qualities I have always wished for in a wife, and I am certain of her devotion and attachment to me.[1]

Gillian Maclaine boarded a Dutch frigate, the *Anthony*, in Rotterdam in the middle of February 1832, and after what he reckoned to be a relatively swift passage to the Indies, arrived off Batavia early in June.[2] For Maclaine personally, and for the business that he had co-founded in Batavia some five years earlier, the voyage was a momentous one. At one and the same time, he found both a wife and a very substantial entry into Dutch official circles in the colony.

Maclaine's projected marriage to Catherina van Beusechem had been the subject, so it would appear, of considerable heart-searching on her future husband's part (of her own feelings, little has survived beyond a formulaic letter to her mother-in-law).[3] There was, of course, the matter of the disparity

---

[1]   GM to AM, Batavia 16.6.1832. Greenfield MSS.

[2]   See *Javasche Courant* 5.6.1832/67: 'Arrived Batavia 2.6.1832 the *Anthonij* from Rotterdam (20.2.1832) De Heer Van Beusechem and family, de Heeren Maclaine, Fraser en Mevrouw Hardy.' The *Anthonij* was one of the small fleet of vessels owned by the great Rotterdam merchant and ship-owner Anthony van Hoboken. See Bram Oosterwijk, *Koning van de Koopvaart. Anthony van Hoboken (1756–1850)* (Rotterdam: Stichting Historische Publicaties Roterodamum, 1983), pp. 153–54. See also 'Register houdende gegevens omtrent Nederlands schepen met besteding Oost Indie, 1828–1832.' NA MK 4172.

[3]   The information and quotations in this and the following paragraphs derive from the 'memo' enclosed in Greenfield MSS. It was sent to his brother Angus, attached to the letter from Gillian to Angus Maclaine, Batavia 16.6.1832. Greenfield MSS (emphases in original).

of their ages, 'she being only 18 and I alas! nearly 34 – nearly double hers'.
More to the point, would his family at Ardtornish be dismayed that he had
not married a fellow Scot?

> – I think I hear my mother or uncle say 'We thought Gillian had <u>Home</u> more
> deeply engraved on his heart than to think of a Foreign connection – or more
> firmness of mind or purpose, than to get married before settling in his native
> country or arranging his affairs – Poor Fellow! He has been captivated by the
> <u>personal</u> attractions of that <u>cunning</u> Dutch girl – merely from being cooped
> up in the same ship with her – on shore he would never have thought of her.

Even so, the pros outweighed the cons. His uncle, in whose household he had
been reared, had married a woman similarly much younger than himself.
Moreover, 'I esteem the Dutch more than any other people after my own
Countrymen – I consider a Dutch girl less a Foreigner than an English girl.'
After listing his bride-to-be's many fine personal qualities – '… her face when
animated strikingly beautiful … Her temper without exception is the most
amiable I have ever met with. Her abilities are above the common – her mind
well cultivated – I am at the moment more attracted by her <u>mind</u> than by her
personal appearance' – and noting that they both shared the same (Calvinist)
religion, he concluded with the comment that:

> I have been advised by Deans and other friends to get married, were it merely for
> prudential reasons – Being a married man will keep me out of the noisy roaring
> Bachelor parties at Batavia, which I always detested – & save me expenses even
> in my house keeping – I hope it will make me a steadier and better man – as a
> man of business it will rather increase than diminish my credit.

One thing, however, was not mentioned in these ruminations, penned on
the high seas and sent to his brother as soon as he arrived back in Batavia.
'Miss Van B has no fortune', he conceded. What he did not say, however,
was that she was a young women with 'connections' that far outweighed
her own and her immediate family's very modest financial circumstances.
Maclaine can scarcely have been unaware of this, given the people with
whom he was intimate in the Netherlands. In particular, apropos the woman
who was subsequently to become his mother-in-law, Maclaine told his
brother that 'Before embarking I had a most flattering description of her
from an old acquaintance of hers, Colonel Nahuijs, and am happy to find
that she equals the description ….'[4] Nahuijs, as a former Resident and man
of influence in colonial circles who had only returned from the Indies a year
earlier, would have been fully conversant with the powers-that-be in Batavia.

---

4   GM to AM, 'Latitude 42 N Lon. 13.12W/ Saturday 3 March 1832'. Greenfield MSS.

Given his evidently close relations with Maclaine, it is inconceivable that he did not inform his friend that his shipboard companions – that is to say, Nicolaas van Beusechem and his immediate family – enjoyed an enviable access to the very highest social and official circles in the colony. Indeed, it was that access that provided the sole rationale for the family's journey to the Indies.

'My Interest at Court': Maclaine's Connections with Colonial Officialdom

The eighteen-year-old Catherina van Beusechem's kin were what in modern-day parlance would be called an 'Empire Family'.[5] Catherina herself came from the town of Gouda in central Holland, where her father was a city official and where the family occupied a house in the elite area of the Westhaven.[6] The extended Van Beusechem clan, however, had strong 'empire' connections. With a background as patricians in state or city service in the Netherlands provinces of both Utrecht and Holland, the family also had close links with the Indies over three generations.

Beginning with Catherina's great-grandfather Godert Ludolph van Beusechem (1717–1803), they had moved back and forth between the Netherlands and the Indies, occupying senior positions in the VOC, marrying variously in the Indies or the Netherlands and sending their (male) children for education 'back home'. Catherina's paternal grandmother, Philippina Cornelia Hartholt (1726–58) was born and buried in the Indies, and had spent most of her married life in Makassar and Ambon in what is now eastern Indonesia. Her grandfather, Ludolph Jan van Beusechem (1747–85), was likewise born in the Indies and was employed and died there. However, he had been educated in Holland, and it was there that he

5   The British-Indian context of a similar phenomenon is extensively discussed – with reference primarily to the late nineteenth and early twentieth centuries – in Elizabeth Buettner, *Empire Families: Britons and Late Imperial India* (Oxford and New York: Oxford University Press, 2004). For a recent discussion of the 'empire family' theme in an early nineteenth-century context, see G. Roger Knight, 'East of the Cape in 1832: The Old Indies World, Empire Families and "Colonial Women" in Nineteenth Century Java', *Itinerario*, 36, 1 (2012), pp. 22–48. Ulbe Bosma, 'Sailing through Suez from the South: The Emergence of an Indies Dutch Migration Circuit, 1815–1940', *International Migration Review*, 41, 2 (summer 2007), pp. 511–36, deals with a slightly later phase of circular 'migration' or, perhaps better said, 'sojourning'.

6   Information from 'Volkstelling Gouda 1830', Gemeente Archief, Gouda. Many substantial houses from the eighteenth century and earlier survive along the *gracht* (canal) that constitutes West- and Oosthaven. However, the Van Beusechem house at *Wijknummer* 58, which may correspond with the present-day number 61, is evidently a house dating from the late nineteenth century and hence must have been rebuilt since the family lived there.

married (1772) his Netherlands-born wife, Catherina Cornelia van Polanan (1753–78), scion of an illustrious Dutch patrician family. The immediate key to the family fortunes, however, was Catherina's childless uncle, the Schiedam-born (1775) Jan Michiel van Beusechem, who had settled permanently in Java – he died in Batavia in 1847 – at the very beginning of the nineteenth century.[7]

Jan Michiel van Beusechem was not only a very rich man but also held an important position in the official world of Batavia. His greatest claim to influence in the colony, however, was his close friendship with Johannes van den Bosch (1780–1844), Governor-General of the Netherlands Indies 1830–34, and subsequently Minister of Colonies in The Hague, a friendship that dated from their time in Batavia at the beginning of the century, prior to which they had travelled together on the same ship from Holland.[8] His intimacy with Van den Bosch was further cemented by the marriage ties that existed in Holland between the Van Beusechem and Van Polanen families: R.G. van Polanen (1757–1833), an influential figure in the political elite of the Netherlands, was also a long-term associate of the later Governor-General.

Jan Michiel van Beusechem himself had married (1803) into probably the richest and most influential of Java's old elite colonial families, the Van Riemsdijks. His wife, Adriana Henriette Louise van Riemsdijk, was a daughter of Vincent Helvetius van Riemsdijk (and granddaughter of Governor General Jeremias van Riemsdijk), a great landowner in the district around Batavia, including Tjimanggies, an estate and mansion that subsequently passed to Van Beusechem (Maclaine's newly acquired in-laws were to stay there after their arrival in the colony in June 1832).[9] His position in the colonial hierarchy of Batavia was no doubt further enhanced by his prominent role in the city's Freemasons, where he was Grand Master (*Voorzittend Meester*) successively of the lodges 'La Virtueuse' and the 'Star of the East'.[10]

Maclaine's newly acquired relative by marriage was (as he explained to his brother):

> … President of the Court of Justice, a man of the highest character here and a bosom friend of our Governor, [and] having no children of his own, has taken

[7]   For the details on his life in this and the following paragraph, see P.A. Christiaans, 'Van Beusechem', *De Indische Navorscher*, 16 (2003), pp. 1–7.

[8]   I am grateful for this information to Angelie Sens of the International Institute for Social History (IISG), Amsterdam. Dr Sens is currently writing a keenly anticipated biography of Van den Bosch.

[9]   V.I. van der Wal, *Indische Landhuizen en hun Geschiedenis* (Batavia: Kolff and Co., 1932), pp. 24, 93.

[10] Christiaans, 'Van Beusechem', p. 3.

the whole family to live with him – and being a man of considerable Prosperity will I hope make them his heirs – the Governor has invited them to spend some time with him at [the Vice-Regal palace at] Buitenzorg [and] they all go there on Monday.[11]

It was not at Buitenzorg, however but at the Governor-General's country residence at Tjipanas high in the mountains to the south, that the newly-weds paid their own respects to Van den Bosch, and '... were received most kindly – On taking leave, our carriage was nearly filled with the Europe roses and other flowers, the Gov. and his Lady presenting them themselves to <u>Mrs. Maclaine</u>'.[12]

The excellent connection to the centre of power that resulted from Maclaine's marriage into the Van Beusechem family extended to Van den Bosch's successor in Java, J.C. Baud: a 'fine fellow', as Maclaine remarked to his mother, 'and a relation by marriage to my wife's family', adding somewhat jocularly that 'my interest consequently at court is just as great as a merchant requires'.[13] His cousin, and eventual successor as the senior partner in the Batavia firm, Donald Maclaine of Lochbuie continued – and if anything improved upon – the family 'tradition'. He married a young woman, the eighteen-year-old, Indies-born Emilie Vincent, one of whose sisters was the wife of a subsequent Governor-General (Jan Jacobus Rochussen), while another was wed to the chief executive (*President*) of the Batavia Office or *Factorij* of the NHM, by far the biggest – and closely state-linked – Dutch company operating in the nineteenth-century Indies.[14] Gillian's own position 'at court' was further consolidated by the fact that his fellow Scot and near-contemporary Alexander Loudon – 'an old Java acquaintance of mine and a very particular friend', Maclaine told his relatives[15] – was also much prized by Governor-General Baud who said that 'he had a Dutch heart', and who

---

11 GM to AM 16.6.1832. Greenfield MSS.
12 GM to MM 25.9.1832. Greenfield MSS.
13 GM to MM 1.5.1833. Greenfield MSS.
14 See P.A. Christiaans, 'Vincent (Van der Parra Breton Vincent)', *De Indische Navorscher*, 2 (1989), pp. 50–53. Nor did the connection stop there. Emilie's older brother Anthony William Adriaan Vincent, 1817–52, the murdered assistant-resident of Ponorogo (Madioen), was married to Antoinette Catharine Pahud, the daughter of the later Governor-General Charles Ferdinand Pahud. Emilie's older sister, Rosalie Antoinette Vincent (1824–1902), was married to Pieter James Gerhard du Puy, of the firm Maclaine Watson and Co. and of MacNeill and Co., also consul of Britain at Semarang, while her other older brother Edward James Elize van de Parra Breton Vincent, 1822–77, bookkeeper of Taylor, Lawson and Co. at Batavia, was married to Anna Catharina Hofland, daughter of the great sugar contractor and estate-owner, Thomas Benjamin Hofland.
15 GM to Marie Maclaine at Ardtornish 19.9.1831. O-M MSS.

evidently did much to advance Loudon's career as a government sugar contractor in the Indies.[16]

Exactly what this kind of intimacy meant for Maclaine himself is harder to judge.[17] Clearly, there were a number of factors at work that did much to alleviate such 'tensions of empire' as existed between the British and the Dutch spheres within which he had to operate. Among these factors there would have been an awareness among senior officials, both in Batavia and in The Hague, that Maclaine and his firm enjoyed connections in the highest quarters. These factors were still on display even after the death of Gillian Maclaine himself, for when his brother Angus travelled both to Holland and Java to claim his brother's legacy, Angus evidently had easy access both to the Minister of Colonies (none other than J.C. Baud) as well as to vice-regal circles in the Indies. Access, indeed, included taking himself to a state ball almost immediately after landing in Batavia ('a crowd dressed "cap-to-toe" in black with stocks and straps, perfect European stiffness and correctness of costume, and thorough contempt for the climate') in July 1846, in order to deliver in person to the Governor-General's plenipotentiary an official communication with whose conveyance he had been entrusted in The Hague.[18]

---

[16] Alexander Loudon, b. Tannadice, Scotland 1789, d. Rotterdam 1839. One-time naval officer and government official under the British occupation 1811–16; administrator of the British-owned Pamanoekan and Tjiassem estate in West Java 1825–29; government sugar and indigo contractor in Pekalongan and Semarang on the north coast of central Java, 1831–38. He took Dutch nationality in 1824. See *Nederlands Patriciaat*, 21 (1933–34), pp. 240–44. For Baud's remark that 'hij heeft een Hollandsch hart' ['he has a Dutch heart'] and 'verdient dan ook aanmoediging' ['deserves … encouragement'], see Baud to Van den Bosch 8.11.1831 in J.J. Westendorp Boerma (ed.), *Briefwisseling tusssen J. van den Bosch en J.C. Baud, 1829–1832 en 1834–1836*, 2 vols (Utrecht: Kemink, 1956), vol. 2, p. 26. Others high up in colonial circles thought rather less well of him. Willem van Hogendorp (Secretary to Commissioner-General Du Bus de Ghesignis in the late 1820s) told his father – in strict confidence since he had enjoyed much hospitality from Loudon on the estate that he managed and did not want him to be damaged by what he went on to say – that 'ik heb bevonden dat hij weinige van zijn landen weet, en veel houdt van grootspreken' ['I found that he knows little about his estate and is much given to boasting'], Willem van Hogendorp to G.K. van Hogendorp 27.3.1828. NA Collectie Van Hogendorp 91.

[17] The evidence is certainly not all one way. The not always reliable Donald Maclaine Campbell, writing some eighty years later as a partner in Maclaine Watson, had picked up a story that in 1832 Maclaine had failed to gain a sugar contract from the Indies government, then in the process of handing out potentially lucrative concessions to manufacture sugar in association with the so-called *Cultuurstelsel* or System of (State) Cultivations. There is no mention of this in Maclaine's extant correspondence. See Donald Maclaine Campbell, *Java: Past and Present*, 2 vols (London: William Heinemann, 1915), vol. 2, p. 917.

[18] Entry for Batavia 23.7.1846 in Angus Maclaine's 'Journal of his Voyage to Batavia on the Overland Mail in 1846', enclosed in AM to William Osborn Maclaine, 26 July 1846. O-M MSS.

Writing of the situation prevailing in Java a decade or so later, the 'company' historian of another of the great Indies firms, Reijnst & Vinju, conjectured that *their* close ties with high official circles in the colony brought readily identifiable benefits in the form of government chartering of their ships and the shipping of government cargoes in company bottoms.[19] Whether Maclaine Watson benefited from similar privileges cannot be ascertained on the basis of existing documentation. In any event, it was probably convenient for Gillian Maclaine personally, as well as for his business venture, that he became so interwoven into Dutch colonial society in the Indies at a time when tensions between Holland and the United Kingdom were again threatening to boil over:

> Business matters go on pretty well [Maclaine reported to his mother nearly twelve months after his return to Java] ... though rumours of a war and consequent <u>panic</u> here has occasioned the present a stagnation of trade. In the British <u>nation</u>, we <u>Dutchmen</u> still confide, but <u>your</u> worthless Whig ministry we detest and wish we could despise. The feeling toward Englishmen here, notwithstanding all that has taken place, is liberal in the extreme and raises my estimate of the Dutch character.[20]

Even so, in Europe if not in Asia, the acrimony between the UK and the Netherlands, occasioned by the British government's support for the Belgian 'rebels' whom the Dutch were attempting to suppress and, in particular, by the Dutch seizure of the Citadel in Antwerp, the main centre of 'rebel' activity, threatened to have major repercussions on the commercial front. Most immediately, the Dutch occupation of the Citadel, and the consequent stoppage of trade along the Scheldt River which it commanded, came near to being a *casus belli* with the British government, which in the end restricted itself 'merely' to blockading the English Channel to Dutch shipping. Before the blockade began in earnest, Maclaine (as we have seen) had already sailed from Rotterdam to Java on a Dutch vessel, the *Anthony*. On its return voyage, however, either attempting to run the blockade or ignorant of it, the ship – belonging to the prominent Rotterdam merchant and ship-owner Anthony van Hoboken – was impounded by the British Navy and held in a southern English port until the 'hostilities' were over.[21] Other Dutch ships, forewarned of impending seizure, made their way into the North Sea via a circuitous – and potentially dangerous – voyage around the north of Scotland.

---

[19] E.C. Godee Molsbergen, *Gedenkboek Reynst en Vinju, 1836–1936* (Batavia: Reynst en Vinju, 1936), p. 8.

[20] GM to MM, Batavia 1.5.1833. Greenfield MSS.

[21] Oosterwijk, *Koning van de Koopvaart*, pp. 185–87.

'Perfectly Independent of Support': Capital Resources for a Mercantile Network

In June 1832, shortly after his return to Batavia, Maclaine was able to announce to his brother that:

> As a house of business we are, you will be gratified to learn, now perfectly independent of support in a pecuniary way either from London or Bengal. Our own capital will I trust carry us on. From the enormous sum I had to pay to the McLachlans and Macintyre I have been fleeced .... My account however will look better before the end of the year, there being no more demands on the part of the insatiable White Lions. It is curious that from the very day we separated from Macintyre we have gone on prosperously and with the dear brought experience we have gained I hope now we may calculate on some years of as good luck as the last.[22]

In Calcutta, the prime site of European commercial activity in Asia at this time, the European business houses run by Maclaine's counterparts and contemporaries drew extensively on locally available funds. Direct investment from the British metropolis appears to have been very limited, although – as the outstanding case of John Palmer and Co. demonstrated – the houses there could draw extensively on the credit of their London associates.[23] The prime source of capital available to such firms took the form not only of the invested savings of the civilian and military personnel of the East India Company but also, and importantly, loans from leading Indian businessmen, who formed part of a very substantial indigenous commercial community both in Calcutta itself and elsewhere in Company territories in the subcontinent. Writing specifically about the Asian associates of Calcutta's 'Prince of Merchants' John Palmer, Anthony Webster has observed that '*Indian* merchants were not only a vital source of capital, they also understood the internal systems of trade and finance which existed in the sub-continent.'[24]

By way of contrast, European merchants in Java operated in the absence of a discernible *indigenous* Javanese capitalist or merchant class. They *did* operate, however, alongside, and in inevitable collaboration with, a substantial

---

[22] GM to AM, Batavia 16.6.1832. Greenfield MSS. The point was reiterated in a letter to his mother more than a year later: 'I am getting on pretty comfortably in matters of business and have no reason to complain ... though now little supported from home. Of late, we have done more for the Finlays than they for us. Macintyre I never hear of, but I believe he is doing well in Calcutta, though quarrelling again with his partners. Mr. Carmichael who went out of the firm a month or two ago is the <u>fourteenth</u> partner with whom Mr. McIntyre has quarreled.' See GM to MM 30.10.1833. Greenfield MSS (emphasis in original).

[23] Webster, *Richest Merchant*, pp. 50ff.

[24] Webster, *Richest Merchant*, p. 78 (emphasis added).

community of locally settled Chinese merchants and capitalists, as well as the Armenians and Arabs who should be similarly designated. Many of the former – Indies-Chinese (or Chinese-Indonesians in modern parlance)[25] – had been established in the colony for several generations. Like their Indian counterparts in Calcutta, they were well versed in the operation of Java's 'internal systems of trade and finance', the critical point being that for much of the nineteenth century Java's leading Indies-Chinese mercantile families were the exclusive farmers of the Indies government's monopoly over the sale of opium, something which gave them unrivalled access to the island's interior as both traders and moneylenders.[26] Some of this capital, at least during the first half of the nineteenth century, undoubtedly helped finance European mercantile enterprises in Java. The Indies-Chinese connections of the East Java-based entrepreneurs J.E. Banck and the brothers Thomas and Benjamin Hofland are cases in point.[27] Maclaine's case was a different one, however, and there is no evidence that he had access to Indies-Chinese, or other locally available, capital.

There was, moreover, no question of his setting up in Java with capital of his own to invest, beyond a small sum of money reluctantly advanced short-term by his uncle John Gregorson, nor evidence that he was able to draw on financial support from mercantile associates in London or Calcutta, apart from the short-term commercial credit necessarily associated with his dealings on their behalf in cotton goods and coffee. In these circumstances, the young merchant (and planter) had experienced great difficulty in amassing the capital necessary to keep his fledgling business afloat. Specifically, his attempts at the degree of primitive accumulation necessary to establish himself on a solid footing were hamstrung – on his reckoning at least – by his high degree of dependence on overseas partners who turned out to be neither trustworthy nor particularly competent in their chosen line of business, and

25 Evolving colonial era racial categorisations and latter-day Indonesian nationalisms denied 'indigenous' identity to such people, despite the fact that many of them were settlers of several generations standing and others were intermarried with the Javanese elite. We should be wary of going down that road, however, even though (until recently at least) terms such as 'ethnic Chinese' and the like have predominated in the relevant historiography.

26 For an introduction to Java's Indies Chinese business communities, see James R. Rush, *Opium to Java. Revenue Farming and Chinese Enterprise in Colonial Indonesia, 1860–1910* (Ithaca, NY and London: Cornell University Press, 1990).

27 For Banck (b. Scheswig 1797, d. The Hague 1857) and his various business partners, both 'European' and Indies Chinese, see Ulbe Bosma and Remco Raben, *Being 'Dutch' in the Indies. A History of Creolisation and Empire, 1500–1920* (Athens, OH: Ohio University Press/Singapore: Singapore University Press, 2008), pp. 126–27; Van Niel, *Java's Northeast Coast*, pp. 368–70; Rochussen to Baud 26.6.1847 and Rochussen to Baud 29.10.1847 in Jhr. Mr W.A. Baud, *De Semi-Officiele en Particuliere Briefwisseling tussen J.C. Baud en J.J. Rochussen, 1845–1851*, 3 vols (Assen: Van Gorkom, 1983), vol. 2, pp. 262, p. 304 fn. 3 and vol. 3, p. 155 fn. 4.

by the declining commercial fortunes of the two main commodities in which he traded.

Indeed, it was only in the 1830s that he had a substantial amount of capital at his immediate disposal, and that was invested (as we saw in the previous chapter) by a former Indies merchant domiciled in Scotland after his return home. Maclaine's own family was in no position to provide him with significant financial backing. His rich and socially well-connected uncle, the recently knighted Lieutenant-Colonel Sir Archibald Maclaine, did indeed intimate when Maclaine visited him at his townhouse in London's West End in 1831 that he could find him a bride wealthy enough to re-finance his operations, but Maclaine demurred. Not even the heady delights of iced champagne and claret at every dinner, liveried servants and a handsome carriage were sufficient to tempt him.[28] Nor is there any evidence that Maclaine's newly acquired and exceptionally well connected Dutch in-laws placed money with him. Maclaine's marriage, as we have seen, had brought invaluable 'connection' into the world of colonial officialdom, but no direct access to capital.

In summary, Maclaine Watson was founded with a miniscule amount of finance, augmented by contacts that linked its founder to commercial (rather than financial) interests in Singapore, Calcutta and London. This was hardly an unusual situation for the 'Scots in the East'. A few decades later, for example, William Mackinnon (the founder of one of the late nineteenth century's major global shipping and commercial conglomerates) established himself in business in India in somewhat similar circumstances.[29] Likewise, when his partnership with James Matheson (in effect) began in 1825, William Jardine, co-founder of the great China Coast firm, was said to have had little more than £3,000 to his name, after twenty-two years as a surgeon for the East India Company, and subsequently as a country trader.[30] Nonetheless, Maclaine's position was a peculiarly, even singularly precarious one. As the preceding two chapters have demonstrated, at various times during the 1820s, his commercial ventures could well have been as short-lived and marginal as those of many of his contemporaries. For a variety of reasons, however, this proved not to be the case. Indeed, during the 1830s the firm began to flourish as never before.

---

[28] 'I spent Sunday last at Gloucester Place with my Uncle Archibald and my new Aunt …. They both told me they live within their income, which I believe to be the case, for I can perceive a good deal of tact in their management. I am much pleased with Mrs. Maclaine. I think I shall continue to like her on further acquaintance. The Colonel looks younger than he did <u>twenty</u> years ago, is as round and fat as an Alderman. He looks forward now to a Major-Generalship, which I trust he may live to enjoy.' GM to AM 31.7.1830; GM to MM, London 15.8.1830. OM MSS (emphasis in original).

[29] Munro, *Maritime Enterprise and Empire*, pp. 19–23.

[30] Le Pichon, *China Trade and Empire*, p. 21.

Maclaine and his Associates: A Network Takes Shape

Gillian Maclaine was far from being a lone operator in the East. On the contrary, he was at the centre of a group of partners, most but not all of them fellow Highlanders, that rapidly developed during the course of the 1830s into a colonial business network that extended to Singapore as well as the three main ports of Java itself. Accordingly, the evolving history of Maclaine Watson in the 1830s was not simply the history of Gillian Maclaine himself. It was also that of a firm that departed radically from its earlier moorings, in the process slewing off its financial connection to the UK and establishing itself as part of an Asian-based mercantile partnership.

For what Maclaine had done was to lay the foundation for a *network*, in the Indies and Singapore, largely independent of metropolitan capital and with its base firmly located in the colonies where it operated. This was, as we shall see subsequently, an arrangement at some remove from what was becoming, by the middle decades of the nineteenth century, the stereotypical or orthodox way of organising commercial relations between colony (albeit, in this case, a Dutch one) and metropole. Given Gillian Maclaine's earlier and bitter experiences with his erstwhile partners in London and what he came to see as their extortionate demands, the form that Maclaine Watson and 'associates' started to take in the 1830s was surely no accident. It was to evolve further in subsequent decades.

Only one of Maclaine's associates was 'family'. This was his cousin Donald Maclaine, of the Lochbuie branch of the clan, who had arrived in Batavia in 1836, scarcely twenty years old and deeply inexperienced in business:

> Donald Lochbuie is a very great acquisition to our little circle, and not only a favourite with us, but also with all our acquaintances. He is a most amiable, sincere, warm-hearted gentlemanly young man, but his education has not been so carefully attended to as it ought to have been – as he himself is now well aware. From his willingness and application I expect much & I hope soon to see him what I wish to make him ... I was very much amused [Gillian remarked to his mother] by some observations in one of your letters about Donald filling Watson's place. In the course of two years more I sincerely hope he will qualify himself to fill the situation of a confidential assistant in our office, [though] a two year apprenticeship may be considered rather a short one ...[31]

Initially more a social than a business acquisition for Maclaine Watson – he cut a fine figure in full Highland rig dancing with the Governor-General De Eerens's wife at a Government House ball[32] – Donald Maclaine eventually became

[31] GM to MM 16.12.1836. Greenfield MSS.
[32] GM to AM 29.12.1837. Greenfield MSS.

senior partner in the firm. Driven possibly by ill-health and certainly by the financial importunity of his debt-ridden Lochbuie kin, he returned to Scotland at the end of the 1850s and died in Edinburgh in 1863, aged forty-seven. He was, however, the only family member to join the firm. Indeed, the only person of Maclaine's Java acquaintance who otherwise qualified as 'kith and kin' was the illegitimate son of his uncle, Sir Archibald Maclaine. The latter evidently thought that the best way to be rid of the inconvenient youth was to send him to the Indies. 'Sir Archibald has saddled his son Mr. Humphrey upon me', Maclaine reported home, 'and he is now in our office, but though willing and very well behaved is of little use.' His cousin judged he might make the grade as a plantation overseer somewhere in the interior, though eventually dispatched him to the firm's business associates further along the coast at Semarang.[33]

Apart from Donald Maclaine and 'squire Humphrey, son of the knight', the other Scots associated with Maclaine Watson were not related to Maclaine, though most were Highlanders. The one with whom Maclaine himself was most closely linked was John McNeill, initially (as we have seen) Maclaine's agent at Semarang and subsequently founder there of McNeill & Co. He was, Maclaine reported to his mother in 1834 'one of the steadiest men of business and finest fellows in Java – and doing well'.[34] Further east, in Surabaya, Maclaine placed Arthur Fraser, the young Scot who had sailed with him to Java on the *Anthony* in 1832, in the mercantile house that subsequently became Fraser Eaton & Co.[35] In Singapore, meanwhile, James Fraser was senior partner in the house of Maclaine Fraser & Co., where Maclaine had first sent him as early as 1828 ('I am sure [he will] give us and our Constituents more satisfaction than Maxwell has done of late')[36] and where he remained – 'a good, steady Scotsman' according to Maclaine's brother who visited in 1846 – for the next two decades.[37]

Moreover, there were yet other Scots, still in the background in the 1830s but who were subsequently become a vital element in the perpetuation of the business. Prime among these was Colin Maclean:

[33] GM to MM 12.2.1836. Greenfield MSS. Archibald Maclaine (1777–1861) had married Elizabeth Brydges (daughter of Captain Brydges of the 4th Dragoons) in 1823. The couple had only one child, who died in infancy.
[34] GM to MM, Batavia 14.1.1834. Greenfield MSS.
[35] 'Young Fraser who came out with me got into a house in Sourabaya, who have already offered to admit him as a partner.' GM to MM 30.10.1833. Greenfield MSS.
[36] GM to MM (undated c.1828). O-M MSS.
[37] Maclaine's brother visited him when passing through Singapore in 1846: 'I had my Tiffin [second breakfast] with Frazer of Maclaine, Frazer & Co., but immediately thereafter the mail brought intelligence to Mrs. Frazer of the death of a Brother, a fine young man who was doing uncommonly well in Rhio island. I therefore would not dine at the house, then a house of mourning, and rejoined my fellow passengers at the Hotel. I slept, however at Fraser's and breakfasted with him next day – a good, steady Scotsman.' AM to Hector Maclaine, Batavia 23.7.1846. O-M MSS.

I have given Colin Maclean a letter of introduction to my Uncle [Maclaine wrote his mother in 1827] which will I know ensure him a welcome reception at Ardtornish .... My good honest friend Colin's looks and address are not in his favour, but he possesses a warm and excellent heart. In his early days he had not the benefit of a good education, but by industry and with the aid of pretty strong natural talents, he has acquired a great deal of useful information. He cannot quote Latin or Greek or even speak English with much elegance or fluency, but few people are gifted with a sounder judgment and I never knew a person possess more honourable feelings and firmer principles. I am sure Angus will be pleased with him and soon discover Colin's <u>latent</u> good qualities.[38]

Maclean was not only a fellow Scot and 'country' trader in the East, with whom Gillian Maclaine (and his then Singapore partner, John Maxwell) had been doing business since at least the mid-1820s. He was also a valued companion, as attested 'by many long [horse] rides through the Highlands of Java'.[39] Maclean's 'natural talents' were to pay substantial dividends for the firm. Indeed, it was Colin Maclean and his descendants who were one of the small group of families, the closely related McNeills prominent among them, who were among the leading figures in the running of Maclaine Watson from the mid-nineteenth century through to the firm's closure in Indonesia in the mid-1960s.[40]

Even so, although the Scots connection was obvious enough, it was by no means an exclusive one. Edward Watson, founding co-partner of the Maclaine Watson business in Batavia in 1827 (whom we met in earlier chapters) is the obvious case in point. He was a Londoner by birth and a 'total stranger' to Scotland when he visited Maclaine's relatives there in the mid-1830s. Watson retired from the firm shortly thereafter, having made a good deal of money in the East and having acquired 'a nice young blooming wife' while 'on leave' in the UK. The lady was heir to perhaps as much as £15,000, 'a circumstance that Watson assures me he was not aware of when he asked her in marriage, but of which the discovery, from my knowledge of him, must have been very agreeable'.[41] Moreover (and as will be discussed in the following chapter), neither during the mid-century decades following Maclaine's death nor subsequently, was Maclaine Watson ever an exclusively 'Scots' enterprise. Instead, it counted both English and Dutch individuals among its leading partners through to the inter-war decades of the twentieth century.

Even so, in explaining how the Maclaine Watson network functioned, during its founder's lifetime, account still needs to be taken of ethnic and

---

[38] GM to MM (fragment, undated c.1827). O-M MSS.

[39] GM to JG (delivered by C. McLean), Batavia 13.12.1827. MacLean MSS.

[40] Crickhowell, *Rivers Join*, pp. 131–38: 'Appendix: The Maclean and McNeill Family Involvement in Maclaine Watson & Co in Java and the East'.

[41] GM to MM 24.8.1835. Greenfield MSS.

cultural propensities. Maclaine's preference for fellow Highlanders as business partners was, perhaps, a reflection of certain Gaelic solidarity. Quite literally, language itself was an issue among people who somewhat self-consciously used a tongue which, in Maclaine's case at least, he appears to have had *to learn*, as a form of bonding. Back in the Javanese Highlands in the early 1820s, for example, he reported conversing in it with John MacMaster, while the two of them were supervising work in a coffee warehouse. Catherine Maclaine, meanwhile, obviously found her newly acquired husband's attachment to Gaelic sufficiently compelling to set about learning it herself: 'at dinner McNeill delighted at hearing Catherine speak a few words of Gaelic', Maclaine recorded during the course of their honeymoon journey through Java in September 1832. 'She now has picked up about 30 or 40 words. In English she now converses with considerable ease and writes the language pretty correctly.'[42]

The larger issue, of course, concerns the extent to which Gaelic, a shared Calvinism (the 'Great Schism' in the Church of Scotland was still a few years away), and an awareness of being part of a Highland 'diaspora' created a basis for trust in business transactions where other certainties were hard to come by. Ties of kith and kin combined with a wider sense of shared ethnicity to create, as one leading authority on 'diaspora' trading networks has remarked, a 'framework that minimizes entrepreneurial risk and provides information flow [and allows] the establishment of transnational connections based on personal relations'.[43] Even so, the fact that Maclaine came from a similar social and cultural background to that of his erstwhile Singapore business partner John Argyll Maxwell (indeed, the two shared a common upbringing in adjacent areas bordering the Sound of Mull) had not stood in the way of a highly acrimonious break-up in which 'trust' was very notably lacking. At least, Maclaine reported to his mother that:

> Poor Maxwell has changed much since I saw him last on Java. He evinced during the time I was settling matters with him at Singapore a most suspicious temper and a most disquieting sourness of disposition. He proposes going home in March next and I really think the sooner he goes the better, for a longer residence in this climate would do his mind harm, for it appears to have suffered more than his bodily health .... My parting with Maxell was rather a cool one, and I do not know whether I shall ever make an attempt to recover our friendship. One thing is certain. I can never agree on any terms to have him as a partner.[44]

---

42 Gillian to MM 25.9.1832. Greenfield MSS.
43 Harlaftis, 'Diaspora Trading Groups', pp. 240–41.
44 GM to MM, Batavia (c.1828). O-M MSS.

'Making Business for Ourselves': The Intra-Asian Country Trade

By the mid-1830s there had been a considerable falling-off in Maclaine Watson's commercial ties with the UK, which had significant ramifications for the way in which the network developed during what turned out to be the final decade of its founder's life. In particular, as Maclaine explained in his letters home, the connection with the great Glasgow textile firm of Finlay & Co., and their trading affiliate in London, which (as we have seen) he had nurtured so carefully during his time in Scotland and London in 1831, proved disappointing:

> I am now obliged to work harder than ever I did, having no commission business from home to depend upon. The Finlays now receive from us more than they give, and my other manufacturing friends appear to have forgotten us. In fact, we are now obliged to make business for ourselves, and as yet have no cause to complain – though there is more anxiety attending it than common agency – as to risk, there is no business properly speaking without it.[45]

It was in these circumstances that Maclaine and his associates, in Singapore as well as in Java itself, found it expedient – and perhaps rather more than that – to shift the core of their business away from the bilateral trade with Europe toward intra-Asian trade. In so doing, they positioned themselves to take advantage of what has been termed 'a new phase in the commercial expansion of Southeast Asia' that had begun around the middle of the previous century.[46] In turn, this expansion was integral to a more general resurgence of intra-Asian commerce that, during the first half of the nineteenth century, in terms of its size was 'probably comparable to Asia's long–distance trade with the West'.[47] From a Western standpoint, at least, the best known of aspect of these developments was the so-called Country Trade.

Designated as such from at least the late 1600s, the Country Trade appears to have originated among South Asian merchants trading eastward across the Indian Ocean, and over time took on an increasingly cosmopolitan character.[48] From the late eighteenth century onward in particular, European trading houses began to participate on a considerable scale in a branch of

---

45 GM to MM 14.1.1834. Greenfield MSS.

46 Anthony Reid, 'A New Phase of Commercial Expansion in Southeast Asia, 1760–1840', in Anthony Reid (ed.), *The Last Stand of Asian Autonomies: Responses to Modernity in the Diverse States of Southeast Asia and Korea, 1750–1900* (New York: St Martin's Press, 1997), pp. 57–81.

47 Kaoru Sugihara, 'The Resurgence of Intra-Asian Trade, 1800–1850', in Giorgio Riello and Tirthankar Roy (eds), *How India Clothed the World: The World of South Asian Textiles, 1500–1850* (Leiden and Boston, MA: Brill, 2009), p. 139.

48 D.K. Bassett, 'British "Country" Trade and the Local Trade Networks of the Thai and Malay States, c. 1680–1770', *Modern Asian Studies*, 23, 4 (1989), pp. 633–40.

commerce that nonetheless remained heavily dependent on indigenous Asian traders and shippers. Cotton goods, whether of Indian or European origin, were of great importance,[49] as was raw cotton and yarn exported from India to China.[50] Southeast Asian goods themselves, fed into the trade en route from Bengal to Canton and vice versa, also played a considerable albeit unquantifiable part. In the 1830s, for example, there was a considerable trade from Batavia to Canton in rice, due to scarcities in southern China,[51] and during that same decade, one of Maclaine's contemporaries went so far as to estimate that the business of 'sending produce [from Batavia] to China, India etc and receiving back returns' might enable a European merchant with £10,000 'employed in this way' to double his capital in two or three years.[52]

Meanwhile, recent research has served to confirm the importance of coastal trade among the Eastern Isles – a trade dominated by non-European shippers and merchants – and, more generally, the key role in commercial development of intra-regional trade *within* maritime Southeast Asia.[53] During Maclaine's lifetime, for example, a significant percentage of the cotton piece goods that arrived in the early 1820s at Batavia and Semarang from the UK were then shipped to 'local' destinations beyond Java itself. For instance, in 1821 the experienced ex-Java trader Robert Addison told a British Parliamentary Committee that although a 'very large proportion' of British goods exported there were 'used on the island of Java', it was also the case that 'a good deal are exported [from Java] to the eastern islands' and that 'I should presume that the islands would take nearly one half'.[54] A decade and a half later, in 1836, a contemporary of Maclaine's (likewise installed at Batavia) referred specifically to the money to be made from the re-export of cotton piece goods from Java 'Eastward and to Sumatra' and added that 'of course the profit is small but it amounts to a commission of 3–5% and if only I can turn a sufficient amount in the year it will pay very well ....'[55]

---

[49] Anthony Reid, 'Southeast Asian Consumption of Indian and British Cotton Cloth, 1600–1850', in Riello and Roy, *How India Clothed the World*, p. 41.

[50] E.g. Heather Sutherland, 'A Sino-Indonesian Commodity Chain. The Trade in Tortoiseshell in the Late Seventeenth and Eighteenth Centuries', pp. 172–99 in Eric Tagliacozzo and Wen-Chin Chang (eds), *Chinese Circulations. Capital, Commodities, and Networks in Southeast Asia* (Durham, NC and London: Duke University Press, 2011); James Warren, *The Sulu Zone 1768–1898: The Dynamics of External Trade, Slavery, and Ethnicity in the Transformation of a Southeast Asian Maritime State* (Singapore: Singapore University Press, 1981).

[51] Broeze, 'The Merchant Fleet', pp. 268–69.

[52] Hugh Mair (Batavia) to Barings, London 27.2.1838. Baring Archive, London. HC 6.2.2.

[53] See Ryuto Shimada, 'The Long-term Pattern of Maritime Trade in Java from the Late Eighteenth Century to the Mid-Nineteenth Century', *Southeast Asian Studies* [Kyoto], 2, 3 (2013), pp. 488–94.

[54] 'Evidence Addison 1821', p. 223.

[55] Hugh Muir (Batavia) to Barings, London 27.2.1836. Baring Archive, London. HC 6.2.2.

By the early nineteenth century, moreover, what can legitimately be called a branch of the Country Trade extended further afield, linking Indian ports, Canton and Southeast Asia to Sydney and other more recently established Antipodean European colonies in Australia and New Zealand. Cargoes included tea, sugar, cotton piece goods, rice and tobacco, and Maclaine Watson was quick to take advantage of the opportunities opened up in the 'Great South Land'. 'I believe I formerly mentioned to you [Maclaine wrote to his brother from Batavia in August 1838] that I have a ship engaged in the trade between this and Australia, which we find a rather profitable one – We dispatched the *Justine* last month ... for Hobart town and Sydney – with liberty to call at the new Settlement of S[outh] Australia.'[56] Moreover, earlier in the same decade, there was already evidence that, even if Maclaine Watson did not yet send their own ships to the Antipodes, they certainly had commercial contacts there. Indeed, it was the apparent disappearance of a pair of such contacts – the brothers Hugh and Neill McLean – into Maori captivity in New Zealand sometime in the course of 1834 that elicited from Gillian Maclaine and *his* brother a strongly worded plea to Lord Aberdeen, the British Foreign Secretary. Aberdeen was enjoined to remember 'that the privilege of a British subject is in modern, as much as the Roman Citizen in ancient time, an immunity from injustice and oppression among Natives, savage or civilized'.[57]

The essential point, however, was that during the 1830s Maclaine Watson became deeply involved in the Country Trade and that, Antipodean connections apart, this involvement took place primarily in Asian waters. 'In business

---

[56] GM to AM, Batavia 18.8.1838. Greenfield MSS.

[57] See New South Wales Governor's Despatches, 1813–1879. Mitchell Library, Sydney MSS A 1272, pp. 869–71: 'Memo Colonial Secretary (with enclosures) 11. 7. 1835. Answered 30.11.1835.' The 'memo' contains part of letter from Angus Maclaine (Ardnamurchan Manse) to Lord Aberdeen, Secretary of State for the Colonies, 24.2.1835, which in turn contains extracts of a letter from Gillian to Angus (undated, but is must have been written sometime in November 1834) concerning the McLean brothers. Gillian Maclaine is quoted as follows: 'A few days ago a respectable looking young man called at my office, and introduced himself as a Mull man. His name is Morrison: he appears to have had a good education and is now settled in Hobart town ... and I believe in good circumstances. He mentioned that poor Hugh McLean and his brother Neill, *after visiting Java* ... [had subsequently] ... fallen into the hands of the Natives ... [of New Zealand], and when he last heard of them were close prisoners, though a ransom had been offered' (emphasis added). 'Hugh McLean I know personally. In his character there was a remarkable combination of steady prudence, great enterprise, kind and honourable feeling. After having comfortably established himself in Van Diemen's Land, he returned to his native land and purchased a vessel, manned her chiefly with his own brothers, bold and hardly seamen, and conveyed his parents and the whole family to his residence in the colony .... *There* [i.e. in Van Diemens' Land/Tasmania] *he betook himself to traffic with the Dutch settlements and other islands in those seas*, in the course of which he found himself in the hands of the savages of New Zealand' (emphasis added).

matters', Maclaine wrote to his mother in July 1833, 'we are doing as well as our neighbours, but our transactions are now chiefly confined to the Country Trade, our consignments [from the UK] having fallen off since I left home'. Evidently, this was more than a temporary phase in the development of the business. Three years later in 1836, for example, Maclaine was pleased to report to his family that 'last year has been a very good one for us, and the success is made more agreeable to me from having originated in some Country operations I planned out and commenced' during the absence overseas of his chief partner, Edward Watson.[58] Indeed, it appears that these 'Country operations' even threatened to swamp the other lines of business in which the firm was engaged. At least, in 1838 Maclaine informed his brother that 'in the course of next year, I intend contracting our Country agency, which is now almost too extensive ....'[59]

Maclaine Watson and Asian Mercantile Networks

Participation in the Country Trade necessitated, of course, involvement in shipping, much of it Asian. Java's own merchant fleet around this time was predominantly in the hands of locally domiciled Chinese and, above all, Middle Eastern entrepreneurs, almost certainly Hadhrami Arabs either born in the Yemen or in the Hadhrami diaspora.[60] Likewise at Singapore, where Maclaine also did significant (albeit unquantifiable) volumes of business through the associated firm of Maclaine Fraser, recent research has emphasised just how extensive during the 1830s was the intra-regional (as well as intra-Asian) trade carried on there through, or in conjunction with, Asian rather than European mercantile networks.[61] It was with these networks that Maclaine Watson would perforce have done business.

To be sure, Maclaine evidently aimed for a degree of self-sufficiency in this respect:

> I have this day made two young men very happy [Maclaine reported home in October 1833] by making one Commander and other Officer of our new Schooner 'Catherina Cornelia', a beautiful little vessel of about 140 tons, mounting 8 guns. The Mate or Officer is a Mr. Taylor, son of a Colonel Taylor of Ayrshire – a most accomplished young man. The Captain – a brother of Capt. Dudman of the Hon. Comp's Service.[62]

---

[58] GM to MM 6.7.1833 and 12.2.1836. Greenfield MSS.
[59] GM to AM 14.12.1838. Greenfield MSS.
[60] Broeze, 'Merchant Fleet', passim; Clarence-Smith, 'Hadhrami Shipping', passim.
[61] Atsushi Kobayashi, 'The Role of Singapore in the Growth of Intra-Southeast Asian Trade, c.1820s–1852', *Southeast Asian Studies* [Kyoto], 2, 3 (2013), pp. 443–74.
[62] GM to MM 30.10.1833. Greenfield MSS.

Far from being an isolated venture, moreover, the commissioning of the *Catherina Cornelia* proved to be the precursor of Maclaine Watson's own small fleet of (presumably) similarly armed ships plying Asian waters. Indeed, by 1840, the year of his fatal voyage to Europe aboard one his company's own ships, the *Regina* (locally constructed from teak), some half dozen sailing ships were registered in Java under the firm's name, and Maclaine himself was a partner in the Javasche Stoombootmaatschappij (Java Steamship Company), which in 1840 launched a paddle steamer, the *Koningin der Nederlanden*, for use in the trade along Java's north coast and elsewhere.[63]

Nonetheless, and despite the fact that in his version of events, as related to his family, such people and networks enjoyed no more than a vestigial existence, it is reasonable to assume that Maclaine's 'Country' ventures remained dependent to a degree, both at Batavia and Singapore, on Chinese and Arab shippers. Maclaine himself was fully aware, as he told a British Parliamentary inquiry in 1831, that in Java 'the commerce of the country [Java]' was carried on 'chiefly by the Chinese' and that 'they trade largely with the eastern islands and with the Malay peninsula'. Significantly, moreover, he was likewise conversant with the fact that Java's Indies-Chinese mercantile community also 'traded ... with Europe'.[64]

For the rest, however, Maclaine's testimony on this score, as contained in his letters home, presumably reflects what he thought would interest his relatives, and perhaps what in modern parlance would be described as 'racial stereotyping'. At least, it may be of significance that his only extensive remarks on the Indies-Chinese were framed when, in reporting his visit to Canton in 1824, he contrasted the 'despotic manner' of those Chinese whom he encountered there, who 'lord it over Europeans', with the behaviour of their Java counterparts, whom he chose to characterise as 'the most servile and cringing creatures imaginable'.[65]

However, this stereotyping was not a universal trait among Maclaine's contemporaries, and their testimony offers evidence not only of the ties that actually existed between the European and Indies-Chinese mercantile communities in early nineteenth-century Java, but also of the commercial implications of such ties. To cite one prime example, in giving evidence to a British Parliamentary Committee in 1830, the retired Java merchant John Deans, formerly partner in the Batavia and Semarang firm of Deans Scott &

63 J. MacLean, 'Macleans in the Former Dutch East Indies in the Period 1819–1849', *Scottish Genealogist*, 19 (1972), pp. 45–47. A decade earlier, in 1825, Maclaine had already bought a ship, the *Soerabaya*, which he renamed the *Caledonia*. See GG in Rade, 10.9.1825/24 NA MK 2487.

64 'Evidence Maclaine 1831', p. 85. For Maclaine's appearance before the Select Committee, see Chapter 4.

65 GM to AM 17.12.1824. O-M MSS.

Co. and subsequently friend and business associate of Maclaine, gave a strikingly different account than that provided by the younger man.

Like his friend, he talked of the 'extensive commercial relations' enjoyed by Chinese settlers and their agents in Java's interior and also of the extensive and long established Chinese junk trade between southeast China and the Indonesian archipelago.[66] This was the common currency of contemporary accounts. Deans went further, however, and explained that during the decade and half that he spent in Java, 'I carried on extensive commercial relations with them ... There are [among them persons] of considerable wealth [and] I have dined with the [wealthy] Chinese merchants at as good a dinner as I could have got anywhere in India.' With its implications of both economic *and* social relationships between substantial but ethnically diverse members of the merchant class, Deans's version of Java – or least of Semarang where he had been principally domiciled – was not so very different from that which has been described as existing in near contemporary Calcutta.[67] As Shinya Sugiyama and Linda Grove have argued (in a more general context), 'Rather than seeing Asian trade as a hostile struggle between "Asia" and "the West", our studies suggest that the relationship was one of collaboration ....'[68]

The precise implications of this collaboration for the evolution during the 1830s of the Maclaine Watson business network is difficult to gauge, not least because of the paucity of direct evidence. The overall context, however, is such as to suggest that, avowedly or not, Maclaine Watson, in common with the rest of the European sector of the mercantile community in Java (and even more so in Singapore), was likely to have been as much engaged with indigenous Asian shippers and traders, in both the Country Trade and local distribution networks, as were its counterparts elsewhere on the maritime fringes of Asia. As will be argued, it turned out to be the vital element in the network's growth, and in the creation of Gillian Maclaine's own personal fortune. To be sure, the network's business was multi-faceted and far from exclusively bound up with intra-Asian commerce. In particular, Maclaine himself evidently maintained a long-standing connection with European plantation enterprise in south central Java which had its origins in the first few months of his arrival in Java in 1820. As we shall see, however, there is reason to believe that this could hardly have been the source of the bumper profits

---

[66]   E.g. Leonard Blussé, 'Junks to Java: Chinese Shipping to the Nanyang in the Second Half of the Eighteenth Century' and (particularly for its historical dimension) Eric Tagliacozzo, 'A Sino-Southeast Asian Circuit: Ethnohistories of the Marine Goods Trade', in Tagliacozzo and Chang, *Chinese Circulations*, pp. 221–58 and 432–54. More generally, see Chan Kok Bun (ed.), *Chinese Business Networks* (Singapore: Prentice Hall, 2000).

[67]   'Select Committee of the House of Lords on the East India Company 1830', *Parliamentary Papers GB* vol. VI, 'Evidence of John Deans', pp. 233–35.

[68]   Sugiyama and Grove, 'Introduction', pp. 6–7.

that the network appears to have enjoyed during the 1830s, for which participation in intra-Asian trade offers an altogether more plausible explanation.

A Multi-faceted Business: Shipping, Insurance, Agency and Commodity Production

In addition to mercantile ventures per se, Maclaine recorded in 1836, 'Our
business, though not extremely extensive, embraces now a very general
Agency, Banking & Insurance.'[69] We have no means of knowing how much
either banking or insurance contributed to the network's profits during the
1830s, or even what they involved at this time in the network's evolving
history. Very much more is known, however, about Maclaine's own, personal
involvement in managing the finances and acting as commercial agent for the
biggest European agricultural entrepreneur operating in south central Java
– a man whom he had known since his own early days as a planter there a
decade or more earlier.

> Since I last wrote you [Maclaine reported to his brother at the close of 1837]
> I was called on business to the Native Provinces to put my friend Dezentje's
> affairs in order ... His plantations are situated in the Morebebo and Merapi
> mountains and the most beautiful I have ever seen. Some of his Bungaloes are
> at an elevation of 4200 feet above sea level and their sites ... well chosen. One
> particularly ... is so desirable a residence that I propose taking Catherine there
> for a month next year. The garden is stocked with European vegetables of every
> description and with peaches, strawberries and apples and the thermometer
> constantly at 64 [degrees]. When there I could not help chanting the old French
> song of 'ou peut on etre mieux' but still there is too much calmness, too much
> serenity for my taste.[70]

It was not European garden produce, however, that was the cornerstone
of Jean Auguste Dezentje's enterprise, but 'an extensive coffee and sugar
plantation with a gross income of upwards of 30,000 pounds a year ... yet I
cannot keep him out of debt. His failing is a too common one to require any
particular description. I have however put him now on an allowance. He has
given me a "carte blanche" to do as I think fit and to make him "in spite of his
head" a rich man.'[71] In the mid-1820s, like Maclaine and his other contemporaries, Dezentje – a man of mixed European-Javanese ethnicity whose
father had been a coachman to the Sushunan of Surakarta – faced eviction

---

69 GM to MM 16.12.1836. Greenfield MSS.
70 GM to AM 29.12.1837. Greenfield MSS. The song to which Maclaine referred is 'Où peut
on être mieux qu'au sein de sa famille'.
71 GM to AM 29.12.1837. Greenfield MSS.

from the Principalities, first by Indies government decree and subsequently by the outbreak of the Java War. Well connected in the Surakarta court (which was largely friendly to the Dutch interest at this point), Dezentje had sidestepped the decree (as we saw in a previous chapter) by having his Surakarta 'landlord', *Pangeran* Buminata, make him administrator instead of lease-holder, and survived the war in situ by fortifying his compound, establishing a small private army and drawing, no doubt, on whatever support that the powerful Buminata was able to afford him.

Dezentje had done more than simply survive, however. Towards the end of the 1820s, he had established a 'sugar works' on his main property at Ampel, situated near Salatiga, in the mountains between Surakarta and Semarang.[72] Initially a fairly rudimentary affair built in the customary 'Chinese' style – cane was crushed in a simple arrangement of two stone, vertically set rollers, set in motion by a pair of water buffalo yoked to an overhead beam and the expressed juice boiled into sugar in open cauldrons set over direct heat – it was the precursor of much more elaborate, 'industrial' systems of manufacture that became widespread throughout the Principalities during the middle decades of the nineteenth century. Output was destined for sale down on the coast at Semarang, some sixty kilometres to the north, whence it was conveyed on carts that Dezentje had built for the purpose.

The centrepiece of Dezentje's operation in Maclaine's time, however, was not so much sugar as coffee. Indeed, it was calculated that by the late 1830s his plantations were producing annually something like one-third (11,000 *picul* or approximately 682,000 kg) of the total coffee output of the entire principality of Surakarta, and that, in total, Dezentje could call on the labour (some of it paid, some of it in the form of corvee) of an 'estate' population of more than 38,000 Javanese peasants.[73] Like Dezentje's sugar, the coffee, carried there by packhorses, was marketed at Semarang, where Dezentje appears regularly to have taken himself on business.[74] By 1828 he was already said by an admiring visitor to have 'laid out an immense sum of money in the plantations, building and stock', and to have shouldered much of the work of management himself, his working day divided by a midday meal ('at noon precisely') followed by a *'meridienne'*.[75] It was a period of somnolence helped along, presumably, by a liberal consumption of alcohol: the same visitor had noted, en route to Ampel, that 'we saw the wreck of a bullock cart which had

---

[72] See the short description of a visit to Ampel in September 1828 in [J.D.P.], 'Native Provinces', pp. 158–62.

[73] Houben, *Kraton and Kumpeni*, pp. 261–63.

[74] [J.D.P.], 'Native Provinces', pp. 159–60.

[75] [J.D.P.], 'Native Provinces', pp. 161–62.

upset in crossing [a dry river bed] … it was laden with gin and many of the cases and bottles were broken … the place smelled like a distillery'.[76]

The 'oriental' and 'feudal' aspects of Dezentje's life at Ampel – he married into court circles in Surakarta and was said to have lived as a Javanese aristocrat – attracted contemporary attention ('his mansion seemed like the seat of a native prince')[77] – and continued to do so into the post-colonial mythologising of the nineteenth-century Indies as a '*tempo doeloe*' (lit. time past) very much on the lines of the legendary, 'pre-capitalist' Ante-Bellum American South. Nonetheless, the essential purpose of Maclaine's visit underlined, as other scholars have noted, the 'modern' and distinctly capitalist commercial and financial relations that existed between mercantile circles in Java's major ports during the mid-century decades and plantation enterprise in island's interior. The story of commodity production in mid-nineteenth-century Java has focused heavily on what took place in the directly ruled territories – the so-called 'Government Lands' – primarily along the island's north coast and in East Java where, initially, the Indies government and its commercial arm, the NHM, dominated the export trade in commodities.[78] Far from being on the fringes of this mid-century burgeoning in the output of sugar, coffee and other world market crops, however, the quasi-autonomous Principalities of south central Java were also well to the fore. Indeed, in so far as it is possible to be certain about these things, coffee production in Surakarta alone appears to have risen ten-fold between 1833 and 1843, and sugar production to have perhaps tripled between 1836 and 1847.[79]

In short, for a period of years in the 1830s, their association with Dezentje meant Maclaine Watson was closely connected to the biggest export-oriented agricultural venture in a key area of colonial economic growth, and gained thereby valuable access to major commodities which, at that date, were otherwise largely monopolised by the Indies government. If bonanza it indeed was, however, it did not last. Late in 1838, some twelve months after Maclaine's visit to his estates in September of the previous year, Dezentje

---

76 [J.D.P.], 'Native Provinces', p. 158.

77 S.A. Buddingh, *Neerlands-Oost- Indie: Reizen… gedaan gedurende de tijdvak van 1852–1857*, 2 vols (Rotterdam: Wijt, 1859–61), vol. 1, p. 227 as quoted in Houben, *Kraton and Kumpeni*, p. 262.

78 During the 1830s and 1840s, under the auspices of the *Cultuurstelsel* or System of (State) Cultivations in force in Java during the middle decades of the nineteenth century, the bulk of the island's output of coffee and exportable sugar (together with indigo) was subject to compulsory delivery to the Indies government and exported on its behalf by the NHM. Commodity production in the Principalities, however, took place outside the sphere of the *Cultuurstelsel*. For a short survey, see Ulbe Bosma, *The Sugar Plantation in India and Indonesia* (Cambridge: Cambridge University Press, 2013), pp. 91–99.

79 Houben, *Kraton and Kumpeni*, p. 264–68. For the parallel situation in Yogyakarta, see Ulbe Bosma, 'Sugar and Dynasty in Yogyakarta', pp. 73–94 in Bosma, Giusti-Cordero and Knight, *Sugarlandia Revisited*.

sounded out the Semarang agent of the NHM to see if they would contract to buy at least some of his coffee. In so doing, he was evidently reaching for a degree of financial backing that Maclaine was either unwilling or, more likely since very large sums of money were involved, unable to provide.

Thereafter, Maclaine Watson's formal connection with the Dezentje enterprise became attenuated, as the entrepreneur began to consign the great bulk of his (notionally) greatly expanded sugar and coffee production to the NHM, who became his financiers on a grand scale. Dezentje was to receive something in excess of one million guilders, and had travelled to Batavia in person to clinch the deal with the NHM's *Factorij* or branch office.[80] Only the coffee already contracted to the Maclaine Watson from the harvests of 1839 and 1840 (in total something in excess of 9,000 *picul* or 558,000 kg) was excluded from the arrangement.[81] As matters turned out, this worked to Maclaine's advantage. Much of Dezentje's projected increase in output, on which his NHM loan had been predicated, proved illusory and by the time of his 'sudden' and unexpected death at the end of 1839 the entrepreneur had amassed huge debts to his new financiers, who lost heavily from their final settlement with his heirs.[82] If Maclaine was himself saved from potentially heavy losses, however, the apparent collapse of his arrangements with Dezentje also severed (albeit temporarily as it turned out) a potentially lucrative connection with the burgeoning commodity production zone of south central Java.

To be sure, Maclaine himself still retained some connections there (inter alia, he continued to be associated with his old Melambong coffee-growing venture),[83] and ties with the Dezentje family continued into the mid-century. In 1846, for example, when visiting Java, Gillian's only brother Angus

---

[80] The details – together with a copy of the contract itself – are in Notulen NHM Factory, Batavia 22.1.1839/436. NA NHMA 4398. In 1839 Dezentje was contracted to consign 4,667 *picul* of coffee to Maclaine Watson and a similar quantity in the following year. Over the four-year duration of his arrangement with the NHM he was contracted to deliver a total of 31,000 *picul* of coffee and 56,000 *picul* of sugar (1 *picul* = 63 kg approx.).

[81] Notulen NHM Factory, Batavia 7.9.1838/427. NA NHMA 4397. The NHM agreed to advance 360,000 guilders against the delivery of 24,000 *picul* of coffee.

[82] Bosma and Raben, *Being 'Dutch'*, pp. 107–10.

[83] In 1833 Maclaine had transferred his coffee plantations in south central Java (Melambong, Dedikan, Semboeng, Sampellan and Djanaran) to one William Brown, after first attempting, unsuccessfully, to sell the leases to the Indies government (GG in Rade 5.11.1832/7 and 17.4.1833/5 N.A Kolonien 2845 and 2847). At around the same time, Maclaine sold his share in the Koeripan estate in the Buitenzorg Residency of West Java to J.J. van Braam, a leading figure in Java's Dutch mercantile community. See GG in Rade, 18.2.1833/20 NA MK 2846. Maclaine evidently maintained a connection with his former enterprises in south central Java, however, and four years later recorded selling 'a coffee plantation belonging to the late Mr Brown who left me executor and guardian of his children'. See GM to AM 29.12.1837. Greenfield MSS.

Maclaine paid a social call at the family's Ampel mansion.[84] All the same, given the history of Maclaine Watson's association with Dezentje during the course of that decade, it would be unwise to assume that the firm's greatly improved profitability in the 1830s resulted primarily or even substantially from its stake in the coffee and sugar output of the Principalities. Some other explanation has to be sought.

Intra-Asian Trade and the Opium Commodity Chain

One strong probability relates to Maclaine Watson's involvement in the Country Trade. During the opening decades of the nineteenth century, as we have seen, the Country Trade became the essential conduit of a newly formed and rapidly expanding commodity chain that linked peasant poppy growers in India to opium importers and consumers several thousand miles by sea to the east. Famously, the trade thereby financed European purchases of Chinese goods, tea above all, destined for the British market, where an addiction to caffeine in this form helped promote a growing addiction to another kind of drug in the Celestial Kingdom. Notoriously, recorded imports of opium into southern China soared between 1809 and 1840 from around 4,000 chests (a chest contained around 120 lb. or about 54 kg) to more than 40,000 chests.[85]

To be sure, it seems probable that the expansion of the trade in a single commodity, however dramatic, has been ascribed too large a role in the growth of intra-Asian commerce during this period.[86] Other commodities

---

84 While in Java in 1846, Angus took the opportunity of travelling through the island – he was issued with a government *Reispass* (travel pass) that entitled him to use the state system of post-horses on the island's high roads – and visited the Principalities after having first sailed along the north coast to the great port of Surabaya. See Lesley Abell and G. Roger Knight, 'Three Countries, Two Brothers, Sugar and Sheep', pp. 57–79 in Susan Magarey and Kerrie Round (eds), *Living History. Essays on History as Biography* (Unley, SA: Australian Humanities Press, 2005).

85 Le Pichon, *China Trade and Empire*, pp. 19–20.

86 E.g. Sugihara, 'Resurgence', pp. 149, 160–61: 'though dominated by Opium, cotton and other Oriental produce took up a significant proportion of [the] ... trade' between India and China, and that 'India's exports to China, depicted in the opium triangle, were only a part, though an important part, of the more complex intra-Asian trading network, the majority of which had little to do with opium ....' His final conclusion is that in 1840 'the opium trade consisted of about 30 per cent [in value] of the recorded intra-Asian trade. The percentage for this particular year was probably below average [due to disruption of the trade by the First 'Opium' War], and should be regarded as such. Even so, it should be clear that opium trade hardly constituted the bulk of inter-Asian trade.' He accepts nonetheless that c.1840 'opium was undoubtedly the largest single commodity in the intra-Asian trade' and that at Singapore in particular (the hub of Maclaine Watson's operations outside the Netherlands Indies) the statistics reveal 'the relatively high share of opium, along with European produce, in the port's trade around that date'.

clearly played a part, as did destinations other than Canton. Nonetheless, in the trade between the Indian subcontinent and southern China, opium would appear to have been dominant. For the most part (but not exclusively, since Turkey and Persia were also sources of varying importance)[87] the Asian opium trade involved the production and sale of the drug in British India and its export to southern China, where an elaborate and large-scale smuggling operation, carried out largely by Country Traders with the connivance of corrupt officials, enabled the commodity to evade the Chinese government's prohibition on its importation. It was in this context, at the beginning of the 1840s, that the commodity became the occasion of the first 'Opium War' between the UK and Beijing that signalled the beginning of a hundred years of British commercial hegemony on the 'China Coast'.[88]

Even so, China was not the only destination for the increasing quantities of opium manufactured in the Indian subcontinent under the auspices of the EIC. During the middle decades of the eighteenth century, for example, 'contraband' opium (i.e. that which escaped the monopolistic pretensions of the Dutch East India Company or VOC) was widely available in East Java and Bali, courtesy of British 'Country' ships,[89] and throughout the nineteenth

---

[87] For a recent discussion, see Masuko Matsui, 'Opium Trade and the Port of Izmir. A Survey for a Comparative and Interactive Analysis', paper presented to the workshop on The Inter-Asian Trade during the 'Long 19th Century': Formation and Dynamics of Regional Commodity Chains, Institute of Humanities, Kyoto University, 26–27 March 2012.

[88] Under the rule of the English East India Company in the subcontinent, opium was a company monopoly: Indian cultivators of poppy had to process their raw material into dry cakes before delivery to EIC agents or contractors, prior to its public sale at EIC auctions in Calcutta. From there, the bulk of it was exported eastward, much of it to Canton, by 'private' merchants rather than by the Company itself, which needed the cash raised from its sale in China to pay for its purchases there, but also needed to circumvent the prohibition placed on its import by the Chinese authorities. See Wright, *East Indian Economic Problems*, pp. 106–65; Michael Greenberg, *British Trade and the Opening of China, 1800–42* (Cambridge: Cambridge University Press, 1951 [1969]), pp. 104–23; Le Pichon, *China Trade and Empire*, pp. 16–20.

[89] See Sri Margana, 'The Formation of a New Frontier: The Conquest of Java's Oosthoek by the VOC in 1768', pp. 184–206 in Nigel Worden (ed.), *Contingent Lives. Social Identity and Material Culture in the VOC World* (Cape Town: Historical Studies Department, University of Cape Town, 2007). Margana (pp. 192–94) reports that low-price opium and cotton was being traded into East Java and Bali by British ships in the 1760s and that the traders involved were Bugis, Chinese, Malays, Javanese, etc. Inter alia, he remarks that: 'The Opium trade around the strait of Bali also involved members of the Javanese elite and Chinese merchants ....
The opium trade was also involving a number of Chinese merchants, including the Captain Chinese of Surabaya, Han Bwee Kong (Han Boeijko in Dutch archive) ....' For a detailed analysis of the role played by opium in regional trade in Southeast Asia in the late eighteenth and early nineteenth centuries, see Anthony Webster, 'British Export Interests in Bengal and Imperial Expansion in Southeast Asia: the Origins of the Straits Settlements', pp. 138–74 in Barbara Ingham and Colin Simmons (eds), *Development Studies and Colonial Policy* (London: Frank Cass, 1987).

century it is safe to assume that at least as much – and very possibly far more – opium entered the Netherlands Indies illicitly than was legally imported by the Dutch authorities for sale to the (Indies-Chinese) opium farmers, the wholesalers of the drug who arranged for its retail distribution throughout the colony.[90] A telling instance, concerning an unknown ship standing off the coast of central Java, was reported by an experienced mercantile traveller in the late 1820s, at the time of the Java War: 'I should rather suppose the vessel to have been a smuggler from Singapore, with opium and British piece goods … A great deal of opium is used at present by the rebels, our native troops and coolies.'[91]

Moreover, opium also found a substantial market among the many communities of migrant Chinese labourers to be found in the *Nanyang* – the region of the 'South Seas' that embraced maritime Southeast Asia – from early in the eighteenth century onward. Brought there to produce commodities such as tin, gambier (an extract from the *Uncaria gambir* vine that is used as a tonic and as an agent in tanning and dyes), gold, pepper and sugar in areas where the local workforce was either sparse or not readily subjugated to the labour involved, these communities of worker-consumers were an significant dimension of the opium commodity chain. Indeed, it has been suggested that this was the point on the chain at which opium consumption made the transition from an elite pastime to a much wider acceptance among the working class. Characteristic of the downward dissemination of commodities in general – in the West, tea, coffee and sugar all travelled a similar route – opium's changed status was integral to the massive growth in its consumption in China itself during the first half of the nineteenth century.[92] The possibilities of a substantial outlet in Southeast Asia itself, however, should not be overlooked.

---

[90] For an extended discussion of opium smuggling in nineteenth-century maritime Southeast Asia, see Eric Tagliacozzo's seminal *Secret Trades, Porous Borders: Smuggling and State along a Southeast Asian Frontier, 1865–1915* (New Haven, CT: Yale University Press, 2009), pp. 186–208. As Tagliacozzo remarks of the second half of the century (p. 187), 'judging by the number of cases surviving in the records, no commodity was smuggled as often and to such profit as opium'. With regard to this latter period, he argues (pp. 187–88) that the great bulk of the region's opium trade was in fact 'illicit', despite the attempts of colonial governments to create and enforce monopolies on its distribution and sale. Tagliacozzo observes of the 1870s (p. 191) that 'Batavia's powers of surveillance and interdiction simply could not live up to the ideal of an indirectly controlled Dutch monopoly on Opium' and 'What the Dutch saw as an unholy alliance between smugglers, [opium] farmers and officials greased the wheels of a massive amount of illegal opium coming into the Indies.' This is situation that is most likely to have been even more pronounced in the first half of the century when colonial surveillance was in its infancy.

[91] [J.D.P.], 'Native Provinces', p. 81.

[92] Trocki, 'Opium as a Commodity', passim.

Maclaine Watson and the Trade in Opium

The importance of the Country Trade to the successful revival of the fortunes of Maclaine Watson during the course of the 1830s emerges quite unambiguously (as we have already seen) from the surviving record. Did this also mean that some at least of the firm's success in the 1830s derived from its participation in the opium commodity chain that had come to be so closely intertwined with the Country Trade? The evidence is largely circumstantial in nature, but leaves open a strong possibility that this was indeed the case. Dealings in opium were not recorded in Gillian Maclaine's letters to his family in Scotland and elsewhere in the UK during the 1830s. Nonetheless, speculations in the drug were critical to the prosperity of many mercantile houses, European and Asian, situated along the Country Trade route from the Indian subcontinent to southern China. It would be surprising if Maclaine Watson had not been similarly engaged.

Gillian Maclaine himself was certainly no stranger to the commerce in opium. Indeed (as we have seen), he had arrived in Java in 1820 with a small investment in a quantity of what he called his 'sleepy commodity', bought in London with money lent by his uncle and almost certainly of Turkish origin, on which he realised a 50 per cent profit when he sold it at Batavia.[93] He evidently had no more moral scruple about trading in the drug than did others of his contemporaries in the Scots diaspora in the East, some of them, like the founders of the great China Coast firm of Jardine Matheson, very eminent indeed. Moreover, and directly to the point, Maclaine's initial business partner in Singapore, John Maxwell, showed himself to be fully conversant both with the opium trade to China that passed through the fledgling entrepot during the course of the 1820s *and* with its Canton terminus. In giving evidence before a British Parliamentary committee in 1830, Maxwell recorded that on his own *last* visit to Canton two years earlier there were thirteen 'opium ships' laying downriver, of which all but two were 'Country' vessels heralding from Calcutta and other Indian ports. Asked about the origin of the opium reaching Canton, Maxwell assured the committee that virtually all of it came from the EIC's territories in the subcontinent, and was always packed in chests bearing the EIC's mark. Revealingly, he went on to observe, 'I have often opened the chests and never found their mark wanting.'[94]

---

[93]   GM to MM 7.8.1820. O-M MSS.

[94]   Select Committee of the House of Lords on the Affairs of the East India Company, *Parliamentary Papers GB* 1830. 'Evidence of John Argyll Maxwell, 16.3.1830', pp. 248–50. Maxwell's familiarity with the opium trade was further underscored by the following exchange: '… you ever known of any country ships proceeding to Chinese ports north of Canton and trading with the natives? – I have heard of several of these adventures. Can you state what the cargoes were that they took? – The cargoes generally consisted of

It is reasonable to assume that if his business partner was so thoroughly familiar with the commerce in opium, so too was Maclaine. Maxwell left Singapore in 1828, but Maclaine's connection there continued through the new firm of Maclaine Fraser. In the absence of anything more than passing observations in Maclaine's personal correspondence, the Singapore firm must be assumed to have played a significant part in Maclaine Watson's Country operations, and, by extension, in the latter's involvement in the opium trade. Such involvement might have taken one – or all – of three forms: 1) engagement in the trade between Bengal and Canton; 2) participation in the regional trade in opium within maritime Southeast Asia itself; and 3) the importation of the drug into Java and its sale there to the Indies government, who acquired it to supply their Indies-Chinese opium farmers, who had a monopoly on its distribution. It is significant, for example, that in 1833 Maclaine Watson were in (unsuccessful) negotiations with the authorities in Batavia to supply them with the drug at a rate that potentially undercut the price charged by the NHM.[95]

There remains, of course, a speculative element in such conclusions. There was nothing speculative, however, about the arrival in the sea roads of Batavia in 1836 of the *Earl of Balcarras*, a recently privatised ex-EIC cargo ship, if a grand vessel of 1,500 tons burden can indeed be so described. Maclaine, always alive to the fact that family members back in Scotland to whom he was writing were far more interested in personalities and events than in the niceties of commerce, described the occasion:

opium, almost altogether …. Did they find any difficulty in effecting sales with the native? – I understood they always effected sales; I did not hear that there were any extra-ordinary difficulties …. Did you understand that the sales that were effected at the northern ports were at a considerable advance upon the Canton prices? – I could not understand that there was a great advance. I heard the parties mention that they found the Chinese dealers there in possession of regular price-currents from Canton, stating the stock in hand of opium …'

95   See NA Collectie Baud 424: 'A comparative statement of charges on Bengal opium as furnished Government by their contract with the factory with those if supplied on the terms proposed by Messrs. Maclaine Watson and Co'.1833 November 23.' There is an identical or similar document (in Dutch) in the Collectie Van den Bosch NA 469: 'Opgaaf van de kosten der levering aan het goevernement van amfioen door de factorij der Nederlandsche Handel Maatschappij vergeleken met de voorwaarden van Maclaine Watson & Co. 1833', which rather suggests that Maclaine had sent copies of the proposal both the GG and his successor. Although it would appear that at a later date the NHM supplied the government with the total wherewithal for its opium farm, 'private' importation of opium and its sale to government still took place in the late 1830s. See Hugh Mair to Barings, London 1.2.1837: 'Turkey opium is imported here [i.e. Batavia]. It is chiefly bought by the Government who have a very profitable monopoly of the drug and the quantity on hand being very small, some brought lately by an American ship sold at 16,000 rupees the chest.' Baring Archive, London HC 6.2.2.

From the nature of our business we are obliged to see and entertain many strangers. During the last eight days we had Capt. [John] Hine and his amiable lady and many others living with us – Capt. Hine is the oldest of the late Company's commanders, now pensioned & owning and commanding the old ... [EIC] ship "Balcarras" ... consigned to us.[96] Mrs. Hine is a daughter of the late Governor Petrie of Prince of Wales Island & a most ladylike woman.[97] I introduced them both to our Governor [Governor-General De Eerens] by whom they were well received. Of such a skipper and such a ship, I feel proud.[98]

From the standpoint of the present argument, however, the point about the *Balcarras* is that it was heavily engaged in the opium trade. Some twenty years earlier, in 1816, and still in EIC colours, it had in effect stood guard over a fleet of some thirty-nine, largely opium-bearing 'Country' ships in the seaway leading to Canton. It was a formidable enough sight for a Chinese artist to have painted it.[99] Subsequent to its privatisation in 1833 (when the EIC lost its monopoly on the China trade), the major stakeholder in the huge vessel was the great Bombay-based Parsee merchant Jamsetjee Jejeebhoy. More than coincidently, Jejeebhoy was heavily involved with Jardine Matheson in their Canton opium smuggling business. Indeed, he was their foremost partner in the subcontinent.[100] In 1836, that is to say, the *Balcarras* would have been heavily laden with opium. Maclaine's share in the cargo would no doubt have included goods – perhaps above all cotton goods – for disposal at Batavia. Even so, bearing in mind the 'core business' of the *Balcarras* and ships like it, it is plausible to suppose that Maclaine's stake in the cargo also included some of the 'sleepy commodity' that was either passing through to the Canton market or was disposed of in Batavia to the Indies government, or was slated for transhipment and sale elsewhere in the region.

The case relating to Maclaine Watson's debt to the trade in opium remains an open one. Even so, Maclaine and his partners made such considerable amounts of money in the 1830s that trade in the drug seems likely to have been a major source of income. Specifically, Maclaine himself had made enough money by the end of 1832 to fully pay off the more than £10,000 sterling that was his share of the accumulated debts of his former (and now

[96] According to Le Pichon, *China Trade and Empire*, p. 470, Appendix IX, the *Earl of Balcarras* was 1,417 tonnes – by any reckoning, a very big ship for the 1830s.

[97] William Petrie (1748–1816) was Governor of Prince of Wales Island (i.e. Penang) from 1812 until his death.

[98] GM to MM 24.8 1835. Greenfield MSS.

[99] Basil Lubbock, *Opium Clippers* (Glasgow: Brown, Son & Ferguson, 1933), p. 31.

[100] On Jardine's 'intimate friends Messrs Jamsetjee Jejeebhoy Sons & Co', and the latter's role as 'principal owner' of the *Earl of Balcarras* (and also of the *Fort William*), see Le Pichon, *China Trade and Empire*, pp. 28, 341–42.

bankrupt) London partners.[101] He and Edward Watson then went on to accumulate sufficient capital for them both to plan to repatriate to the UK by the end of the decade (in Watson's case without mishap, while in Maclaine's case, as we shall see, ending in shipwreck and death in the Indian Ocean). 'Since I returned to Java', Maclaine informed his Aunt Mary Gregorson (née Maclaine of Lochbuie, 1800–80) at the end of 1839, 'providence has blessed my labours and from a pecuniary point of view my ambition has been more than gratified'.[102]

Indeed, by the late 1830s Maclaine had accrued enough capital in Batavia not only to plan his imminent retirement but also to finance an ambitious land purchase scheme in the newly founded colony of South Australia, designed amongst other things to set up his brother as a sheep-farmer with large holdings on the (then) fringe of the city of Adelaide. By this date, wool was fast becoming the major commodity exported from the Antipodes along a chain of production, manufacture and distribution that began with the dispossession of aboriginal hunters and gatherers in the coastal and subsequently inland regions of the continent, and their replacement by sheep-farming enterprises owned and manned by newly arrived Europeans. The chain continued, via the intermediary of colonial wool dealers and the seaborne shipment of the bales of fleeces, in the proletarian mill towns of the UK and continental Europe, before terminating among distributors and consumers of woollen cloth in Europe, the Americas and, though to a lesser extent, Asia.[103]

Earlier in the same decade, meanwhile, it might be reasonably supposed that Maclaine Watson had the money to invest in opium ventures, since Maclaine's rich Scots friend John Deans, head of the erstwhile Java firm of Deans, Scott and Co., had supplied him some £15,000 in 1831–32 and, so it would appear, another £20,000 sterling a couple of years later.[104] It was perhaps more than coincidental that Deans's former business partner, Robert Scott, was well-versed in the opium trade and ended his career in the Indies as an 'opium agent' for the NHM, the state-backed company that inter alia (c.1825 onward) ran much of the business of importing opium into the

---

[101] GM to JG 4.9.1830. O-M MSS and GM to MM 17.7.1832. Greenfield MSS.

[102] GM to Mrs Gregorson 26.12.1839. Greenfield MSS.

[103] For the information about Angus Maclaine in this and the following paragraphs, see G. Roger Knight and Lesley Abell, '"So Like Home": Angus Maclaine (1799–1877), Sheep Farmer and Sojourner in South Australia', *Journal of the Historical Society of South Australia*, 33 (2005), pp. 40–56.

[104] GM to MM 6.1.1832. Greenfield MSS. See also Palmer to Maclaine 5.6.1832. Palmer Eng. Lett. c 121, pp. 290–92: 'J[ohn] D[eans] tells me of some project between you, and I wish well to it for both your sakes.' It would also appear that two years later, Deans placed a further £20,000 at Maclaine's disposal. See GM to AM 19.9.1834. Greenfield MSS.

Indies.[105] Even more to the point, according to Deans's own account, during his years in the East prior to 1828, he himself 'had a great deal to do in the opium trade at Java'.[106]

The Fatal Voyage, March–May 1840

> We have made up our minds to go home in February in a splendid new ship belonging to the Firm and Capt Ross – and filled up by the latter with every convenience for our accommodation and comfort. This new craft is called the 'Regina' and carries about 350 tons of cargo. MacNeill has not yet arrived – but as I hear he was to sail from Holland the 6 July, we may now daily look for him.[107]

There was some delay, and as a result it was not until the middle of March 1840 that Gillian and Catherina Maclaine, their two children, Catherina's widowed mother and her two still unmarried sisters, together with a number of Indonesian servants, boarded the vessel for the return voyage to Scotland. For two years or more Maclaine had been letting his relatives know that he was proposing to repatriate – 'I am well and happy here', he wrote to Scotland in 1836, 'but I never look upon this land, fair and fertile as it is, as a home. Neither does Catherine ....'[108] His decision was no doubt made easier by the death of his father-in-law in Batavia early in 1839, an event that left him in effect the head of his joint Scots-Dutch family, not fabulously rich, but certainly with that 'independency' that had eluded him hitherto and with enough capital to establish himself, as had long been his ambition, as a landed proprietor in the Highlands. Indeed, as early as 1836 he had been negotiating (unsuccessfully) to buy an estate on Morvern.[109] 'My wish to become a proprietor of lands in the highlands', he had informed Angus in 1837, 'is as strong as ever.'[110]

The *Regina* had been carefully fitted out for their exclusive use. The ship was not large. Its displacement was some 350 tons at a time when many sailing ships on the route from Java to Europe would have been twice that size. It was however, in the charge of a richly experienced captain: James Clunies Ross had a long career in the Country Trade and was one of Gillian's most trusted associates. On 17th March 1840, a number of senior members of the

---

[105] See Robert Scott to Willem van Hogendorp, (undated c.1827) and 10.2.1827; 13.3.1828, GM to Willem van Hogendorp 13.3.1828. NA Collectie Van Hogendorp190.

[106] 'Evidence Deans 1830', p. 237. Deans was probably alluding to his dealings in opium on behalf of the Indies government.

[107] GM to AM 8.10.1839. Greenfield MSS.

[108] GM to MM 16.12.1836. Greenfield MSS.

[109] GM to MM 24.8.1835. Greenfield MSS.

[110] GM to AM 30.1.1837. Greenfield MSS.

firm saw the family aboard at Batavia. Last sighted two days later sailing west from Anjer into the Indian Ocean between the islands of Java and Sumatra, neither the *Regina* nor its passengers were ever seen or heard of again. It must be presumed that the vessel went down in a hurricane somewhere in the vicinity of Mauritius, where it was said that other vessels were likewise lost in a storm at around the same time.[111] Catherina's two brothers, who had opted to remain in the Indies, were all that was left of Gillian's immediate Dutch family. The youngest of them, a boy of ten when his family had arrived in Java in 1832, Ludolph Jan van Beusechem, died there some eighty years later.

On Gillian's side of the family, his mother had already died in 1836, four years before his departure from Java. His only sibling, Angus Maclaine had decided, before his brother's death, to become a sheep-farmer in South Australia (where Gillian, as we have seen, had bought land). By eeric coinci-dence, just at the time in April–May 1840 that his brother and his family were lost at sea somewhere between Java and the Cape of Good Hope, Angus Maclaine himself would have been on board ship either approaching Cape Town or actually in the Indian Ocean itself on his way to South Australia. However, it was not until February 1841 that he became aware of the disaster when letters reached him from Edward Watson, Maclaine's erstwhile business partner who had relocated to England some three years previously. Angus was now no longer simply the manager of his brother's South Australian properties: he had become Gillian's sole heir. He returned to Scotland in the late 1840s, and died there, unmarried, in 1877.[112]

Before that, however, the ties linking the founders of Maclaine Watson to the Batavia firm had long since ceased. Gillian Maclaine died in 1840 and during the decade that followed his brother withdrew from Maclaine Watson the capital that he had inherited. Edward Watson, it may be presumed, had likewise severed his connection. Even so, and we shall see in the following chapter, the firm remained very much a going concern. Indeed, over the next century it gained and retained a position among the very biggest export–import businesses operating on Java.

---

[111] Understandably, there was a flurry of correspondence c.1840–41 concerning the possible fate of the *Regina* and its passengers, preserved in the Greenfield MSS. See e.g. Edward Watson to JG 20.5.1841. One early report from Finlay Hodgson in London mentioned one possible 'favourable circumstance', viz. that the *Regina* had diverted to the Cocos Islands, where its captain (Ross) had a brother, to deliver stores. See Finlay Hodgeson & Co. to JG 31.8.1840. Greenfield MSS. The stretch of the Indian Ocean around Mauritius had a long-held bad reputation at the wrong time of the year: in 1809, for example, 'four homeward-bound East Indiamen disappeared without trace off Mauritius, only a year after the similar loss of three ships in the central zone of the ocean'. Bowen, 'Britain in the Indian Ocean Region and Beyond', p. 53.

[112] Knight and Abell, 'Angus Maclaine', passim.

Six

CONCLUSION: MACLAINE'S LEGACY, COMMODITIES AND TRADE ON A COLONIAL 'PERIPHERY', 1840–1964[1]

The commercial network that Gillian Maclaine established in Southeast Asia was part of what has been identified as an '… expatriate maritime business community that was deeply embedded in … imperial territories'.[2] Nonetheless, the commodity chains – coffee, cotton goods and (most probably) opium – in which Maclaine Watson was enmeshed were global as well as imperial in character, and the dynamics that drove their commercial (and plantation) ventures had at least as much to with world markets as with 'empire' per se. At same time, moreover, the Maclaine Watson network remained a *partnership* of *family* businesses whose structure set it apart from a dominant contemporary trend (if such indeed it was) toward the evolution of the 'visible hand' of a centralised, formal hierarchy of impersonal control and management. One closely associated characteristic was that the network likewise remained outside the web of metropolitan control and direction that, classically, constituted a hallmark of late-era imperialism. Instead, the network's continued existence for well over a century after its founder's death not only demonstrates the vitality and relative autonomy of developments on the so-called 'colonial periphery'. It also underscores, while complicating somewhat, a variety of ongoing analyses of the long-term significance of the *intra-Asian* mercantile activity (as distinct from bilateral, inter-continental trade between Asia and 'the West') in which the network was predominantly engaged. On these several counts, it can be argued that Gillian Maclaine left behind him a quite singular enterprise.

---

[1] I would like to thank Anne Booth and Thomas Lindblad for their valuable comments on an earlier draft of this chapter.

[2] Michael B. Miller, *Europe and the Maritime World. A Twentieth Century History* (Cambridge: Cambridge University Press, 2012), p. 15.

A Network of Family Firms and the Scots' Diaspora

Gillian Maclaine became the co-founder of Maclaine Watson in Batavia in 1827, when the new firm supplanted the earlier business of Gillian Maclaine & Co., in which he had been partner with associates in London and Calcutta. The new firm had no such ties, but was closely linked in Southeast Asia with two other firms in Java and one in Singapore, all three of which Maclaine had played some part in establishing. The resultant Maclaine Watson 'network' – in Batavia Maclaine Watson itself, McNeill & Co. in Semarang, Fraser Eaton in Surabaya and Maclaine Fraser in Singapore – functioned throughout is existence as a network of mercantile firms with interlocking memberships but with no obvious 'head office'. To a remarkable degree, it remained a partnership of family businesses in which many but by no means all the partners came from inter-related Scots families. Inside the network, a number of factors worked to create cohesion and commercial success, not least of which were kinship and a degree of trust – and of corporate knowledge – bred among people, most of whom had worked together, in various locations, over several generations.

Given the ethnicity of many of the people involved in its operations over the nearly 150 years of its existence, it is possible to envisage the network as held together by the shared cultural norms and close family ties of the Scots' 'diaspora' that provided most of the partners over several generations.[3] As will be argued, however, matters were not quite so simple, and 'diaspora' is not necessarily the best term to describe the situation. Many of the partners were sojourners rather than permanent settlers (though one of the key Java partners – see below – established a Eurasian Indies branch of the family) and circulated fairly freely, at least after the formal establishment of a London office in the 1880s, between metropolis and colony. Moreover, as a British firm in the Netherland Indies, the Maclaine Watson partners culti- vated excellent relations – of necessity perhaps – in Dutch colonial circles, as well as establishing a significant bridgehead in metropolitan Holland and taking on a number of Dutch (and English) partners who played a significant role in developing the business. We can begin, however, with the coterie of Scots families, already associated with Maclaine during his time in Java, who undeniably played a key role in running and perpetuating Maclaine Watson after its founder's death. Indeed, family continuity was a hallmark of the network's operations.

Among those families were the descendants of John McNeill, who had joined forces with Maclaine in the 1820s and subsequently founded McNeill & Co. in Semarang, at that time Java's second major port city and gateway

---

[3]   See list of partners in *One Hundred Years*, pp. 4–7.

to the populous and agriculturally rich 'principalities' of south central Java. Equally prominent among the enduring Scots dynasties involved in running the Maclaine Watson enterprise, however, was that founded by Colin Mclean, who had initially worked for Gillian Maclaine as a 'country captain' in the 1820s and who became related to the McNeill family through marriage.[4] Successive generations of both families remained among the partners in the Maclaine Watson network down to the end. One descendent, Neil McLean, was a partner throughout the 1870s,[5] and some sixty years and several generations later a trio of McLean family members were active in one part or other of the Maclaine Watson network throughout the 1930s.[6] During the post-war years, one of the latter continued as a partner, as did R.G. Macindoe, another of the 'old hands' from the interwar decades (and likewise a relative through marriage to the McNeill and McLean connection).[7] Indeed it was they and a number of fellow Scots expatriates who continued in the management of Maclaine Watson until the Indonesian government took control of the Batavia/Jakarta the end of the business in 1964.

Even so, there was nothing exclusive about Maclaine Watson's long-standing Scots connection. As one prominent analyst of diaspora-based commerce has remarked, although 'kinship is obviously an important ingredient in merchant networks, ... its importance can be exaggerated',[8] and neither kinship nor ethnicity precluded the participation in the firms that made up the Maclaine Watson network of Netherlanders, or even of the occasional Sassenach, including, of course, co-founder Londoner Edward Watson. Watson – 'a perfect stranger to Scotland' was how Maclaine described him[9] – had left the firm by the end of the 1830s, but another Englishman, John Lewis Bonhote (1805–67) remained a key figure in Maclaine Watson throughout the mid-century decades. Son of the gentleman head clerk and bookkeeper of Gillian Maclaine's erstwhile London employers (and later business partners) the McLachlan brothers, whom Maclaine had befriended during his 'apprenticeship' in the City, John Lewis Bonhote arrived in Batavia

4 For this and what follows, see Crickhowell, *The Rivers Join*, pp. 131–35.
5 J. Rogge, *Het Handelshuis Van Eeghen* (Amsterdam: Van Ditmar, 1949), p. 249.
6 The individuals concerned were N.M. Mclean, L.M. Mclean and N.G. Mclean. See *Handboek voor Cultuur-en Handelsondernemingen in Nederlandsch Indië* [Handbook of Plantation and Mercantile Enterprises in the Netherlands Indies, hereafter HCHO] (Amsterdam: De Bussy, 1888–1940), 50 (1938), p. 1230 and 42 (1930), p. 1618.
7 School of Oriental and African Studies, University of London, Papers of John Swire and Sons (hereafter JSS) plus relevant identifying numbers from Elizabeth Hook, *A Guide to the Papers of John Swire and Sons Ltd., London* (London: The Library, School of Oriental and African Studies, 1977), Swire/SOAS JSSI box 2821. Minutes of the AGMs Swire and Maclaine, 1947–1970.
8 Markovits, *Indian Merchants*, p. 26.
9 GM to AM 23.10.1832. Greenfield MSS.

to join Maclaine Watson at the end of the 1820s.[10] He had early made a good impression. By 1836 Maclaine was already describing him as 'my right hand' man and with the imminent departure to patria of Edward Watson, informed his mother that 'I propose admitting our hardworking and faithful assistant Bonhote as a Partner on a small share in Jan. 1837 – to which his devoted attention to my interest for the last two years gives him a just claim – not to mention his abilities as a man of business which are very superior.'[11] With Maclaine's consent, he attempted – though without success – to woo his boss's sister-in-law,[12] though he did eventually become senior partner in the firm: even before that time, Maclaine had reckoned him 'perhaps the most thoroughbred man of business in the colony ...'[13] It was with Bonhote that Angus Maclaine stayed, at 'a large and commodious' house in the prime European quarter of the city, with a deep ninety foot verandah running its entire breadth, when he arrived in Batavia in 1846. He was there to settle his late brother's affairs and, more specifically, to negotiate the withdrawal of his capital from the firm. His host, he concluded, 'though exceptionally contentious and sometimes difficult to do business with is, has ever been considered a man of his word, and is decided enough in his action'.[14] Other members of the family, Malcolm Bonhote and Thomas Bonhote were also in Batavia in the 1840s, but the latter subsequently retired to London where he appears to have represented Maclaine Watson's interests for a decade or more.[15]

It was the continuing Dutch connection, nonetheless, that far outweighed the English presence in the longer term. Indeed, it looks very much as if the network was careful to maintain the 'Dutch' side to its business as a hedge against any difficulties caused by its location betwixt two empires. Maclaine Watson and its associates had established an important foothold in Dutch colonial circles early on, when first Gillian Maclaine and subsequently his cousin Donald Maclaine of Lochbuie made very good marriages to quite exceptionally well-connected Dutch (colonial) women.[16] Of greater long-term importance, however, were ties that saw the establishment in Holland itself of branches of Scots families closely linked, both commercially

---

[10] My thanks to Peter Christiaans of the Centraal Bureau voor Genealogie (CBG), The Hague, for the information about Bonhote's period in Java.

[11] GM to MM, Great River St (i.e. Kali Besar), Batavia 9.8.1836 and GM to MM 12.2.1836. Greenfield MSS.

[12] GM to AM 29.12.1837. Greenfield MSS.

[13] GM to AM 29.12.1837. Greenfield MSS.

[14] AM to William Osborn Maclaine 26.7.1846. O-M MSS.

[15] See, for example, the references to Thomas Bonhote's London-based association with the Maclaine Watson network in Fraser Eaton to Van Eeghen 3.9.1858; Fraser Eaton to Van Eeghen 18.6.1859; Fraser Eaton to Van Eeghen 2.2.1860 and Maclaine Watson to Van Eeghen 5.4.1870. Archief Handelshuis Van Eeghen, Amsterdam Stadsarchief [hereafter ASVE], 447.

[16]

and/or in terms of kinship, to the Maclaine Watson enterprise. Hence the McNeill family – long-standing, cross-generational partners in the network – had their Dutch branch, while the Frasers (inter alia of Fraser Eaton in Surabaya) had also established themselves in Rotterdam by the 1860s, doing business there as A.C. Fraser & Co. in partnership with the very substantial Dutch firm of Suermondt.[17]

At least as revealing of its placement in the Indies, however, was the Maclaine network's long-term association with significant figures in the Dutch business world. Early in the twentieth century, for example, two of the network's Java-based partners – themselves related through marriage to the McNeills and the McLeans – came from the Loudon family, a patrician clan whose Scots origins had been subsumed into a Dutch identity during the middle decades of the nineteenth century and who went on to become very big in Dutch-Indies business circles. Gillian Maclaine had been a close friend of the family patriarch, Alexander Loudon, back in Java in the 1820s and 1830s. His direct descendants included a Governor-General who had, prior to that, been Minister of Colonies in The Hague.[18] Commerce and finance, however, proved to be the Loudon's real forte and Jonkheer Hugo Loudon (1860–1941) – a key clan member in the early twentieth century and a cousin of the men who worked with Maclaine Watson – was *Commissaris-President* of the Deli Maatschappij (the biggest plantation company operating on Sumatra) and one of the founders, and one-time *Directeur*, of Royal Dutch (Shell).[19]

By far the most immediately important of Maclaine Watson's 'Dutch' connections, however was Gerhard Herman Miesegaes,[20] remembered these days (if at all) as the ancestor of the celebrated mid-twentieth-century millionaire rock music promoter Stanley Miesegaes, but in his day a well-known Dutch businessman who, together with his son, played a major role in the development of the Maclaine Watson network. Born in Westphalia, but subsequently domiciled in the Netherlands, the elder Miesegaes made his first appearance in the network in 1859 as the agent for Fraser Eaton in the 'sugar'

---

17 See Gemeentearchief Rotterdam, Inventaris no. 468.0.1, 'Familie Suermondt/A.C. Fraser & Co'.

18 The individuals concerned were J.H. and W.F. Loudon, both partners in the network in the interwar decades. J.H. (1868–1952) took out British citizenship and died in retirement at Olantigh House (where he had lived from c.1912), a substantial mansion and famous garden near the Kent (UK) town of Wye. His widow, the Surabaya-born Louise Wilhelmena Fuchter, died there in 1964. See *HCHO* 42 (1930), p. 1618 and 50 (1938), p. 1230; 'Loudon' in *Nederlands Patriciaat*, 21 (1933–34), pp. 240–49; and 'Olantigh' in Wikipedia (accessed 8/10/2014); Crickhowell, *Rivers Join*, pp. 131–32.

19 Arjen Taselaar, *De Nederlandse Koloniale Lobby. Ondernemers en de Indische Politiek, 1914–1940* (Leiden: Research School CNWS, 1998), p. 71.

20 Gerhard Herman Miesegaes, b. Bremen 2.5.1833, d. London 13.4.1913.

town of Pasuruan, some sixty kilometres from their base at Surabaya and in the heart of the booming *Oosthoek* sugar belt from which they drew most of their supplies of the commodity.[21] Subsequently moving first to Surabaya itself and then on to Batavia, by 1880 Miesegeas was in the UK, where he established Maclaine Watson's London office (see below) and apparently did a great deal to stave off the potentially disastrous effects for his firm of the great sugar 'crisis' of 1884, when the world price of industrially manufactured sugar suddenly dropped by about 40 per cent.[22] He presumably remained based there until his death in 1913. A brief obituary notice appearing in the *Straits Times* – the man obviously enjoyed an international reputation – hailed him as the 'oldest member of the well-known firm of Messrs.' Maclaine, Watson ... [who had] lived for many years in Java and was amongst other things a conspicuous figure in the sugar business. In spite of his age (he was 80 when he died) he took part in the business of the firm to the last. In 1911 he celebrated the fiftieth year of his partnership.'[23]

Extended residence in London did not mean, however, any significant diminution of ties between the Miesegaes family and their 'native' Holland. When Gerhard Herman's son August Friederich Miesegaes died (either on holiday or in retirement) in Switzerland in 1938, he was memorialised by no less a figure in Dutch business circles than E.J. Heldring (inter alia, long-serving *president* of the mighty NHM) as 'my old friend, ... I became acquainted with him during my time in the Indies in 1898 and subsequently saw him many times both in England and here [in the Netherlands]'.[24] Born in Surabaya in 1863, the younger Miesegaes had at one time been '*chef*' of Fraser Eaton and was said to have subsequently occupied a similar position in Maclaine Watson's London office. During the interwar decades he was among the partners in Maclaine Watson's Batavia concern, still operating, as it had done for decades, out of premises on the Kali Besar West in the city's still-prime commercial quarter. Another member of the family, G.H. Miesegeas 'the second' (possibly August Friederich's son) was also active in the firm between the wars, both as partner in the London-based Maclaine Sugar Company (see below) founded in 1930,[25] and, toward the end of the decade, partner in Maclaine Watson Batavia itself.[26] Nonetheless, although

---

[21]   Fraser Eaton to Van Eeghen 17.11.1859. ASVE 447.

[22]   Rogge, *Van Eeghen*, p. 249.

[23]   *The Straits Times* 30.4.1913, p. 30. Online at: eresources.nlb.gov.sg/newspapers/.../straits-times1913 (accessed 14/8/2014).

[24]   Joh. De Vries (ed.), *Herinneringen en dagboek van Ernst Heldring 1871–1954*, 3 vols (Utrecht: Nederlands Historisch Genootschap, 1970), vol. 1, p. 524; vol. 2, pp. 832, 1299.

[25]   *HCHO* 50 (1938), p. 834.

[26]   For evidence of the presence of AFM and GHM ('the second') on the various boards of the Maclaine Watson network, see e.g. *HCHO* 42 (1930), p. 1618 and *HCHO* 50 (1938), p. 1230.

the network evidently maintained metropolitan connections – with both the UK and the Netherlands – both on an individual and corporate level, such links did not equate with metropolitan direction or control.

A Singular History: Colonial Orphans, Metropolitan Parents and the Provenance of Capital

Gillian Maclaine & Co., the first Batavia commercial concern in which Maclaine was engaged, was founded in 1822 in partnership (as we have seen) with overseas mercantile interests in Calcutta and London. Its successor, Maclaine Watson & Co., founded five years later in 1827, had no such connections and became the template for the network's trajectory for the remaining 150 years of its existence. The extent of the Maclaine Watson's independence from metropolitan control and finance and the degree of its local entrenchment in the Indies first needs to be referenced, however, to the global context of the evolving matrix of trade and empire in the late imperial era. Increasingly, during the course of the nineteenth century, one of the correlates of European imperial ascendency was the erosion of the relative autonomy of European colonial mercantile activity and its subjection (albeit to varying degrees) to the control and direction – either commercial or financial or both – of a metropolitan parent. It did so, amongst other things, because of the way in which such control, fuelled by economic growth and consequent expansion of capital resources in certain parts of Northern Europe and North America, was facilitated by developments in communications and transport.[27]

In relation to developments in Asia itself, it has been argued that the mid-century decades saw 'a revolution in the organisation of *British* firms … and in the nature of British economic relations'. The 'revolution' involved the replacement of an earlier generation of quasi- autonomous European mercantile houses with a new breed of enterprise that was much more in thrall to metropolitan financial and commercial interests than had been the case with their immediate predecessors: 'while this curtailment of independence was not total, it did mean that the new firms had to be much more responsive to the needs of their London parents, who in many cases had supplied [their] capital ….'[28] The business historian S.D. Chapman put the matter even more succinctly, noting that British mercantile houses in mid-nineteenth century India commonly had 'close connection with the City of London or with wealthy families in Glasgow and Liverpool'.[29] The

---

27 E.g. Darwin, *The Empire Project*, p. 63.
28 Webster, *The Twilight*, pp. 10–14 and 91–92 (emphasis added).
29 Chapman, *Merchant Enterprise*, p. 113.

assumption appears to be that much the same held good, though perhaps at a rather later date, for the nexus between metropolis and colony in relation to the *Dutch* empire in Asia, especially after the collapse in the mid-1880s of the world price for industrially manufactured sugar – the empire's key export by that date – ostensibly undermined much of the existing autonomy of the Java-based merchants and manufacturers who until then had constituted the empire's key capital resource.[30]

One particular manifestation of this changing nexus was the evolution of the 'managing agency system', whereby Western enterprises in the Indian subcontinent and Southeast Asia – in the Indies as well as in British Malaya to its north – acted as agents for metropolitan commercial or finance capital in the ownership and management of plantation ventures geared to the production of world commodities such as rubber, tea and coffee. Sometimes locally based, their subordination to metropolitan interests remained a defining characteristic.[31] Much the same can be said of the large-scale Dutch trading houses (the so-called 'big five') that grew up in the Indies during the late colonial era: for the most part, they were metropolitan based or the colonial offshoots of metropolitan businesses.[32] To be sure, the usefulness of

---

[30] The assumption has not gone unquestioned. See e.g. Bosma, 'Sugar and Dynasty in Yogyakarta', pp. 89–92. For the mid-century 'Indies' bourgeoisie in general, see Knight, *Sugar Steam and Steel. The Industrial Project in Colonial Java, 1830–1885* (Adelaide: Adelaide University Press, 2014), pp. 133–76.

[31] E.g. Nicholas J. White, *Business, Government and the End of Empire. Malaya, 1942–1957* (Kuala Lumpur: Oxford University Press, 1996), p. 23: '… the Straits merchant's "expert knowledge" of local investment opportunities was fed back to "the centre of a global information network", the City of London, where syndicates were formed and companies floated' whose assets and investments were then managed by the agency businesses in Singapore. In the Straits Settlements, immediately to Java's north, their number famously included such firms as Guthries and Harrisons & Crosfield (e.g. Chapman, *Merchant Enterprise*, pp. 107–08; Geoffrey Jones and Judith Wale, 'Diversification Strategies of British Trading Companies: Harrisons & Crosfield, c.1900–c.1980', *Business History*, 41, 2 (1999), pp. 69–101; J. Thomas Lindblad, 'British Business and the Uncertainties of Early Independence in Indonesia', *Itinerario*, 37 (2013), pp. 147–64), while in Java itself during the second half of the nineteenth century a number of similar firms (*'administratie kantoren'*) grew up – among them Tiedeman & Van Kerchem and Anemaet & Co. – in connection with the sugar industry, to the (overseas) owners of which they provided both management and technical services. Harrisons & Crossfield, however, were London-based. Guthrie & Co., based in Singapore, would be a more promising point of comparison with the Maclaine Watson network, but acted for much its history in partnership with the London-based firm of Scott and Co. (see e.g. J. Thomas Lindblad, *Foreign Investment in Southeast Asia in the Twentieth Century* (Basingstoke: Macmillan Press, 1998), especially pp. 43–47).

[32] In the Indies, the sole potentially comparable, Indies-based and large-scale trading enterprise was Geo. Wehry, with a head office in the port city of Surabaya (Howard Dick, *Surabaya, City of Work* (Athens, OH: Ohio University Press, 2002), p. 248; Claver, *Dutch Commerce and Chinese Merchants*, pp. 389–40). Other major trading companies in late colonial Indonesia were

any such dichotomy between 'colonial' and 'metropolitan' capital may itself be queried. Inter alia, it fails to take sufficient cognisance of the fact that enterprises might be initiated in the metropolis but then achieve a degree of colonial entrenchment that renders redundant any easy classification of their operations.[33] Even so, the singularity of the Maclaine Watson network still stands out.

First and foremost – and to espouse the relevant jargon – it was quite explicitly *not* the subordinate agent of metropolitan 'core' capital operating on a colonial 'periphery'. The network's activities did not fit the 'managing agency' model, nor did it resemble in terms either of its prime business or its mode of finance the other big European mercantile houses of the late colonial Netherlands Indies. On the former count, at times there were indeed contrary indications: in the 1860s, for example, one of the 'Java' Frasers (of Fraser Eaton in Surabaya) became 'chief agent' in Batavia for the Nederlandsch Indisch Stoomvaart Maatschappi (Netherlands Indies Steam-Transport Company) or NISM, newly launched in Holland under the patronage of the UK-based Mackinnon mercantile and shipping conglomerate in an attempt by the latter to muscle in on the steam-packet business in the Indies. Along with Fraser himself, Maclaine Watson took shares in the new company.[34] Again, some forty years later, c.1900, members of the Maclaine network were to be found acting for overseas capital, notably as Netherlands Indies chief representative (*hoofdvertegenwordiger*) for the two light railway (*stoomtram*) companies which operated in East Java but were based in Amsterdam.[35] Even so, these appear to have been exceptional developments. For the most part, an examination of contemporary business directories reveals that virtually all the enterprises with which the Maclaine Watson network was concerned during the late colonial era – they included coffee and tea estates in Java, as well as stakes in local shipping and transport companies – had their seat of business

unambiguously headquartered in the Netherlands, viz. Internatio (Rotterdam), Borsumij (Arnhem), Lindeteves and Jacobson van den Berg (Amsterdam, with a Chief Representative or *Hoofdvertegenwoordiger* in the Indies). See e.g. Inventaris van het Archief van Lindeteves-Jacoberg NV (1860) 1889–1979, Nationaal Archief, Den Haag, 2.18.23. For a brief and now rather dated, but still reputable, summary, see G.C. Allen and Audrey G. Donnithorne, *Western Enterprise in Indonesia and Malaya* (London: Allen & Unwin, 1957), pp. 53–63. For more recent work touching on the subject, see Lindblad, *Foreign Investment*, pp. 84–88 and Nicholas J. White, 'Surviving Sukarno: British Business in Post-Colonial Indonesia, 1950-1967', *Modern Asian Studies*, 46 (2102), pp. 1277–315.

[33] On this score, see in particular, Lindblad, *Foreign Investment*, pp. 1–7 and Lindblad, 'Corporate Structure and Profit in Colonial Indonesia, 1920–1930', (as yet unpublished) paper prepared for the international workshop 'Foreign Capital in Colonial Southeast Asia: Profits, Economic Growth and Indigenous Society', Leiden, 16–17 December 2014.

[34] See Munro, *Maritime Enterprise and Empire*, pp. 74–75.

[35] *HCHO* 16 (1904), pp. 600, 607.

(their '*zetel*' in Dutch terminology) in one or other of the main cities of the Indies, and not in either the Netherlands or the UK.[36]

Moreover, such involvements were a rather minor part – most of them were in fairly modestly capitalised enterprises – of the Maclaine Watson network's overall business. That business was first and foremost in the sugar trade, a fact that differentiated the network from the much more diverse mercantile business carried on by the Dutch 'big five'. Indeed, it meant that the nearest comparable business in late colonial Indonesia was not a European firm but rather the Chinese-Indonesian firm of Kian Gwan, the sugar-manufacturing and sugar-exporting arm of the Oei Tiong Ham Concern (OTHC), the major Southeast Asian business and manufacturing conglomerate founded in Semarang, central Java, during the 1880s.[37] It is a comparison to which we shall return later.

These several dimensions of the network's business activities underline the colonial autonomy of the Maclaine Watson network. From its establishment in the late 1820s, it continued to operate as a network firmly based in 'the East', and – despite the opening of a London office during the course of the 1880s – headquarters continued to be located in Batavia/Jakarta through to the firm's dismantlement in the mid-1960s. Significantly, the London office, in Fenchurch Street in the City, was established by an individual (G.H. Miesegaes) who was already long connected on Java with Maclaine Watson and its associates on the island and, as far as can be judged, this custom of 'repatriating' some of the network's Java-based partners to Fenchurch Street continued through into the mid-twentieth century. It represented, it may be suggested, a formalisation and extension of arrangements for having Maclaine Watson's interests represented in London (a representation that had begun, as we have seen, with Thomas Bonhote some decades earlier) rather than an assertion of metropolitan control over the network's activities.

Indeed, all the signs are that the network's commercial activities were conducted on essentially autonomous lines, without the long-term or direct provision of capital from outside sources. It would have been standard

---

[36]   The situation of the network c.1900 onwards emerges fairly clearly from the *HCHO* data. See e.g. *HCHO* 16 (1904), pp. 661, 642; *HCHO* 35 (1923), p. 1222 and *HCHO* 50 (1938), p. 863.

[37]   On the OTHC, see the ongoing work of the Dutch scholar Peter Post, e.g. 'Chinese Business Networks and Japanese Capital in South East Asia, 1880–1940: Some Preliminary Observations', pp. 154–75 in R.A. Brown (ed.), *Chinese Business Enterprise in Asia* (London and New York: Routledge, 1995); Liem Tjwan Ling, 'Sugar Jing: Oei Tiong Ham', pp. 135–47 in Yoshihara Kunio (ed.), *Oei Tiong Ham Concern: The First Business Empire of Southeast Asia* (Kyoto: Kyoto University, The Centre for Southeast Asian Studies, 1989); Howard Dick, 'Oei Tiong Ham', pp. 272–81 in John Butcher and Howard Dick (eds), *The Rise and Fall of Revenue Farming* (New York: St Martin's Press, 1993).

commercial practice, of course, for the network to have drawn on credit made available short term by the overseas firms with whom it traded. Like any other contemporary mercantile firm involved in the commodity trade with Europe, the Maclaine Watson network had a number of 'correspondents' in both the UK and the Netherlands. Inter alia, they obviously retained a connection – presumably primarily in relation to consignments of British cotton goods from Finlay's mills – with the London and Glasgow house of Finlay Hodgeson with whom Gillian Maclaine had forged close links back at the beginning of the 1830s. Yet those links were not substantial. Indeed after an initial excitement – the Finlays want to 'keep me for themselves', Maclaine had confided to his mother in 1831, regretting that he had met with them a decade earlier[38] – consignments rapidly dropped off. There is no indication, moreover, that Finlay Hodgeson ever became the conduit for the channelling of metropolitan funds into the network's activities in Asia.[39] Other major commercial connections – ones that continued into the twentieth century – included the Amsterdam mercantile house of Van Eeghen, with whom Maclaine Watson, Fraser Eaton and McNeill & Co. were in regular and extensive correspondence during the 1850s and 1860s, and the UK firm of Butterfield and Swire, owners amongst others of the great Taikoo sugar refinery in Hong Kong (see below) to which the network shipped vast quantities of Java sugar from the 1880s through to the 1930s. Credit from such sources did not equate, however, with any degree of financial control.

What remains at issue, therefore, is the provenance of the capital with which the network *did* work. It is not one that is easily resolved. As we saw in an earlier chapter, by the close of the 1820s Gillian Maclaine had divested himself of his earlier links to overseas commercial capital and had subsequently 'struck out alone' with the help of considerable sums of money lent by a fellow Scot, the repatriated veteran Indies merchant John Deans Campbell. Maclaine was hence enabled to rebuild his stake in the Batavia partnership after having used up all his own resources to buy his way out of the financial morass created by the bankruptcy of his erstwhile London partners. In consequence he was able to declare by the middle of 1832 that his Java business was 'now perfectly independent of support in a pecuniary way either from London or Bengal' and that 'our own capital will I trust carry us on'.[40]

38 GM to MM, London 12.3.1831. Greenfield MSS.
39 The firm's history ([Brogan], *James Finlay*, pp. 43, 171, etc.) though making several mentions of Finlay's commercial links with Maclaine Watson – a point reiterated in the network's own centenary volume (*One Hundred Years*, p. 9) – contains no suggestion that the network was financed by the Glasgow concern.
40 GM to AM, Batavia 16.6.1832. Greenfield MSS.

How far this continued to be the case, however, is a subject on which the existing documentation is largely silent. Maclaine Watson, like the other firms in the network, never transformed into a limited liability company (Dutch: *naamloze vennootschap* or NV) when this became possible in the Indies late in the nineteenth century. As a result there were no published annual reports to shareholders containing information about the company's capital resources and their provenance.[41] It appears reasonably safe to conclude, nevertheless, that the Maclaine Watson network operated independent of its commercial connections, essentially with its own accumulated stock of capital rather than with that supplied by overseas associates, partners or principals. Even so, there is no way that the network could have financed from its own resources, inter alia, what developed into huge purchases of Java sugar, and there are strong pointers to the fact that it did so with the support of the Javasche Bank (Java Bank) or DJB, the colony's premier financial institution and supplier of capital to a wide variety of mercantile enterprises there. Documented instances of Maclaine Watson's dealings with DJB begin at least as early as 1872 and continue until the late 1920s (when the credit involved was an impressive 40 million guilders) and beyond.[42] Such indications as do exist, in short, strongly suggest that the Maclaine Watson network belonged to the category of companies operating in Asian colonies – and there were many of them – which, though owned and operated by European expatriates, were not controlled from headquarters located in the metropole or elsewhere and worked with capital accessed within the colony, often ploughing back their profits to expand the enterprise.[43] In this sense, the Maclaine Watson network adhered to a common enough pattern. What made it unique among European mercantile concerns in the Indies, however, was the sheer size of its operations and the extent of the network's intra-Asian reach.

Through Sweetness to Wealth: The Maclaine Watson Network and the Java Sugar Industry

The extent of that reach, it may be argued, was accounted for – in part at least – by the fact that the absence of a directing or controlling metropolitan

---

[41] The often invaluable, annually appearing *HCHO* is silent on this score, since its compilers were dependent on information supplied them by the firms concerned.

[42] I am grateful for this information to the Dutch scholar Dr Alexander Claver.

[43] I am indebted here to Professor Anne Booth (SOAS, London), and in particular to remarks appearing in her as-yet-unpublished 'Growth, Industrialization and the Role of Foreign Capital: Asian Colonies, 1900–42', paper prepared for the international workshop 'Foreign Capital in Colonial Southeast Asia: Profits, Economic Growth and Indigenous Society', Leiden, 16–17 December 2014.

'parent' enabled the Maclaine Watson network to 'escape' from its initial moorings in the bilateral trade with Europe and to relocate firmly within an intra-Asian mercantile context. In the process, it developed over the decades into the largest European sugar-trading concern in Southeast Asia and, as such, took a prime position in the intra-Asian rather than intercontinental trade in that commodity. Conversely, the very fact of its heavy engagement in sugar – a highly particular albeit highly important branch of international commodity trade – may well have helped protect the network from the metropolitan takeover that was the story of many contemporary colonial businesses: specialisation of this kind, and the local knowledge on which it was predicated, it has been suggested in another context, might well have enabled such firms to survive the 'onslaught' of metropolitan finance capital and have formed a barrier against takeover.[44]

The Maclaine Watson network's development into one of Asia's most prominent sugar traders only began well after Maclaine himself was dead, even though it was in a sense foreshadowed by his engagement in the Country Trade during the final decade of his life. Initially, indeed (and as will have been apparent from the analysis in the foregoing chapters) the network of 'Maclaine' firms was only marginally connected with sugar and was located, first and foremost, along commodity chains in cotton goods and coffee predicated primarily on bilateral commercial ties with Europe and North America. It was these commercial ties that had brought Gillian Maclaine himself to Java in the first place – and subsequently kept him there. Already by the 1830s, however, things had begun to change, and the network, as we have seen, came to owe much of its success to its engagement in the intra-Asian Country Trade and, quite possibly, to its participation in the highly lucrative commerce in opium from the Indian subcontinent through maritime Southeast Asia to southern China, for which the Country Trade was the vital conduit. The big switch to sugar came later, and initially brought the Maclaine Watson network firmly back within the orbit of bilateral trade with Western Europe and North America, where Java's sugar rapidly expanding sugar production found its main outlet between the 1840s and 1880s. Towards the end of the nineteenth century, however, the East–West commodity chains that had hitherto characterised the international sugar economy underwent a radical transformation, one that was to have a profound impact on network's subsequent development.

During the middle decades of the nineteenth century, beginning in the 1830s, Java had become a major producer-exporter of industrially manufactured cane sugar to world markets. Toward the end of the period, indeed, the Dutch colony overtook Brazil to rank, after Cuba, as the world's second

---

[44] Jones, 'British Imperialism and the Argentine', pp. 437–44.

largest exporter of the commodity. To an extent, it did so on the basis of the expanded output of some hundred or so factories operated in part by (mostly) expatriate Europeans and Indies-Chinese (Chinese-Indonesians in modern parlance) working on contract to the Indies government and its commercial agent the NHM. They did so under the auspices of the so-called *Cultuurstelsel* or System of (State) Cultivations inaugurated in the directly ruled 'Government Territories' of Java in 1830 and not fully dismantled until late in the century. Yet, by no means all of the island's mid-century output of industrially manufactured sugar was supplied by these state contractors, and the burgeoning of Java's exports of the commodity was also fuelled by several score of manufacturers, many of them Indies-Dutch, operating 'privately' in the Government Territories and in the quasi-autonomous Principalities of south central Java, where Maclaine himself had set up as a planter (of coffee) within a few months of his arrival in the colony in 1820.[45]

It was long-standing connections in the Principalities that brought Maclaine Watson initial access to Java's sugar production as early as the 1830s, but the major development dated from around the mid-century when, c.1860 it was said that, along with two other Java-based Dutch firms, Maclaine Watson virtually controlled the export-commodity trade between the Principalities and the port of Semarang.[46] Along with coffee, sugar would have been very much to the fore. It was not only from the Principalities, however, that the firm found its supplies of the commodity. During the 1850s the Indies government had begun to free up the trade in sugar produced under the auspices of the *Cultuurstelsel* which it had previously reserved for export by the NHM. It began both to auction quantities of sugar and other *Cultuurstelsel* commodities at Batavia (rather than have them all shipped for sale in the Netherlands) and to allow contracting manufacturers to place a proportion of their output directly on the open market. The upshot was not only to give mercantile houses like Maclaine Watson ready access to ever larger amounts of what was fast becoming Java's key commodity but also to encourage them to invest in the expansion of its production. During the 1850s and 1860s the network hence came to own several sugar factories and became active in providing financial backing for a number of others. Indeed, around 1870, the network's three Java-based firms were said to have had something of a stranglehold on the purchase of the commodity from the factories of West Java (Cirebon) and in the prime sugar districts of East Java that stretched along the coast eastward of the great port-city of Surabaya.[47]

---

[45] For a recent overview, see Bosma, *The Sugar Plantation*, pp. 91–99.

[46] Houben, *Kraton and Kumpeni*, p. 287.

[47] J.H. Schmiedell, *Gedenkblatter zum 50-Jahrigen Bestehen der Firma Erdmann & Sielcken in Java, 1875–1924* (np. nd. [1924]), p. 3.

Within this context, it looks as if the Maclaine Watson partners opted for a strategy of limiting their direct backward investment in sugar manufacture per se in favour of one that kept the bulk of their (limited) capital fluid enough to take full advantage of the commercial opportunities offered by concentrating on the purchase of the commodity at source, largely from manufacturers with whom they had financial ties. Rather than moving into fully-fledged ownership, that is to say, they concentrated on providing working capital to sugar factories in return for consignment of their output. Hence, despite the fact that throughout its history the network did indeed own (or have a direct financial stake in) a number of sugar factories, its holdings in the colony's sugar manufacturing sector were hardly commensurate with the vast quantities of sugar in which the network traded. There were around 160 or more sugar factories established in the colony by the early twentieth century, of which Maclaine Watson and associated firms had a (by no means exclusive) financial stake in no more than eight.[48] At the same time, however, in one key dimension, Maclaine Watson did indeed enjoy a high degree of intimacy with the production as well as the trade in sugar. By the early twentieth century, the island's industry had become globally unique in terms of the degree of its dependency on chemical fertiliser, and the Maclaine Watson network stood out as one of Java's main suppliers of that indispensible commodity.[49]

Despite this role in provisioning the industry with a vital input into the production process, the essential point, nonetheless, is that Maclaine Watson remained, first and foremost, a network of sugar traders, whose access to Java's sugar output was articulated less through direct participation in production per se than through consignment contracts involving the short-term financing of the manufacturers' annual production costs and, independent of this, the purchase of sugar either at source or from the 'speculators' who played such a large role in the colony's sugar market.[50] In so doing, they acted much in line with an industry in which, at a quite early date, manufacturing had become divorced from the export trade in sugar. Though some mercantile firms, including those in the Maclaine Watson network itself, also had a modest direct stake in sugar manufacture, the overall structure of the Java industry was one in which sugar buyers and exporters formed a quite separate entity from the firms who manufactured the commodity.[51]

---

[48] Details of the network's financial interest in Java's sugar factories are to be found in successive annual volumes of the *HCHO* from 1888 onward. See under Maclaine Watson, MacNeill & Co. and Fraser Eaton & Co.

[49] G. Roger Knight, *Commodities and Colonialism. The Story of Big Sugar in Java, 1885–1940* (Leiden and Boston, MA: Brill, 2013), p. 67.

[50] On the latter, see Tio Poo Tjiang, *De Suikerhandel van Java* (Amsterdam: De Bussy, 1923), pp. 59–67.

[51] Tio, *Suikerhandel*, remains as a virtually unique attempt at analysis.

During the opening years of the twentieth century, in its prime role as a network of traders and as a major participant in the international trade in sugar, Maclaine Watson was vitally impacted upon by developments in the world sugar economy – and its associated commodity chains – which saw it radically transformed by the growing market for industrially manufactured sugar in Asia itself.[52] In the face of competition from European beet sugar manufacture, sales of Asian (and New World) sugar in the West shrank dramatically. Dutch Java – previously by far the biggest of Europe's suppliers of Asian sugar – was particularly affected. Through a combination of factors, however, the island's manufacturers were able to redirect their still-expanding output to markets for industrially manufactured sugar that were opening up in Asia, predicated on the stimulation of demand inherent in the dramatically reduced 'world price' for this form of the commodity that continued to hold in the wake of 'sugar crisis' (see above) of 1884.

It was within this context that the Maclaine Watson network's continued focus on sugar propelled it away from inter-continental and into intra-Asian trade to an ever-increasing degree. To be sure, the development was not an uninterrupted one. At the very end of the nineteenth century and for several years thereafter Maclaine Watson devoted most of its attention to the North American market where Java sugar covered much of the shortfall left in refinery supplies by the (temporary) cessation of exports from war-torn Cuba, while later still the network was the prime conduit for the supply of Java sugar to the UK during the First World War, where it filled the (huge) gap left by the termination of imports from Germany and Austria-Hungary.

Even so, the secular trend was toward Asian rather than Western markets and, in the culmination of developments that had begun late in the nineteenth century, by the inter-war decades the Maclaine Watson network was first and foremost an *Asian* sugar trader, dealing in the sale of the commodity in a variety of markets extending from the Indian subcontinent through to Japan. The single most critical development, however, had taken place as early as the 1880s, with the forging of ties with the large, newly established Taikoo sugar refinery in Hong Kong.[53] Taikoo had been opened early in the decade by the UK-based China-Coast firm of Butterfield and Swire to produce not only for Chinese consumption but also – and initially more importantly – for sale on the rapidly expanding Japanese market for the white, crystalline 'pure' form of the commodity. Though initially drawing on raw sugar produced in the adjoining mainland regions, Taikoo soon began to take most of its supplies from Java, where the Maclaine Watson network became the main conduit

---

[52] For this and the following paragraph, see the extended discussion in Knight, *Commodities and Colonialism*, pp. 17–52.

[53] Knight, *Commodities and Colonialism*, pp. 23–30.

(though they probably also participated in the export of Java sugar to Japan's own refineries when these began to operate late in the 1890s).

The Maclaine network's connection with Taikoo proved an enduring one. To be sure, Swire's was not averse to trying its luck with other Java exporters: in 1898, for example, they cheerfully informed Maclaine Watson that the '*Hupeh* [one the refinery's dedicated sugar carriers] leaves in a few days for Java, to load a full cargo from your neighbours'.[54] In the long term, however, Taikoo's relation with the Maclaine Watson remained close. From sometime in the 1890s onward, for example, Maclaine sent a 'regular wire of quotations' to Hong Kong, and for their part Swire's were prepared to concede that Maclaines were '… better placed to coordinate big orders quietly … [without] disturbing the market unduly' than were some of the smaller Java operators. Nonetheless, and quite categorically, the Maclaine network remained independent of Swires and Taikoo, even to the extent of supplying raw sugar to the refinery of their greatest rivals, the Hong Kong firm of Jardine Matheson. Nor did their ongoing connection with Taikoo prevent the network from developing – c.1936 onward – its own source of refined sugar in Java itself,[55] and selling it on the China market, where the network had its own agents.[56] Even so, it was Taikoo that still remained their prime connection on the China Coast throughout the inter-war decades, all the more so after the closure of Jardine's Hong Kong refinery at the close of the 1920s.[57]

The Maclaine network's large-scale involvement in the intra-Asian sugar trade was not confined, however, to doing business in Hong Kong, China and Japan or to the trade in *raw* sugar alone. They also exported to South Asia vast quantities of a quasi-refined form of the commodity known as Factory White which was the mainstay of their subcontinental business (as it was also for that of their Chinese-Indonesian competitors), where its importation compensated for, and partly explained, the fact that prior to the 1930s India had little to match huge, industrialised refinery capacity of contemporary East Asia. Factory White was produced at source, by various chemical processes, in the same factories that manufactured raw sugar, though from the early twentieth century onward it was usual, in the case of the Java producers, for factories to

---

54 For this and subsequent references to Maclaine Watson's relations with Taikoo in this paragraph, see Knight, *Commodities and Colonialism*, p. 30.
55 See 'Jaarverslagen NV Cultuur Maatschappij Pandji & Tandjoongsarie, Gevestigd te Surabaja', 1920–1953, Biblioteek Koninklijk Instituut voor de Tropen/Royal Tropical Institute, Amsterdam, L 2827.
56 E.g. Butterfield & Swire London to Butterfield & Swire, Hong Kong 19.2.1937. Refinery Letters 1937 JSSV 1/9/box 27.
57 E.g. BS London to BS Hong Kong 1.1.1937, Refinery Letters 1937 JSSV 1/9/box 27 Swire SOAS.

specialise exclusively in one form of the commodity rather than produce both. Of a lesser quality than the produce of sugar refineries, it had the advantage of being substantially cheaper. In Europe it found its main outlets among conserve and cake manufacturers, but in Asia – and particularly in South Asia – it was marketed in great quantities to direct consumers.[58]

Throughout the subcontinent, the Maclaine Watson network's long-term associates were Ralli Brothers, one of the largest European commercial enterprises in India. Indeed, it was in conjunction with Ralli that the network set up the Maclaine Sugar Company in 1930 (it continued in operation until 1937) to handle their sugar business.[59] Inter alia, the international scale of the Sugar Company's dealings embroiled Maclaine Watson with NIVAS (Nederlandsch Indisch Vereeniging voor de Afzet van Suiker), the quasi-governmental Dutch agency set up in 1932 as a single-seller organisation for the Java sugar industry. Accusing NIVAS of setting its prices too high, the Maclaine Sugar Company, in a thoroughly global fashion, sought (inter alia) to remedy the situation by supplying the Indian market with refined sugar from UK producers.[60]

From the late nineteenth century onward, in short, the Maclaine Watson network played a key role in the Java sugar trade. During the mid-1880s, for example, in conjunction with one other 'friendly' firm, it was credited with purchasing – presumably at knock-down prices because the local market was so bad – more than 50 per cent of the Java sugar harvest,[61] while in one particular year early in the twentieth century the network was reputed to have bought up as much as two-thirds of the Java sugar crop.[62] Despite being very big indeed, however, Maclaine Watson was far from having a monopoly on the business of exporting Java's industrially manufactured sugar. More specifically, during the closing decades of the century they had been joined by three European newcomers and by two major Chinese-Indonesian firms, Kian Gwan/OTHC (see above) and the likewise Semarang-based firm of Kwik Hoo Tong (KHT).[63] Kian Gwan/OTHC, in particular, was a significant enough presence in the international sugar trade during the opening decades of the twentieth century to have competed with Maclaine Watson

---

[58] Knight, *Commodities and Colonialism*, pp. 32–38.

[59] NA Archief NIVAS 518: 'Maclaine Sugar Co. 1930–1937'.

[60] NA Archief NHMA 2949: 'Maclaine Watson 1933–35'.

[61] Jaarverslag NHM Factorij Batavia 59 (1884), p. 7; 60 (1885), p. 7; 61 (1886), p. 8; 62 (1887), pp. 10–11. NA NHMA 4552.

[62] See Keuchenuis to DJB Surabaya, Samarang 6.3.1908/19, Archief Bank Indonesia/De Javasche Bank. Agentschapsarchieven. C. Surabaya, 5183 (copy kindly supplied to the author by Dr Alexander Claver).

[63] Peter Post, 'The Kwik Hoo Tong Trading Society of Semarang, Java: A Chinese Business Network in Late Colonial Asia', *Journal of Southeast Asian Studies*, 32 (2002), pp. 279–96.

in supplying the British market during the First World War. Indeed, the head of the conglomerate, Oei Tiong Ham himself, gained some fame at this time as Java's 'sugar king', perhaps because of the sheer novelty of an *Asian* businessman supplying the British with a vital commodity.[64]

Despite some early signs of collaboration between them – c.1900, for example, one of the Maclaine Watson companies shared positions on the board of a big sugar factory in north central Java with representatives of OTHC[65] – competition between Maclaine Watson and the colony's two major Chinese-Indonesian sugar traders (and their Japanese associates) appears in general to have been intense. In 1930s, for instance, the network may have been part of a push to keep Kian Gwan/OTHC out of the inner councils of NIVAS.[66] Rivalry with *European* firms – Erdmann & Sielcken and Wellenstein Krause (both companies were registered in the Indies) and the Rotterdam-based Internatio (Internationaal Crediet-en Handels-Vereeniging 'Rotterdam') – was altogether more qualified. The latter firm had no apparent connection with the Maclaine Watson network, but the cases of Erdmann and Wellenstein were rather different. Back in the 1880s, the head of the latter firm had been related through marriage to two of the senior partners in the Maclaine Watson network, a fact that suggests that rivalry was perhaps mingled with co-operation.[67] This was certainly the case in the twentieth century, when, in the interwar decades, Maclaine, Erdmann and Wellenstein formed what was referred to at the time as 'the combine'.

Nonetheless, throughout the First World War and subsequently during the 1920s and 1930s, it was the Maclaine Watson network that remained consistently at the forefront of the colony's sugar purchasers. In 1921, the network's sugar purchase was only exceeded in quantity by that of Suzucki, the Japanese

---

64 Onghokham, *The Thugs, the Curtain Thief and the Sugar Lord. Power, Politics and Culture in Colonial Java* (Jakarta: Metafor, 2003).

65 See *HCHO* 16 (1904), p. 691 under 'Sf. Pakkies'. It is noteworthy in this context, however, that less than two decades earlier Maclaine Watson had categorically denied (to DJB) that they had money on loan from the great Semarang businessman Be Biauw Tjoan (on whom see Rush, *Opium to Java*, pp. 77–78, 93–95). See Notulen Vergadering Directie DJB, 26.11.1884, Archief Bank Indonesia/De Java Bank, DJB 52, no. 57: 256–57 (copy kindly supplied to the author by Dr Alexander Claver).

66 Inter alia, the 'combine' appears to have succeeded – in conjunction with the Dutch interests who ran it – in keeping Kian Gwan out of the inner councils (*daglijksche bestuur*) of NIVAS, quite probably to the detriment of NIVAS's sales in East Asia, where Kian Gwan was very well connected in political as well as business circles. See e.g. 'Dossier inzake raffinaderijen in China' in NA NIVAS 537.

67 Victor August Wellenstein, the founder of Wellenstein Krause, was the brother-in-law of the heads of both Maclaine Watson in Batavia and their Fraser Eaton associates in Surabaya. See C. Fasseur, 'Wellenstein, Edmund Peter (1880–1934)', in *Biografisch Woordenboek van Nederland*. Online at: http://resources.huygens.knaw.nl/bwn/BWN/lemmata/bwn3/wellenstein (accessed 12/11/2013).

conglomerate that did very big business in Java prior to its collapse in 1927, and marginally exceeded, in turn, the purchase that year by the Chinese-Indonesian KHT concern and was more than double that of Kian Gwan. At the end of the decade, and following the withdrawal of most Japanese capital from the Java sugar market, the network's purchases were far in excess of any other buyer. In 1929, at over 600,000 tonnes, they were almost twice as large as that of Kian Gwan, and a similar situation held good in 1930.[68] At the end of the 1930s, by which time the Java industry had a made a substantial, albeit only partial, recovery from the impact of the inter-war depression, the Maclaine network's dominance of the market was even more pronounced. Its purchase amounted to around 20 per cent of the absolute total of Java sugar sold in 1939, was approached in terms of quantity only by the Dutch Internatio concern, and far exceeded that of Kian Gwan.

An Asian *Context: Maclaine Watson and the Growth of Intra-Asian Trade*

With the important exception of the period of the First World War, when the network (as we have seen) exported huge amounts of Java sugar to the UK, its leading role as an exporter of Java's sugar placed Maclaine Watson firmly within the orbit of intra-Asian trade. Bilateral commercial ties with Europe or North America were largely, though rarely completely, in abeyance. In short, for long stretches of its history, the Maclaine Watson network was not only an Asia-based mercantile enterprise but also one whose essential business was carried out along intra-Asian commercial circuits. Like Kian Gwan and its parent company OTHC, Maclaine Watson participated significantly in the modern-era development of commerce among the various regions of Asia: not only were they based in 'the East', but their commercial activities – just like those of their Kian Gwan counterpart – took place predominantly in an Asian context.

What was also important in this context, moreover, was not sugar alone but also the Maclaine Watson network's role as leading agent in the Netherlands Indies for a variety of shipping companies, and as an agent there for the provision of the maritime insurance that was likewise an essential lubricant for commercial transactions between the major Asian ports. The commercial directories of the time provide the vital (if tantalisingly abbreviated) information.

---

[68] These figures in this paragraph derive from date in the Jaarverslagen (annual reports) of the Verenigde Javasuiker Producenten or VJSP (United Java Sugar Producers Association) 1918–1931, NA VJSP 18 and from the Jaarverslagen (annual reports) of the Nederlandsch Indische Vereeniging voor de Afzet van Suiker or NIVAS (Netherlands Indies Association for the Sale of Sugar), 1932/3–1940/41, NA NIVAS 15.

They demonstrate that during the inter-war decades an integral, albeit lesser, part of the network's business was its agency for insurance companies and major international shipping lines. A score or more of insurance companies (mostly with UK bases) were represented in the Indies by Maclaine Watson, and for a short time in the 1920s the network ran its own insurance company, The London and Java Assurance Company, based in Surabaya with Fraser Eaton and McNeill & Co. as its board members (*commissarisen*).[69] Among the shipping lines that the firm represented, the inevitable P&O and other metropolitan firms such as the Ocean Steam Ship Company of Liverpool[70] were predominantly engaged in the inter-continental trade between Asia and Europe or North America. The remainder, however, were primarily involved in intra-Asian commerce. Two of the firms that the network represented in the Java ports around 1922 were Japanese – Kishimoto Kisen Kaisha and Nanyo Yusen Kaisha.[71] Others, including for example the Asiatic Steam Ship Company that dominated the Java–India run, although often registered in Europe or North America, were likewise predominantly or exclusively active in Asian waters and in intra-Asian trade, as well as in the closely associated trade between Asia and the Antipodean ports.[72]

Even so, it was its extensive involvement in the burgeoning of the intra-Asian trade in industrially manufactured sugar from the 1880s onward that constitutes the core of the Maclaine Watson network's importance to the present argument. The full import of intra-Asian trade for the economic history of modern Asia – and, indeed, for the so-called 'Asian Miracle' of the late twentieth century – is something that has become of increasing concern to scholars during the last few decades.[73] It did so initially in the context of East Asia and the mercantile activity of the Chinese 'diaspora', but subsequently came to embrace the Indian subcontinent as well. Emphasis here has been (well) placed on the indigenous, Asian dimension of this development. The present argument, however, is that it was not only indigenous Asian merchants and shippers who were crucially involved (prior to the Second World War) in the expansion of intra-Asian trade but also European ones, of which – in regard to maritime Southeast Asia – the Maclaine Watson network was a prime instance. Increasingly (though never completely) divorced from bilateral trade with Europe from the late nineteenth century onward, the

---

[69] *HCHO* 35 (1923), p. 1358.

[70] *HCHO* 35 (1923), pp. 1820 and 1822.

[71] *HCHO* 35(1923), pp. 1814 and 1817.

[72] See inter alia, *One Hundred Years*, pp. 12–13.

[73] The classic thesis of the distinguished Japanese historian Kaoru Sugihara (e.g. Sugihara, *Japan, China and the Growth of the Asian International Economy*) is briefly discussed in the first chapter of this book. For a developed approach, see e.g. Shigeru Akita and Nicholas J. White (eds), *The International Order of Asia in the 1930s and 1950s* (Farnham: Ashgate, 2010).

network participated in the very extensive early twentieth century intra-Asian trade in sugar just are surely as did its great Chinese-Indonesian contemporary, OTHC/Kian Gwan. The latter was almost certainly more heavily capitalised than the Maclaine Watson network, and was more directly involved in the production of sugar, with half a dozen or so factories whose total capacity was well in excess of the few owned by Maclaine Watson. All the same, the comparison is potentially fruitful, not least because of the emphasis it throws on family firms and on the binding ties of shared ethnicity and/or cultural background. It seems doubtful if the partners in the Maclaine Watson network would have relished being placed in a similar category to Chinese business in early twentieth-century Southeast Asia, but for the historian writing almost a century later, the comparison is inescapable. Equally inescapable in this context, however, and perhaps rather more to the tastes of the network's Scots partners, is a reminder that the intra-Asian commercial activity that from the late nineteenth century onward arguably formed such an important foundation of Asian economic modernity was a cosmopolitan rather than exclusively indigenous Asian development. Far from being an outsider to this commerce, Maclaine Watson, through its role as a major supplier (in one form or another) of a key commodity from Java to other Asian centres, actively participated in its expansion. In short, viewed in the long term Gillian Maclaine's legacy was a significant one, not only from the perspective of imperial history but also from that of the broader narrative of economic development in Asia in general.

BIBLIOGRAPHY

Primary Sources: Documents

Nationaal Archief, Den Haag, The Netherlands
Archief Hoofdkantor Nederlandsche Handel-Maatschappij
Archief Ministerie van Koloniën
Archief Nederlandsch-Indische Vereeniging voor de Afzet van Suiker (NIVAS)
Archief van Lindeteves-Jacoberg NV
Archief Vereenigde Javasuiker Producenten (VJSP)
Collectie Baud
Collectie Schneither
Collectie Van den Bosch
Collectie Van Hogendorp

National Archives of Scotland, Edinburgh, UK
Papers of Maclaine of Lochbuy

National Archives UK, Kew
Probate Records
Records of the Office of the Commissioners of Bankrupts and Court of
    Bankruptcy

Bibliotheek Koninklijk Instituut voor de Tropen/Royal Tropical Institute,
Amsterdam, The Netherlands
Jaarverslagen NV Cultuur Maatschappij Pandji & Tandjoongsarie

Gloucestershire Archives, Gloucester, UK
Papers of the Osborne and Maclaine Families of Thornbury and Mull

The Bank of England, London, UK
Court of Directors Minutes 1830–31

Baring Archive, London, UK
East Indies; India and Indian Ocean

Bodleian Library, Oxford, UK
Letter books of John Palmer

Cambridge University Library, Cambridge, UK
Jardine Matheson Archive

School of Oriental and African Studies, University of London, UK
Papers of John Swire and Sons

Bank Indonesia, Jakarta, Indonesia
Arsip/Archief Bank Indonesia/De Java Bank

Stadsarchief, Amsterdam, The Netherlands
Archief Handelshuis Van Eeghen

Gemeentearchief, Gouda, The Netherlands
Volkstelling Gouda

Mitchell Library, Sydney, Australia
New South Wales Governor's Despatches, 1813–1879

Gemeentearchief, Rotterdam, The Netherlands
Archief Familie Suermondt/A.C. Fraser & Co.

Papers in Private Possession, UK
Greenfield MSS
McLean MSS
McMaster MSS

Primary Sources: Published

Parliamentary Papers GB
Select Committee of the House of Commons on the means of improving and
    maintaining Foreign Trade – East Indies and China, 1821, vol. VI
Select Committee of the House of Lords on the East India Company, 1830,
    vol. VI
Select Committee on the China and the Affairs of the East India Company,
    1831–1832, vol. VI

Newspapers, Contemporary Journals and Directories
Bataviasche Courant
Glasgow Herald

Javasche Courant
Pigot's New Commercial Directory for Scotland
Pigot's Ayrshire Directory
[Regeerings] Almanak en Naamregister van Nederlandsche Indie
The Asiatic Journal and Monthly Intelligence
The County Directory of Scotland
The Gentleman's Magazine
The Law Advertiser
The Straits Times

Secondary Sources

Abeysekere, Susan, *Jakarta. A History* (Singapore: Oxford University Press, 1987)

Akita, Shigeru and Nicholas J. White (eds), *The International Order of Asia in the 1930s and 1950s* (Farnham: Ashgate, 2010)

Allen, G.C. and Audrey G. Donnithorne, *Western Enterprise in Indonesia and Malaya* (London: Allen & Unwin, 1957)

Bair, Jennifer, 'Global Commodity Chains: Genealogy and Review', pp. 1–34 in Jennifer Bair (ed.), *Frontiers of Commodity Chain Research* (Stanford, CA: Stanford University Press, 2009)

Bassett, D.K., 'British "Country" Trade and the Local Trade Networks of the Thai and Malay States, c. 1680–1770', *Modern Asian Studies*, 23, 4 (1989), pp. 625–43

Baud, W.A., *De Semi-Officiele en Particuliere Briefwisseling tussen J.C. Baud en J.J. Rochussen, 1845–1851*, 3 vols (Assen: Van Gorkom, 1983)

Bickers, Robert, 'Shanghailanders: The Formation and Identity of the British Settler Community in Shanghai 1843–1937', *Past and Present*, 159 (1998), pp. 161–211

Blussé, Leonard, 'Junks to Java: Chinese Shipping to the Nanyang in the Second Half of the Eighteenth Century', pp. 221–58 in Eric Tagliacozzo and Wen-Chin Chang (eds), *Chinese Circulations. Capital, Commodities and Networks in Southeast Asia* (Durham, NC and London: Duke University Press, 2011)

Blussé, Leonard, 'Batavia 1619–1740: The Rise and Fall of a Chinese Colonial Town', pp. 73–96 in Leonard Blussé, *Strange Company. Chinese Settlers, Mestizo Women and the Dutch in VOC Batavia* (Dordrecht: Foris Publications, 1986)

Boase, Frederic, *Modern English Biography* [1892–1921], 6 vols (London: Frank Cass, 1965), vol. 2

Boomgaard, Peter, 'The Non-Agricultural Side of an Agricultural Economy: Java, 1500–1900', pp. 20–24 in Paul Alexander, Peter Boomgaard and Ben White (eds), *In The Shadow of Agriculture. Non-Farm Activities in the Javanese Economy, Past and Present* (Amsterdam: Royal Tropical Institute, 1991)

Booth, Anne, 'Growth, Industrialization and the Role of Foreign Capital: Asian Colonies, 1900–42', Paper prepared for workshop 'Foreign Capital in Colonial Southeast Asia: Profits, Economic Growth and Indigenous Society,' Leiden, 16–17 December 2014

Bosma, Ulbe, 'Het Cultuurstelsel en Zijn Buitenlandse Ondernemers', *Tijdschrift voor Sociale en Economische Geschiedenis*, 2, 2 (2005), pp. 3–28

Bosma, Ulbe, 'Sailing through Suez from the South: The Emergence of an Indies Dutch Migration Circuit, 1815–1940', *International Migration Review*, 41, 2 (summer 2007), pp. 511–36

Bosma, Ulbe, 'Sugar & Dynasty in Yogyakarta,' pp. 73–94 in Ulbe Bosma, Juan Giusti-Cordero and G. Roger Knight (eds), *Sugarlandia Revisited: Sugar and Colonialism in Asia and the Americas, 1800 to 1940* (with a preface by Sydney W. Mintz), International Studies in Social History (London and New York: Berghahn Publishers, 2007)

Bosma, Ulbe, *The Sugar Plantation in India and Indonesia* (Cambridge: Cambridge University Press, 2013)

Bosma, Ulbe and Remco Raben, *Being 'Dutch' in the Indies. A History of Creolisation and Empire, 1500–1920* (Athens, OH: Ohio University Press/ Singapore: Singapore University Press, 2008)

Bowen, H.V., 'Britain in the Indian Ocean Region and Beyond: Contours, Connections and the Creation of a Global Maritime Empire', pp. 45–67 in H.V. Bowen, E. Mancke and J.G. Reid (eds), *Britain's Oceanic Empire: Atlantic and Indian Ocean Worlds c.1550–1850* (Cambridge: Cambridge University Press, 2012)

Bowen, H.V., *The Business of Empire: The East India Company and Imperial Britain, 1756–1833* (Cambridge: Cambridge University Press, 2006)

Bowen, H.V., E. Mancke and J.G. Reid (eds), *Britain's Oceanic Empire: Atlantic and Indian Ocean Worlds c.1550–1850* (Cambridge: Cambridge University Press, 2012)

Breman, Jan, *Koloniaal Profijt Van Onvrije Arbeid: Het Preanger Stelsel Van Gedwongen Koffieteelt Op Java* (Amsterdam: Amsterdam University Press, 2010)

Broeze, Frank, 'The Merchant Fleet of Java, 1820–1850', *Archipel*, 18 (1979), pp. 251–69

Broeze, Frank, 'A Scottish Merchant in Batavia (1820–1840). Gillean Maclaine and Dutch Connections', pp. 393–414 in Ina Baghdiantz McCabe, Gelina Harlaftis and Ionna Pepelasis Minoglou (eds), *Diaspora Entrepreneurial Networks. Four Centuries of History* (Oxford and New York: Berg, 2005)

[Brogan, Colm], *James Finlay and Company Limited. Manufacturers and East India Merchants* (Glasgow: Jackson Son and Company, 1951)

Brown, R.A. (ed.), *Chinese Business Enterprise in Asia* (London and New York: Routledge, 1995)

Buettner, Elizabeth, *Empire Families: Britons and Late Imperial India* (Oxford and New York: Oxford University Press, 2004)

Bulbeck, David, Anthony Reid, Lay Cheng Tan and Yiqi Wu, 'Southeast

Asian Exports Since the 14th Century. Cloves, Pepper, Coffee and Sugar', Data Paper Series, Sources for the Economic History of Southeast Asia, Institute of Southeast Asian Studies, Singapore, 1998

Butcher, John and Howard Dick (eds), *The Rise and Fall of Revenue Farming* (New York: St Martin's Press, 1993)

Campbell, Donald Maclaine, *Java: Past and Present*, 2 vols (London: William Heinemann, 1915)

Campbell, R.H., 'The Making of the Industrial City', pp. 23–44 in T.M. Devine and Gordon Jackson (eds), *Glasgow*, 2 vols (Manchester: Manchester University Press, 1994), vol. 1.

Carey, Peter, *The Power of Prophecy: Prince Dipanagara and the End of an Old Order in Java, 1785–1855* (Leiden: KITLV Press, 2007)

Chan Kok Bun (ed.), *Chinese Business Networks* (Singapore: Prentice Hall, 2000)

Chapman, Stanley, *Merchant Enterprise in Britain: From the Industrial Revolution to World War I* (Cambridge: Cambridge University Press, 1992)

Christiaans, P.A., 'Van Beusechem', *De Indische Navorscher*, 16 (2003), pp. 1–7

Christiaans, P.A. 'Vincent (Van der Parra Breton Vincent)', *De Indische Navorscher*, 2 (1989), pp. 50–56

Clarence-Smith, William Gervase, 'The Coffee Crisis in Asia Africa and the Pacific, 1870–1914', pp. 100–19 in William Gervase Clarence-Smith and Steven Topik, *The Global Coffee Economy in Africa, Asia and Latin America, 1500–1989* (Cambridge: Cambridge University Press, 2003)

Clarence-Smith, William Gervase, 'The Rise and Fall of Hadhrami Shipping in the Indian Ocean, c1750–c1940', pp. 227–58 in David Parkin and Ruth Barnes (eds), *Ships and the Development of Maritime Technology across the Indian Ocean* (London: Routledge-Curzon, 2002)

Clarence-Smith, William Gervase, 'The Impact of Forced Coffee Cultivation on Java, 1805–1917', *Indonesia Circle*, 64 (1994), pp. 214–64

Claver, Alexander, *Dutch Commerce and Chinese Merchants in Java. Colonial Relationships in Trade and Finance, 1800–1942* (Leiden and Boston, MA: Brill, 2014)

Colley, Linda, *The Ordeal of Elizabeth Marsh* (London: Harper Collins, 2007)

Constable, Phillip, 'Scottish Missionaries, "Protestant Hinduism" and the Scottish Sense of Empire in Nineteenth and Early Twentieth Century India', *The Scottish Historical Review*, 86, 2 (2007), pp. 278–313

Cooke, Anthony, *The Rise and Fall of the Scottish Cotton Industry* (Manchester and New York: Manchester University Press, 2010)

Creutzberg, P., *Changing Economy in Indonesia; A Selection of Statistical Source Material from the Early 19th Century up to 1940; Vol 1: Indonesia's Export Crops 1816–1940* (The Hague: Nijhoff, 1975)

Crickhowell, Nicholas, *The Rivers Join: The Story of A Family* (Victoria, BC: Trafford Publishing, 2009)

Currie, Jo, *Mull. The Island and Its People* (Edinburgh: Birlinn, 2000)

Curry-Machado, Jonathan, 'Preface ... and Introduction', pp. viii–x, 1–14 in J. Curry-Machado (ed.), *Global Histories, Imperial Commodities, Local Interactions* (Basingstoke: Palgrave Macmillan, 2103)

Curtin, Philip D., *Cross-Cultural Trade in World History* (Cambridge: Cambridge University Press, 1984)

Darwin, John, *The Empire Project. The Rise and Fall of the British World System* (Cambridge: Cambridge University Press, 2012)

Devine, T.M., *Scotland's Empire* (London: Allen Lane, 2003)

Devine, T.M., *To the Ends of the Earth. Scotland's Global Diaspora, 1750–2010* (London: Allen Lane, 2011)

Dick, Howard, 'Oei Tiong Ham', pp. 272–81 in John Butcher and Howard Dick (eds), *The Rise and Fall of Revenue Farming* (New York: St Martin's Press, 1993)

Dick, Howard, *Surabaya, City of Work* (Athens, OH: Ohio University Press, 2002)

Enk, E.C.M. van, 'Britse Koopleiden en de Cultuurs op Java. Harvey Thompson (1790–1837) en Zijn Financiers' (PhD dissertation, Vrije Universiteit, Amsterdam, 1999)

Farnie, D.A., *The English Cotton Industry and the World Market 1815–1896* (Oxford: Clarendon Press, 1979)

Fasseur, C., 'Wellenstein, Edmund Peter (1880–1934)', in *Biografisch Woordenboek van Nederland*, online at: http://resources.huygens.knaw.nl/bwn/BWN/lemmata/bwn3/wellenstein (accessed 12/11/2013)

Fernando, M.R., 'Coffee Cultivation in Java, 1830–1917', pp. 157–72 in W.G. Clarence-Smith and S. Topik (eds), *Global Coffee Economy* (Cambridge: Cambridge University Press, 2003)

Fisher, D.R. (ed.), *The History of Parliament: the House of Commons 1820–1832* (James Mackilllop), 7 vols (Cambridge: Cambridge University Press, 2009). Online at: www.historyofparliamentonline.org

Furber, Holden, 'The Overland Route to India in the Seventeenth and Eighteenth Centuries', *Journal of Indian History*, 29 (1951), pp. 105–33

Gaskell, Philip, *Morvern Transformed. A Highland Parish in the Nineteenth Century* (Cambridge: Cambridge University Press, 1980)

Gereffi, Gary, Miguel Korzeniewicz and Roberto D, Korzeniewicz, 'Introduction: Global Commodity Chains', pp. 1–14 in Gary Gereffi and Miguel Korzeniewicz (eds), *Commodity Chains and Global Capitalism* (Westport, CT: Praeger, 1994)

Gevers Deynoot, W.T., *Herinneringen eener Reis naar Nederlandsch Indie in 1862* (The Hague, Nijhoff, 1864)

Graaf, Ton de, *Voor Handel en Maatschappij. Geschiedenis van de Nederlandsche Handel-Maatschappij, 1824–1964* (Amsterdam: Boom, 2012)

Grace, Richard J., *Opium and Empire. The Lives and Careers of William Jardine and James Matheson* (Montreal & Kingston: McGill-Queen's University Press, 2014)

Greenberg, Michael, *British Trade and the Opening of China, 1800–42* (Cambridge: Cambridge University Press, 1951 [1969])

Grove, Linda and Mark Selden, 'Editor's Introduction: New Perspectives on China, East Asia and the Global Economy', pp. 1–11 in Takeshi Hamashita, Linda Grove and Mark Selden (eds), *China, East Asia and the Global Economy* (London and New York: Routledge, 2008)

Haan, F. de, 'Personalia der Periode van het Engelsch Bestuur over Java, 1811–1816', *Bijdragen tot de Taal-Land-en-Volkenkunde*, 92 (1935), pp. 477–681

Haggerty, S., A. Webster and N. White (eds), *Empire in One City: Liverpool's Inconvenient Imperial Past* (Manchester: Manchester University Press, 2008)

Handboek voor Cultuur-en-Handelsondernemingen in Nederlandsch-Indië (Amsterdam: De Bussy, 1888–1940)

Harlaftis, Gelina, 'Diaspora Trading Groups: From Diaspora Traders to Shipping Tycoons: The Vagliano Bros', *Business History Review*, 81, 2 (Summer 2007), pp. 240–41

Hook, Elizabeth, *A Guide to the Papers of John Swire and Sons Ltd., London* (London: The Library, School of Oriental and African Studies, 1977)

Hopkins, Terence K. and Immanuel Wallerstein, 'Commodity Chains: Construct and Research', pp. 17–20 in Gary Gereffi and Miguel Korzeniewicz (eds), *Commodity Chains and Global Capitalism* (Westport, CT: Praeger, 1994)

Horn, Nico van, 'Het Indische handelshuis Bauermann in de negentiende eeuw', *NEHA-jaarboek voor economische, bedrijfs- en techniekgeschiedenis*, 60 (1997), pp. 137–58

Houben, Vincent, J.H., *Kraton and Kumpeni. Surakarta and Yogyakarta 1830–1870* (Leiden: KITLV Press, 1994)

Jackson, Gordon and David M. Williams (eds), *Shipping, Technology, and Imperialism: Papers Presented to the Third British-Dutch Maritime History Conference* (Aldershot: Scholar Press/Brookfield, VT: Ashgate, 1996)

[J.D.P.], 'Journal of an Excursion to the Native Provinces in 1828, during the War with Dipo Negoro', *Journal of the Indian Archipelago and East Asia*, 8 (1854) [Nendeln/Liechtenstein, Kraus Reprint, 1970], pp. 1–19, 136–57, 225–46

Jones, C., 'British Imperialism and the Argentine, 1875–1900: A Theoretical Note', *Journal of Latin American Studies*, 12, 2 (1980)

Jones, Geoffrey, 'Alfred Chandler and the Importance of Organization', *Enterprise and Society*, 9, 3 (2008), pp. 419–21

Jones, Geoffrey, *The Evolution of International Business. An Introduction* (London: Routledge, 1995)

Jones, Geoffrey and Judith Wale, 'Diversification Strategies of British Trading Companies: Harrisons & Crosfield, c.1900–c.1980', *Business History*, 41, 2 (1999), pp. 69–101

Junghuhn, F., *Terugreis van Java naar Europa met de zoogenaamde Engelsche Overlandpost, in de Maanden September tot October 1848* (Zalt-Bommel: Joh, Norman & Zoon, 1851)

Knaap, Gerrit, *Shallow Waters, Rising Tide; Shipping and Trade in Java around 1775* (Leiden: KITLV Press, 1996)

Knight, G. Roger, *Commodities and Colonialism: The Story of Big Sugar in Indonesia, 1880–1942* (Leiden: Brill, 2013)

Knight, G. Roger, 'Descrying the Bourgeoisie: Sugar, Capital and the State in the Netherlands Indies, c. 1840–1884', *Bijdragen tot de Taal-, Land- en Volkenkunde*, 163, 1 (2007), pp. 52–83

Knight, G. Roger, 'East of the Cape in 1832: The Old Indies World, Empire Families and "Colonial Women" in Nineteenth Century Java', *Itinerario*, 36, 1 (2012), pp. 22–48

Knight, G. Roger, 'John Palmer and Plantation Development in Western Java during the Earlier Nineteenth Century', *Bijdragen tot de Taal-, Land- en Volkenkunde*, 131, 2 & 3 (1975), pp. 309–37

Knight, G. Roger, 'From Plantation to Padi-Field: The Origins of the Nineteenth Century Transformation of Java's Sugar Industry', *Modern Asian Studies*, 14, 2 (1980), pp. 177–204

Knight, G. Roger, 'Rescued from the Myths of Time: Toward a Reappraisal of European Mercantile Houses in Mid-Nineteenth Century Java, c. 1830–1870', *Bijdragen tot de Taal-, Land- en Volkenkunde*, 170 (2014), pp. 313–41

Knight, G. Roger, *Sugar Steam and Steel. The Industrial Project in Colonial Java, 1830–1885* (Adelaide: Adelaide University Press, 2014)

Knight, G. Roger, 'Technology, Technicians and Bourgeoisie: Thomas Jeoffries Edwards and the Industrial Project in Sugar in Mid-Nineteenth Century Java', pp. 31–52 in Ulbe Bosma, Juan Giusti-Cordero and G. Roger Knight (eds), *Sugarlandia Revisited: Sugar and Colonialism in Asia and the Americas, 1800 to 1940* (with a preface by Sydney W. Mintz), International Studies in Social History (London and New York: Berghahn Publishers, 2007)

Knight, G. Roger and Lesley Abell, '"So Like Home": Angus Maclaine (1799–1877), Sheep Farmer and Sojourner in South Australia', *Journal of the Historical Society of South Australia*, 33 (2005), pp. 40–56

Knight, G. Roger and Lesley Abell, 'Three Countries, Two Brothers, Sugar and Sheep', in Susan Magarey and Kerrie Round (eds), *Living History. Essays on History as Biography* (Unley, SA: Australian Humanities Press, 2005), pp. 57–79.

Kobayashi, Atsushi, 'The Role of Singapore in the Growth of Intra-Southeast Asian Trade, c.1820s–1852', *Southeast Asian Studies* [Kyoto], 2, 3 (2013), pp. 443–74

Korthals-Altes, W.L., *Changing Economy in Indonesia: General Trade Statistics, 1822-1940 v.12A: Selection of Statistical Source Material from the Early 19th Century up to 1940* (Amsterdam: KIT, 1992)

Kossmann, E.H., *The Low Countries, 1780–1940* (Oxford: Clarendon Press, 1978)

Kraan, Alfons van de, 'Anglo-Dutch Rivalry in the Java Cotton Trade, 1811–30', *Indonesia Circle*, 68 (1996), pp. 35–64

Kunio, Yoshihara, (ed.), *Oei Tiong Ham Concern: The First Business Empire of Southeast Asia* (Kyoto: Kyoto University, The Centre for Southeast Asian Studies, 1989)

Kynaston, David, *The City of London. Volume 1. A World of its Own, 1815–1890*, 4 vols (London: Pimlico/Random House, 1995)

Lamb, Rebecca, *MacQuoid of Waniassa* (Canberra ACT: Waniassa Publications, 2006)

Le Pichon, Alain, *China Trade and Empire. Jardine Matheson & Co. and the Origins of British Rule in Hong Kong, 1827–1843* (Oxford and New York: Oxford University Press for the British Academy, 2006)

Liem Tjwan Ling, 'Sugar Jing: Oei Tiong Ham', in Yoshihara Kunio (ed.), *Oei Tiong Ham Concern: The First Business Empire of Southeast Asia* (Kyoto: Kyoto University, The Centre for Southeast Asian Studies, 1989), pp. 135–47

Lindblad, J. Thomas, 'Corporate Structure and Profit in Colonial Indonesia, 1920–1930, Paper prepared for workshop 'Foreign Capital in Colonial Southeast Asia: Profits, Economic Growth and Indigenous Society', Leiden, 16–17 December 2014

Lindblad, J. Thomas, *Foreign Investment in Southeast Asia in the Twentieth Century* (Basingstoke: Macmillan, 1998)

Lindblad, J. Thomas, 'British Business and the Uncertainties of Early Independence in Indonesia', *Itinerario*, 37 (2013), pp. 147–64

Lubbock, Basil, *Opium Clippers* (Glasgow: Brown, Son & Ferguson, 1933)

McCabe, Ina Baghdiantz, Gelina Harlaftis and Ionna Pepelasis Minoglou (eds), *Diaspora Entrepreneurial Networks. Four Centuries of History* (Oxford and New York: Berg, 2005)

[Maclaine Watson], *The First One Hundred Years. 1827–1927. Maclaine Watson & Co. MacNeill & Co. Fraser Easton & Co* (nd, np [1927])

MacLean, J., 'Macleans in the Former Dutch East Indies in the Period 1819–1849', *Scottish Genealogist*, 19 (1972), pp. 45–47

MacLeod, Norman, *Morvern. A Highland Parish*, edited by Iain Thornber (Edinburgh: Birlinn, 2002)

Magarey, Susan and Kerrie Round (eds), *Living History. Essays on History as Biography* (Unley, SA: Australian Humanities Press, 2005)

Mansvelt, W.F.M., *Geschiedenis van de Nederlandsche Handel-Maatschappij*, 2 vols (Haarlem: Druk van J. Enschedé, 1924–26)

Margana, Sri, 'The Formation of a New Frontier: The Conquest of Java's Oosthoek by the VOC in 1768', pp. 184–206 in Nigel Worden (ed.), *Contingent Lives. Social Identity and Material Culture in the VOC World* (Cape Town: Historical Studies Department, University of Cape Town, 2007)

Markovits, Claude, *The Global World of Indian Merchants, 1750–1947* (Cambridge: Cambridge University Press, 2000)

Matsui, Masuko, 'Opium Trade and the Port of Izmir. A Survey for a Comparative and Interactive Analysis', Paper presented to the workshop on 'The Inter-Asian Trade during the "Long 19th Century": Formation and Dynamics of Regional Commodity Chains', Institute of Humanities, Kyoto University, 26–27 March 2012

Miller, Michael B., *Europe and the Maritime World. A Twentieth Century History* (Cambridge: Cambridge University Press, 2012)

Molsbergen, E.C. Godee, *Gedenkboek Reynst en Vinju, 1836–1936* (Batavia: Reynst en Vinju, 1936)

Munro, J. Forbes, *Maritime Enterprise and Empire. Sir William Mackinnon and his Business Network, 1823–1893* (Woodbridge: The Boydell Press, 2003)

Onghokham, *The Thugs, the Curtain Thief and the Sugar Lord. Power, Politics and Culture in Colonial Java* (Jakarta: Metafor, 2003)

Oosterwijk, Bram, *Koning van de Koopvaart. Anthony van Hoboken 1756–1850* (Rotterdam: Stichting Historische Publicaties Roterodamum, 1983)

Parker, James G., 'Scottish Enterprise in India, 1750–1914,' in R.A. Cage (ed.), *The Scots Abroad* (London: Croom Helm, 1985), pp. 191–219

Philips, C.H., *The East India Company, 1784–1834* (Manchester: Manchester University Press, 1961)

Porter, Andrew, '"Gentlemanly Capitalism" and Empire: The British Experience since 1750?', *The Journal of Imperial and Commonwealth History*, 18, 3 (1990), pp. 265–95

Post, Peter, 'Chinese Business Networks and Japanese Capital in South East Asia, 1880–1940: Some Preliminary Observations', pp. 154–75 in R.A. Brown (ed.), *Chinese Business Enterprise in Asia* (London and New York, Routledge, 1995)

Post, Peter, 'The Kwik Hoo Tong Trading Society of Semarang, Java: A Chinese Business Network in Late Colonial Asia', *Journal of Southeast Asian Studies*, 32 (2002)

Reid, Anthony, 'A New Phase of Commercial Expansion in Southeast Asia, 1760–1840', in Anthony Reid (ed.), *The Last Stand of Asian Autonomies: Responses to Modernity in the Diverse States of Southeast Asia and Korea, 1750–1900* (New York: St Martin's Press, 1997)

Reid, Anthony (ed.), *The Last Stand of Asian Autonomies: Responses to Modernity in the Diverse States of Southeast Asia and Korea, 1750–1900* (New York: St Martin's Press, 1997)

Reid, Anthony, 'Southeast Asian Consumption of Indian and British Cotton Cloth, 1600–1850', pp. 31–52 in Giorgio Riello and Tirthankar Roy (eds), *How India Clothed the World: The World of South Asian Textiles, 1500–1850* (Leiden and Boston, MA: Brill, 2009)

Riello, Giorgio and Tirthankar Roy (eds), *How India Clothed the World: The World of South Asian Textiles, 1500–1850* (Leiden and Boston, MA: Brill, 2009)

Rogge J., *Het Handelshuis Van Eeghen* (Amsterdam: Van Ditmar, 1949)

Rush, James R., *Opium to Java. Revenue Farming and Chinese Enterprise in Colonial Indonesia, 1860–1910* (Ithaca, NY and London: Cornell University Press, 1990)

Schmiedell, J.H., *Gedenkblätter zum 50-Jährigen Bestehen der Firma Erdmann & Sielcken in Java, 1875–1924* (np., nd. [1924])

Shimada, Ryuto, 'The Long-term Pattern of Maritime Trade in Java from the Late Eighteenth Century to the Mid-Nineteenth Century', *Southeast Asian Studies [Kyoto]*, 2, 3 (2013), pp. 475–97

Singh, S.B., *European Agency Houses in Bengal, 1783–1833* (Calcutta: Firma Mukhopadhyay, 1966)

Smith, E.A., *George IV* (New Haven, CT and London: Yale University Press, 1999)

Sugihara, Kaoru, 'An Introduction', pp. 1–20 in K. Sugihara (ed.), *Japan, China and the Growth of the Asian International Economy, 1850–1949* (Oxford: Oxford University Press, 2005)

Sugihara, Kaoru, 'The Resurgence of Intra-Asian Trade, 1800–1850', pp. 139–72 in Giorgio Riello and Tirthankar Roy (eds), *How India Clothed the World: The World of South Asian Textiles, 1500–1850* (Leiden and Boston, MA: Brill, 2009)

Sugiyama, Shinya and Linda Grove, 'Introduction', pp. 1–14 in S. Sugiyama and L. Grove (eds), *Commercial Networks in Modern Asia* (Richmond: Curzon, 2001)

Sutherland, Heather, 'A Sino-Indonesian Commodity Chain. The Trade in Tortoiseshell in the Late Seventeenth and Eighteenth Centuries', pp. 172–201 in Eric Tagliacozzo and Wen-Chin Chang (eds), *Chinese Circulations. Capital, Commodities, and Networks in Southeast Asia* (Durham, NC and London: Duke University Press, 2011)

Sutherland, Heather and Gerrit Knaap, *Monsoon Traders; Ships, Skippers and Commodities in Eighteenth-Century Makassar* (Leiden: KITLV Press, 2004)

Tagliacozzo, Eric, *Secret Trades, Porous Borders: Smuggling and State along a Southeast Asian Frontier, 1865–1915* (New Haven, CT: Yale University Press, 2009)

Tagliacozzo, Eric, 'A Sino-Southeast Asian Circuit: Ethnohistories of the Marine Goods Trade', pp. 432–54 in Eric Tagliacozzo and Wen-Chin Chang (eds), *Chinese Circulations. Capital, Commodities, and Networks in Southeast Asia* (Durham, NC and London: Duke University Press, 2011)

Tagliacozzo, Eric and Wen-Chin Chang (eds), *Chinese Circulations. Capital, Commodities, and Networks in Southeast Asia* (Durham, NC and London: Duke University Press, 2011)

Tarling, Nicholas, *Anglo-Dutch Rivalry in the Malay World 1780–1824* (Cambridge: Cambridge University Press, 1962)

Tarling, Nicholas, 'The Palmer Loans', *Bijdragen tot de Taal-, Land-en Volkenkunde*, 119 (1963), pp. 161–88

Tarling, Nicholas, 'The Prince of Merchants and the Lion City', *Journal of the Malaysian Branch of the Royal Asiatic Society*, 36, 1 (1964), pp. 20–40.

Taselaar, Arjen, *De Nederlandse Koloniale Lobby. Ondernemers en de Indische Politiek, 1914–1940* (Leiden: Research School CNWS, 1998)

186 *Bibliography*

Tio Poo Tjiang, *De Suikerhandel van Java* (Amsterdam: De Bussy, 1923)
Topik, Steven, 'Historicizing Commodity Chains. Five Hundred Years of the Global Coffee Commodity Chain', pp. 37–62 in Jennifer Bair (ed.), *Frontiers of Commodity Chain Research* (Stanford, CA: Stanford University Press, 2009)
Topik, Steven and William Gervase Clarence-Smith, 'Introduction. Coffee and Global Development', pp. 1–17 in William Gervase Clarence Smith and Steven Topik (eds), *The Global Coffee Economy in Africa, Asia and Latin America, 1500–1989* (Cambridge: Cambridge University Press, 2003)
Trocki, Carl A., 'Opium as a Commodity in the Chinese Nanyang Trade', pp. 84–104 in Eric Tagliacozzo and Wen-Chin Chang (eds), *Chinese Circulations. Capital, Commodities, and Networks in Southeast Asia* (Durham, NC and London: Duke University Press, 2011)
Trocki, Carl A., *Opium, Empire and the Global Political Economy* (London and New York: Routledge, 1999)
Van Niel, Robert, *Java's Northeast Coast 1740–1840* (Leiden: CNWS Publications, 2005)
Vries Joh, de (ed.), *Herinneringen en dagboek van Ernst Heldring (1871–1954)*, 3 vols (Utrecht: Nederlands Historisch Genootschap, 1970)
Wal, V.I. van der, *Indische Landhuizen en hun Geschiedenis* (Batavia: Kolff and Co., 1932)
Wallerstein, Immanuel, *World-Systems Analysis: An Introduction* (Durham, NC: Duke University Press, 2000)
War Office (Great Britain), *A List of the Officers of the Army and Royal Marines on Full and Half-Pay with An Index* (London: War Office, 1820)
Warren, James, *The Sulu Zone 1768–1898: The Dynamics of External Trade, Slavery, and Ethnicity in the Transformation of a Southeast Asian Maritime State* (Singapore: Singapore University Press, 1981)
Webster, Anthony, 'British Export Interests in Bengal and Imperial Expansion in Southeast Asia: the Origins of the Straits Settlements', pp. 138–74 in Barbara Ingham and Colin Simmons (eds), *Development Studies and Colonial Policy* (London: Frank Cass, 1987)
Webster, Anthony, *Gentlemen Capitalists: British Imperialism in Southeast Asia, 1770–1890* (London and New York: Tauris Academic Studies, 1998)
Webster, Anthony, 'Liverpool and the Asian Trade, 1800–1850. Some Insights into a Provincial Commercial Network', in S. Haggerty, A. Webster and N. White (eds), *Empire in One City: Liverpool's Inconvenient Imperial Past* (Manchester: Manchester University Press, 2008)
Webster, Anthony, *The Twilight of the East India Company 1813–1858* (Woodbridge and Rochester, NY: The Boydell Press, 2009)
Webster, Anthony, *The Richest East India Merchant. The Life and Business of John Palmer of Calcutta, 1767–1836* (Woodbridge: The Boydell Press, 2007)
Westendorp Boerma, J.J. (ed.), *Briefwisseling tusssen J. van den Bosch en J.C. Baud, 1829–1832 en 1834–1836*, 2 vols (Utrecht, Kemink, 1956)
Whatley, Christopher A., 'Labour in the Industrialising City, c. 1660–1830',

pp. 361–82 in T.M. Devine and Gordon Jackson (eds), *Glasgow*, 2 vols (Manchester: Manchester University Press, 1994)

White, Nicholas J., *Business, Government and the End of Empire. Malaya, 1942–1957* (Kuala Lumpur: Oxford University Press, 1996)

White, Nicholas J., 'Surviving Sukarno: British Business in Post-Colonial Indonesia, 1950–1967', *Modern Asian Studies*, 46 (2012), pp. 1277–315.

Wright, H.R.C., *East Indian Economic Problems in the Age of Cornwallis and Raffles* (London: Luzac & Co., 1961)

Wurtzburg, C.E., *Raffles of the Eastern Isles* (London: Hodder and Stoughton, 1954)

Young, James, *A Short Memoir of James Young, Merchant Burgess of Aberdeen, and Rachel Cruickshank, His Spouse, and of Their Descendants* (Aberdeen: J. Craighead & Co., 1861), online at: archive.org › eBooks and Texts (accessed 04/01/2014)

INDEX

WORLDS OF THE EAST INDIA COMPANY

Printed and bound by CPI Group (UK) Ltd, Croydon, CR0 4YY

24/04/2025

14661366-0001